British English Pronunciation Roadmap

Book 1

VOWELS

written, designed and illustrated by

Ashley Howard

Copyright © 2015 Ashley Howard. All rights reserved.

Ashley Howard has asserted his moral right to be identified as the author of this work.

All rights reserved. No part of this publication, including the accompanying audio, may be reproduced, stored in a retrieval system, or transmitted in any form or by any means — electronic, mechanical, photocopying, recording, or otherwise — without the prior written permission of the copyright holder, except in the case of brief quotations used in reviews or critical articles.

A catalogue record for this book is available from the British Library.

ISBN: 978-0-9933602-1-3

Published by Ashley Howard, United Kingdom.

Contents

Chapter	Page
Before You Explore...	1
My Pronunciation Roadmap	6
How to Navigate Each Page	8
How to Download the Audio Examples	9
Speech Anatomy	10
Vowel Sounds	12
Take the next step...	103
How do I Integrate these New Habits into Live Speech?	104
Bonus Section: Practice Pages	105
Bonus Section: Practice Pages - Answers	124
Additional Resources	130
Bibliography and Recommended Reading	132

before you explore...

> **Complete the Series...**

This is Book 1 in a 3 part series that enables you to master pronunciation and intonation in British English. So once you mastered vowels complete the series with *Book 2 - Consonants* and *Book 3 - Intonation*.

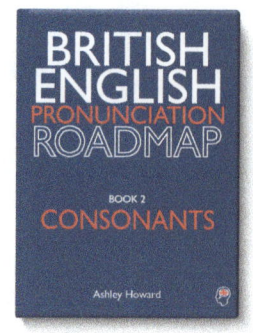 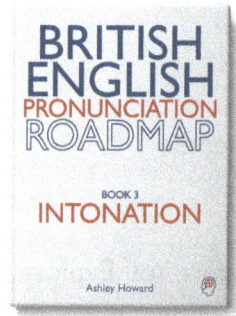

> **What is an accent?**

Everyone has an accent – even if it is considered neutral or region-less. And there are too many to count, partly because accents constantly evolve. An accent is heard primarily in the way we pronounce our words, how we stress them, and the intonation we use to convey emotion, attitude and intention. It reveals something about us and we all make associations, rightly or wrongly with the way a person speaks. More importantly, everybody modifies their accent – it's true. We make slight adjustments depending on whom we're with and what we're talking about. For example, talking to friends and family makes most people talk in a more relaxed and casual way whilst when talking to certain colleagues or addressing people in authority, most people talk in a slower, more considered way – this is, in a way, changing one's accent.

> **Why change an accent?**

Accents are wonderful! They are as unique as the lives we live. They are part of our identity and represent our cultural diversity and heritage. But some people, for practical, personal or professional reasons, want to change or modify their accent. As one client said, "my accent speaks louder than my words...". During our lives we reinvent ourselves all the time, by dressing differently, changing our hairstyle, moving house or country, learning a new skill, changing behaviours, profession or lifestyle, and so changing one's accent is within our transformational capacity. Learning another accent isn't about eliminating your current accent – those neural pathways will always remain – but simply having choice. This takes time and practice, but it means that you are in control of how you want to be perceived in the world.

> **Is it even possible?**

Yes! I have worked with countless clients over many years and they have all achieved great success, but it's true that some people find it really easy and straightforward and some find it challenging. Whilst accent is very much part of who we are and how we interact with the world around us, it is also just a physical habit – you don't think about how to speak, you just think about what you want to say – it's part of your muscle memory. Think of this roadmap process in two stages. Firstly, it involves getting the new sounds into your muscle memory. This includes various aspects: conscious awareness of what you current do and what you are aiming for; imitation; daily repetitive practice; and understanding patterns. The second stage is integrating these new habits into live speech. This aspect is the real moment of transformation, which takes courage, commitment and a willingness to change.

> **How long is it going to take?**

It's a necessary and relevant question, but an impossible one to answer. Learning an accent is, as I've said, about

before you explore...

acquiring a new habit and building muscle memory. This takes as long as it takes. Learning to drive is as much to do with comprehension and exposure, as it is to do with muscle memory. Some people can pass their driving test within an intensive week of fifteen lessons, and some people take a year with thirty sessions, or more. You can control your level of commitment and practice – and this can make a huge difference. Also, successfully changing just one word is success and progress! So it's a bit like a jigsaw – celebrate every new piece that fits together, take your time and enjoy the process.

> Who is this book for?

This book is designed to help anyone, for whatever reason, who wants to learn a 'standard southern' British English accent – also known as RP (see below). You might speak English as a second language and simply want to sound like the people around you. You might teach English as a second language or be a fellow voice coach seeking a resource for how to help your students with their pronunciation and intonation. You might be a native English speaker with a regional accent who wants it softened. You might even be an actor who needs to learn a standard British accent for an audition or part.

> What is an RP accent?

RP stands for Received Pronunciation. Today, it refers to a standard British English accent associated with the south of England. The word 'received' used to mean something being accepted or approved, and so this accent was considered the most well-received or the most 'standard' pronunciation of British English. It was therefore set apart from regional accents.

Every language has their own version of RP – their own standard accent – as well as their regional accents. All accents have their positive and negative stereotypes and associations. Amongst native English speakers, RP is most typically associated with privilege, wealth, power and intellect – in the early twentieth century some described it as 'Public School Pronunciation' (Daniel Jones *English Pronouncing Dictionary* CUP 1917). It is an accent often associated with the current monarch, those in certain professions and positions of authority and some British actors. As with all stereotypes, they are just that, stereotypes, a fixed, simplified and often inaccurate belief about a group of people. RP or standard southern British English is spoken by a large variety of people from many walks of life.

Thankfully, every accent evolves and adapts to the changing socio-cultural-political landscape, which is influenced by many factors. So the accent that you can learn through this book is more of a typical modern RP – it is a neutral, region-less, standard southern British accent, still used to transcribe the pronunciation of British English words in dictionaries.

> Fearless, playful imitation is essential

We learn our first language through imitation. We listen to and watch those around us and mimic their sounds, exploring with fearless playfulness the ways in which our *tongue, lips* and *soft palate* move in order to accurately reproduce their sounds. In contrast, learning a second language is primarily through spelling. Some written languages are more phonetic, so what's written is more reliable in terms of pronunciation. British English is not one of these languages, so the first way to engage with this process of changing your accent towards modern RP is to develop a reliance on your ears by listening to the audio in each section, imitating the sounds with fearlessness and playfulness, and paying attention to the sensation of the way each sound feels in your mouth.

before you explore...

> Deprogramming the spelling

When exploring a new vowel sound, a client once said, "my eyes are controlling my mouth", which is to say that the spelling is trying to dictate the way to say the word. This is part of the challenge with the British English language. What you see is not necessarily what you should say. For examples, you're probably quite aware that in the English language there are five vowel letters, however, in terms of pronunciation, there are actually nineteen vowel sounds. So these five vowel letters are used in various combinations to represent this larger number of sounds. Sometimes the vowel letters accurately describe the consonant sounds, as in 'bad', 'pet', 'got' and 'seek' but sometimes they do not, as in 'sergeant', 'foetus' and 'thorough' and 'sieve'. So, exploring vowel sounds is a lot to do with deprogramming the spelling and focusing on the sounds instead of the letters.

> Using phonetic symbols to check the pronunciation

Some people are familiar with phonetics, which is a symbol system for writing sounds. If you've ever been confused by the strange symbols next to a word in a dictionary, they're phonetic symbols. So every sound has a single symbol. There is a symbol for the 'a' sound in 'cat' and the 'or' sound in 'shore'. Each vowel page has the relevant phonetic symbol and you can also use the *Phonetic Symbols (p.130)* as a reference. This makes it possible for you to consult a reliable dictionary and actually see how to pronounce the word. There are also specialised pronunciation dictionaries. In fact, the online Oxford Dictionary not only has phonetic transcriptions but also audio examples of words – so you can see and hear how to pronounce them in R.P. They also have an app called *The Oxford Advanced Learner's Dictionary*, which offers the phonetic transcription and audio examples without needing to connect to the internet – which might be useful for on-the-go, 'location-less' reference.

> Do I need to know the phonetic symbols to use this book?

Thankfully you do not need to know phonetics in order to successfully use this book. As I said, I have given the relevant phonetic symbols in the top right hand corner of each of the vowel and consonant sound page, so that you are able to cross-reference and clarify the pronunciation of other words with the words and examples given for each vowel sound. However, in this book, I have focused on comprehension, listening and imitation: there are detailed descriptions of each sound and pattern, with audio examples of every word and phrase. With imitation and daily practice, you will be able to understand, develop your ear and experience the sensation of what it's like to pronounce words differently.

> 20 minute coaching sessions

I have attempted to make this book feel as if I am there with you, coaching you through every section. So it is very thorough, albeit a bit wordy at times. One suggestion is that you treat each new consonant sound like a twenty minute coaching session. Set aside this time to explore the pages that focus on the new sound, discover your habits and follow the guidance on each page. This means that it can fit in with your life style and commitments and you can pick it up and put it down accordingly.

before you explore...

> 'I'll put a thought on it'

Whilst discussing the process of integrating new pronunciations into live speech, another client I was coaching said to me, 'I'll put a thought on it', referring to a new sound he had learnt for a particular word. He explained that when speaking, he would be actively 'thinking' about what he might say, in order to catch the word with the new sound in it, hoping to change it in the moment. Of course, at the beginning, it tends to be that you catch the word after it is spoken, but the more he caught it, the more able he felt to catch it before speaking.

> Creating a word bank

Another client created a folder of notes on their phone, so that throughout the day they could identify what the sort of language and common phrases they used frequently. They would then check these words in a pronunciation dictionary, notice whether or not any of these words contained vowels or consonant sounds that they had been working on with me, and then changed them where necessary. This enabled them to make the integration of their new habits immediately into live speech, without having to play the guessing game of when the new habits would be needed.

Whilst I have offered you many everyday words and phrases and many practice sentences to help you get started, creating a word bank of words that you tend to use is invaluable. And when working on vowel sounds in the first book in this three part series, words can be grouped into words that contain the same vowel sounds, or into what are known as lexical sets – which is to say that if the vowel in the primary stressed syllable of a word rhymes with another word, they belong in the same group. For example, 's<u>aw</u>', 'b<u>o</u>red' and 'en<u>o</u>rmous' would be in the same lexical group because the main vowel sound rhymes. You can do the same for consonants in book two: find words that have the same initial consonants ('do', 'does', 'don't'), the same medial consonant ('ladder', 'bolder', 'hiding') and the same final consonants ('side', 'called', 'had') and group them together. This way, you can focus your practice on words that feature whatever new sound you are learning.

> Make your intentions known

It can feel easier to reinvent yourself in front of new people, but when in front of your friends, family or colleagues, it might feel more challenging. Many people that I have coached express an anxiety about what people will think of them if they change their pronunciation. We all tend to pigeonhole each another based on the clothes that we wear, the music that we like, where we live, where we were educated, what profession we are in etc… When we change anything about ourselves, there is a very natural fear about acceptance. Making those around you aware of your intention to work on your speech and accent may dissolve some of this anxiety and help to create a conversation about why and how you intend to do it, which makes them part of your process rather than obstacles to your progress.

> Proprioception

In the sections of vowels and consonants, you will be asked to notice what your lips, tongue, jaw and soft palate are doing. Arguably, you may never have considered the position and movement of your tongue or lips unless you have accidentally bitten them, or your jaw, unless it aches or is painful - and you may never have even heard of your soft palate, let alone considered what it's doing in speech. You will slowly become more and more conscious of what these parts of your speaking anatomy are doing, but there is still a heavy reliance on what it called proprioception: your body's ability to sense, feel and notice what it is doing. This is where recording

before you explore...

yourself and using a mirror become almost vital to practicing and exploring effectively. Your body's internal sense of these parts will strengthen but may take time, so be patient.

> '...it's percolating'

I had a client once whose response to the question 'how has it been going this week?' (which I tend to ask at the beginning of most coaching sessions), was 'it's percolating'. He seemed quite happy with this idea: that just like coffee, his new skills and habits were slowly permeating into his everyday speech. Some aspects of the learning might be really immediate and transformative, and some may take time to percolate. Set goals, but be generous to yourself.

> Your pronunciation 'roadmap'

Once you know your habits and how to change them, you no longer need to look at each section. It's a bit like navigating around a new place. Once you've discovered where each new road or path or corridor leads to, the more you travel along them, the more familiar they become until you can navigate without thinking. So think of the process of exploring this book, like exploring the roadmap of pronunciation. You are where it all starts, and the destination is clearer and more confident British English pronunciation. Go to the *My Pronunciation Roadmap (p.6)* and tick the relevant sections as you travel through the book. I hope you enjoy your journey!

> Who is the Author?

Ashley Howard is an experienced British Voice Coach trained at the Royal Central School of Speech and Drama in MA Voice Studies (2007). He did a further two years of training with Kristin Linklater author of *Freeing the Natural Voice* 2007. The three books series *British English Pronunciation Roadmap* is a distillation of thousands and thousands of hours of coaching, with hundreds and hundreds of clients and students from almost every country and every language. For more info on Ashley, visit www.ashleyhoward.me

Disclaimer:

The information in this book has been compiled by way of general guidance in relation to the specific subjects addressed, but is not a substitute for individual professional guidance on specific circumstances. Please consult a medical professional before beginning any physical exercises or speech related exercises, particularly if you have known specific issues that may influence their general safety and efficacy. If you engage in the exercises in this book, you agree that you do so at your own risk, are voluntarily participating in these activities, assume all risk of injury to yourself, and agree to release and discharge the author and publisher from any and all claims or causes of action, known or unknown, arising out of the author or publisher's negligence.

My Pronunciation Roadmap

The inspiration for the name of this book came from a session I had a long time ago when a client of mine was talking about navigating around a new city to which he had recently moved. At the end of the session he said, 'knowing which sound to use in which word is becoming a little easier', to which I replied, 'yea, it's a bit like navigating around the new city in which you're now living - without a roadmap it can feel a bit overwhelming. So think of this process a bit like getting a roadmap to your new pronunciation'. It seemed to be a perfect comparrison.

It's also true that when learning anything new, there is a sort re-mapping of the roadmap inside the brain - where new synaptic connections are made. These synaptic connections take time to establish. In the same way that learning a new route or journey takes repetition and repetition before it becomes something that you can do without thinking, so these new pronunciations take time and practice before they become second nature.

So, over the page is your very own pronunciation roadmap. If you've already had a personalised assessment from me, then your journey is all mapped-out and you just need to follow the path to clearer and more confident speech. If you chose to work alone, you'll discover, sound by sound, which ones apply to you and you can tick each one accordingly. and your roadmap will emerge. This way, you'll be able to navigate the book and practice more specifically on the things that will deliver the most change for you.

Get a personalised assessment of every vowel, consonant and aspect of intonation to find out how well you're doing, exactly what to focus on and what you need to do to speak in this accent accurately and naturally:

https://www.ashleyhoward.me/pronunciation-evaluation

My Pronunciation Roadmap

Consonants

R	☐	p.15	S and Z	☐	p.41	K and G	☐	p.71
Rhotic / Non-Rhotic	☐	p.19	TH	☐	p.45	SH and ZH	☐	p.75
M	☐	p.22	NG	☐	p.49	DG and CH	☐	p.78
P and B	☐	p.24	N	☐	p.54	H	☐	p.83
W	☐	p.28	L	☐	p.57	Consonant Clusters	☐	p.85
F and V	☐	p.31	T and D	☐	p.61			
Yod	☐	p.35	Syllabic Consonants	☐	p.66			

ONLY available in my second book — CONSONANTS

Vowels

SCHWA	☐	p.17	THOUGHT, NORTH, FORCE	☐	p.48	NEAR	☐	p.74
NURSE	☐	p.21				DRESS	☐	p.78
GOAT	☐	p.26	CHOICE	☐	p.53	FACE	☐	p.82
BATH, PALM, START	☐	p.31	TRAP	☐	p.57	SQUARE	☐	p.86
STRUT	☐	p.35	MOUTH	☐	p.61	GOOSE	☐	p.90
PRICE	☐	p.39	FLEECE	☐	p.65	FOOT	☐	p.94
LOT, CLOTH	☐	p.43	KIT	☐	p.70	CURE	☐	p.98

Word Stress, Relationships between Words and Intonation

Syllable stress	☐	p.174	Syllable/stress timed	☐	p.208	Apologising	☐	p.224
Compound words	☐	p.177	Resting rhythm	☐	p.208	Ongoing thought	☐	p.225
Dates, times, money	☐	p.180	Mono/polysyllabic words	☐	p.210	Listing	☐	p.225
Primary/secondary stress	☐	p.182	Short/long vowels	☐	p.211	Naming places, people...	☐	p.226
Unstressed syllables	☐	p.183	Phrasing	☐	p.211	Parenthesis	☐	p.227
Prefixes & Suffixes	☐	p.186	Asking a question	☐	p.221	Quoting/paraphrasing	☐	p.227
Linking/intrusive sounds	☐	p.195	Rhetorical	☐	p.222	Irony/sarcasm/satire	☐	p.229
Elision & contractions	☐	p.198	High Rise Tone	☐	p.222	Expanding a statement	☐	p.229
Assimilation	☐	p.199	Responding to questions	☐	p.222	Antithesis	☐	p.230
Weak forms	☐	p.202	Statements, commands...	☐	p.224	but... or... so...	☐	p.231

ONLY available in my third book — INTONATION

How to Navigate Each Page

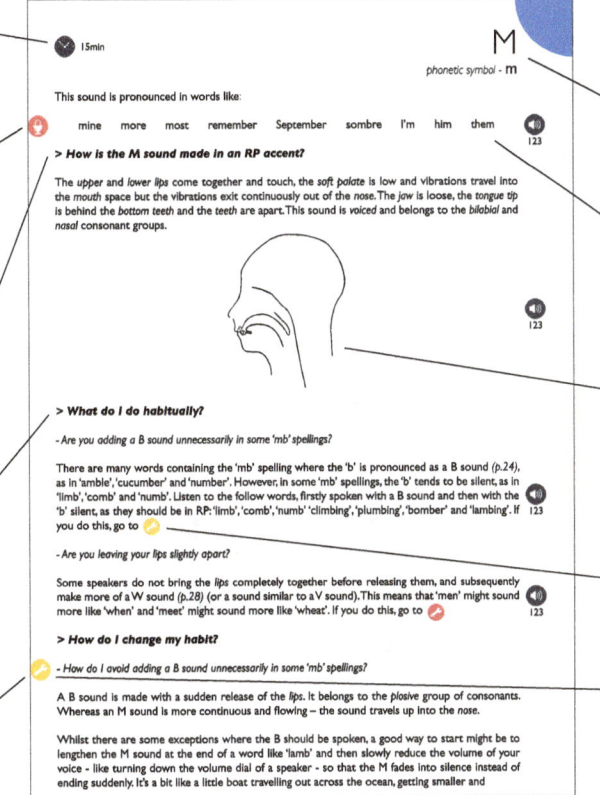

How much time to set aside for each sound

The red icon of a mic suggests that you could record yourself saying the words before exploring the sound. This will enable you to compare yourself to the audio example and discover your habit

Explanation of how and where the sound is made and whether it is voiced or voiceless

Identify your habit by reading aloud the examples, listening to the audio examples and comparing to your recording

Use the relevant subsection to help change your specific habit

There is a list of words and the most typical spellings for each sound. Record yourself saying the words then imitate and practice with the audio examples to help guide you to the new pronunciation

There are also practice sentences for each sound. Again, record yourself saying the sentences then imitate and practice with the audio examples to help guide you to the new pronunciation

The target sound under which is its phonetic symbol for reference

Words that contain the target sound

A drawing of the position of the tongue, soft palate and also the lips (when relevant)

At the end of each *What do I do habitually?* section, there is a coloured icon of a spanner. It suggests that you go straight to the same coloured icon in the *How do I change my habit?* section to help you 'fix' your habit

The grey icon of a speaker indicates an audio example along with its track number

This green icon of a pencil indicates that there is further practice material for this sound

How to Access the Accompanying Audio

Your purchase of this book includes free access to the accompanying audio to help you hear, imitate and practice. Listen privately on your phone, tablet, or computer in any podcast app.

> How To Unlock Your Audio?

Open the camera of your smart phone to scan the following QR code or visit the following webpage and following the instructions:

https://www.ashleyhoward.me/book-one-audio

Enter your email address accurately on the sign-up page.

You will then receive an email with your a private link (check your junk and spam folders).

Tap/click the link to open the audio in your favourite podcast app (works with Apple Podcasts, Spotify, Overcast and most podcast apps).

To start using the audio, cross reference the audio track numbers in the book with the same numbers used in the podcast app you're using.

Please remember that your private audio feed is provided free for purchasers of this book only. Please keep your link private and do not share it online. The audio is copyright © 2015 Ashley Howard. All rights reserved.

> Need any help?

For any help or technical support reach out at: ashley@ashleyhoward.me

Speech Anatomy

This is just a reference page, so refer to it when prompted.

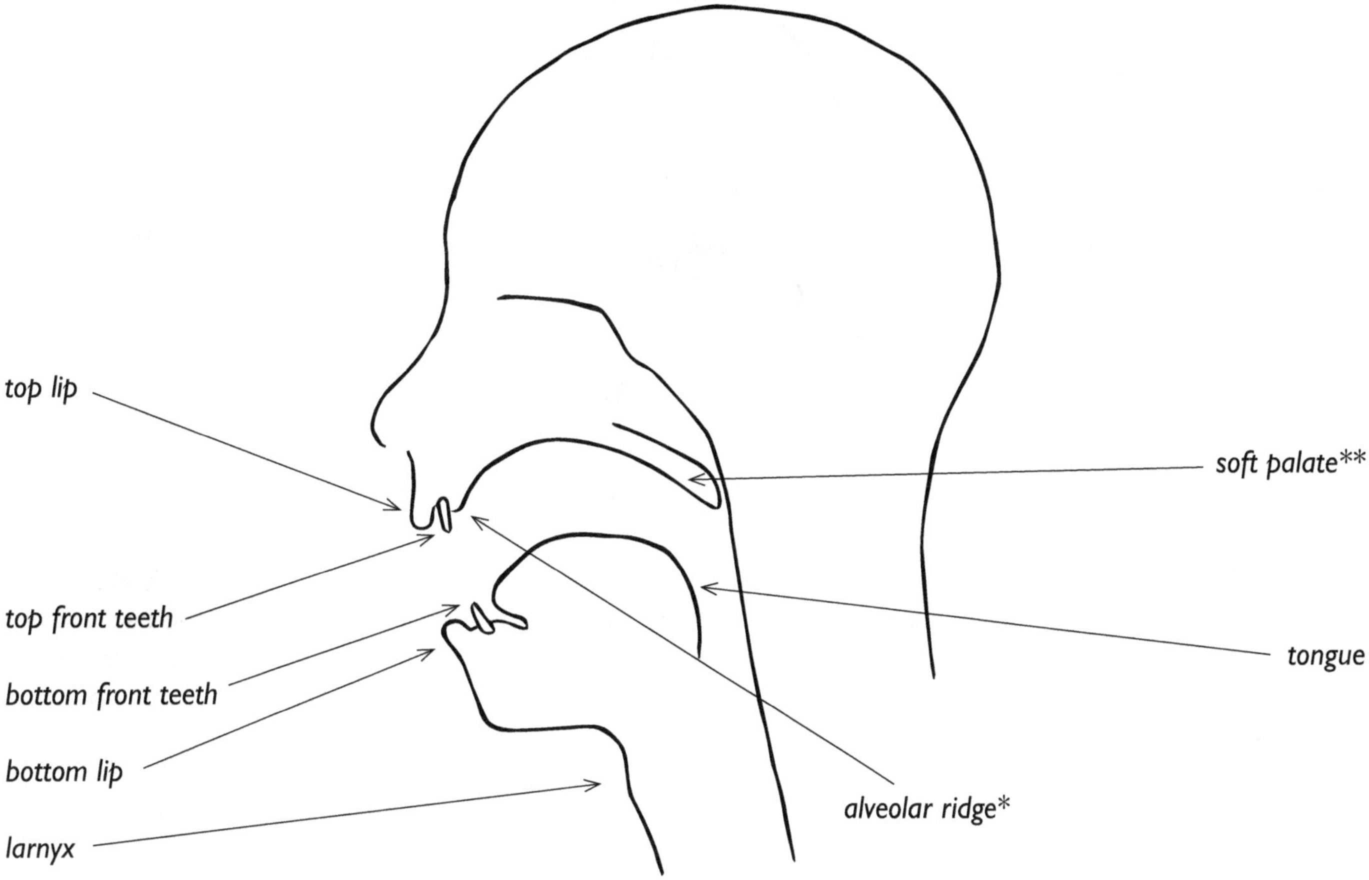

*Diagram labels: top lip, top front teeth, bottom front teeth, bottom lip, larynx, soft palate**, tongue, alveolar ridge**

* Alveolar ridge – The shape and prominence of the *alveolar ridge* can vary from person to person. To find this ridge, put the *tip of your tongue* on the back of your *upper front teeth* and then very slowly slide the *tongue tip* up and backwards along the *roof of your mouth* and you should feel a little bumpy ridge less than a centimetre away from your *upper teeth*. If you went further back, you would then feel the main curve of the *roof of your mouth*. The *tongue tip* should NOT touch the ridge, but simply be curling up towards it.

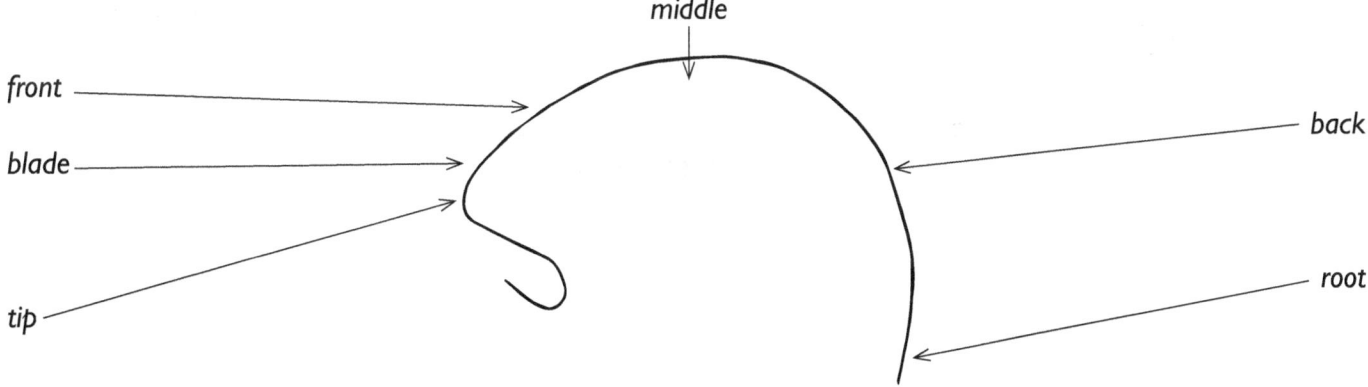

Tongue Divisions – As you can see, for the purpose of speech and articulation the tongue can be divided into different sections and each part can be used to make contact with different parts to make different sounds. Familiarise yourself with the following sections, which will be referred to, especially in the consonant section: *tip*, *blade*, *front*, *middle* and *back*.

Speech Anatomy

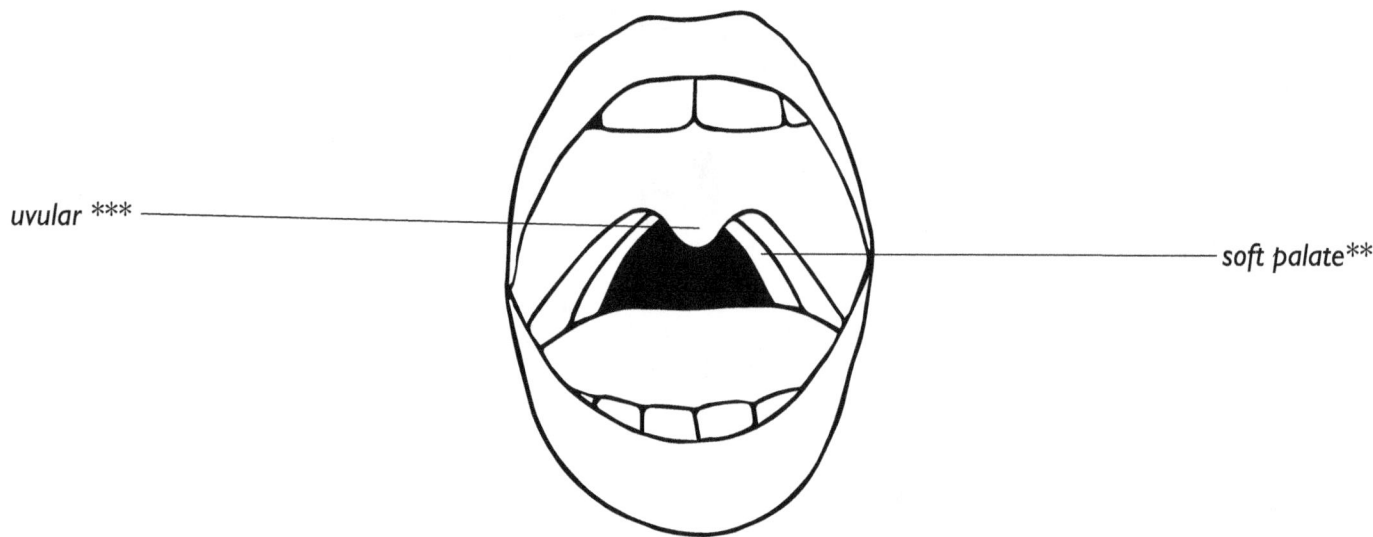

** Soft Palate – The *soft palate* is the part of the *roof of the mouth* towards the back that is soft. When you look into the *back of your mouth* you might see the *uvular* (the dangly thing in the middle at the back) which comes out of the *soft palate* but is not the *soft palate*. The *soft palate* is behind the *uvular*. One of its jobs in speech is to direct the vibrations of your voice into the *mouth* or *nose*. In speech there are four positions that it tends to be in:

1. When it is lifted high it blocks the entrance to the *nose*, and all the vibrations exit through the *mouth*.

2. When it is dropped low and the *back of the tongue* is raised so that they touch, all the vibrations travel through the *nose*.

3. When it is lifted high and the *back of the tongue* is raised so that they touch, the vibrations gather behind the *back of the tongue* and can only release once either the *tongue* or *soft palate* releases down.

4. When it is dropped low and the *back of the tongue* is also low the vibrations travel through the *nose* and the *mouth* (which produces a nasal quality to speech – some languages like French have certain vowel sounds that are nasal).

*** Uvular – the *uvular* is the dangly thing in the middle at the back that we often see when cartoon characters scream. It has no real function in speech. It seems to stimulate the gag reflex.

Vowels

My Pronunciation Roadmap

SCHWA	p.17	THOUGHT, NORTH, NEAR			p.74	
NURSE	p.21	FORCE	p.48	DRESS	p.78	
GOAT	p.26	CHOICE	p.53	FACE	p.82	
BATH, PALM, START	p.31	TRAP	p.57	SQUARE	p.86	
STRUT	p.35	MOUTH	p.61	GOOSE	p.90	
PRICE	p.39	FLEECE	p.65	FOOT	p.94	
LOT, CLOTH	p.43	KIT	p.70	CURE	p.98	

12

before you explore...

a b c d **e** f g h **i** j k l m n **o** p q r s t **u** v w x y z

As you are probably aware there are a total of twenty-six *letters* in the English Language, twenty-one of which are described as consonants and five as vowels: 'a', 'e', 'i', 'o' and 'u'. However, in terms of pronunciation, there are actually nineteen vowel *sounds* (twenty-five depending on how you look at them). So these five vowel *letters* are used in various combinations to represent this larger number of vowel *sounds*. Sometimes, the same vowel sound can be represented by different spellings: 'p<u>oo</u>r', 'p<u>ou</u>r', 'p<u>aw</u>' and 'p<u>o</u>re', for example, are actually pronounced with the same vowel sound *(p.48)*. Equally, the same spelling can be pronounced with different vowel sounds, as with 'ear' in words like 'w<u>ear</u>', '<u>ear</u>th', 'h<u>ear</u>' and 'h<u>ear</u>t'. So exploring vowel sounds is a lot to do with deprogramming the spelling and focusing on the sounds instead of the letters.

One way to describe the difference between vowel sounds and consonant sounds might be to say that vowel sounds are made by the articulators moving into different shapes and where vibration can always pass between them without any obstruction, as in vowel sounds like OO or AH or EE, whereas consonant sounds are made by the articulators touching or almost touching, as in consonant sounds like P or T or F or V. For this reason, vowel sounds are subtler. For example, you'll be asked to notice whether the tongue is *high*, *mid* (in the middle) or *low*, and *forward*, *centre* or *back*. In contrast, consonant sounds may by slightly simpler to understand and change, because you can actually feel the difference between, say, the *lips* coming together and releasing for a P sound in comparison to the *tongue tip* touching the *hard palate* for a T sound.

> How might I approach vowel sounds?

Treat each page like an actual coaching session: each page suggests how long to set aside. Take your time it. Read each part, record yourself when recommended and listen to the audio examples. Where appropriate, use a mirror to see what your habit might be. Play with each exercise and by the end you will hopefully know and feel what to aim for, what your habit is, how to change it and how to practice the new habit.

There are three aspects of vowel sounds that make a real difference in how they sound:

> *Length* – the duration of the sound.
> *Lips* – the shape of your lips.
> *Tongue* – the position and shape of your tongue.

> Length – the duration of the sound

Vowel sounds can be grouped into sounds that are *short* and sounds that are *long* in duration. The vowels in each group are all the same length, although some can feel slightly longer or shorter if they are followed by certain consonant sounds (which is explained in each section when relevant). Each of the pages in this section suggests the required length for each specific vowel sound, and gives exercises to assist you. When prompted, it might be useful to record yourself saying the words or sentences given. Listen back and compare yourself to the audio examples, and then use the exercises to guide you towards the correct length of the sound.

Short   k<u>i</u>t, dr<u>e</u>ss, tr<u>a</u>p, str<u>u</u>t, l<u>o</u>t, f<u>oo</u>t, comm<u>a</u>
Long   fl<u>ee</u>ce, n<u>ur</u>se, b<u>a</u>th, th<u>ough</u>t, g<u>oo</u>se, f<u>a</u>ce, pr<u>i</u>ce, ch<u>oi</u>ce, g<u>oa</u>t, m<u>ou</u>th, n<u>ear</u>, squ<u>are</u>, c<u>u</u>re

before you explore...

Changing the *length* of a vowel sound not only impacts on the pronunciation (and sometimes the meaning) of the word, but also the *rhythm* of speech *(book 3 - Intonation)* If a phrase has many words with long vowel sounds that are made short, the flow and rhythm of the phrase will sound very different.

> Lips – *the shape of your lips*

Vowel sounds can be grouped into sounds that are made with the *lips spread* (smiling), the *lips rounded* (pouting), or the *lips neutral* (resting in a relaxed, open position). Each of the pages in this section suggests the required *lip* shape for each specific vowel sound, and gives exercises to assist you. For this reason, it is essential to use a mirror to help you see as well as hear and feel the differences. When prompted, it might be useful to record yourself saying the words or sentences given. Listen back and compare yourself to the audio examples, and then use the exercises to guide you towards the correct length of the sound.

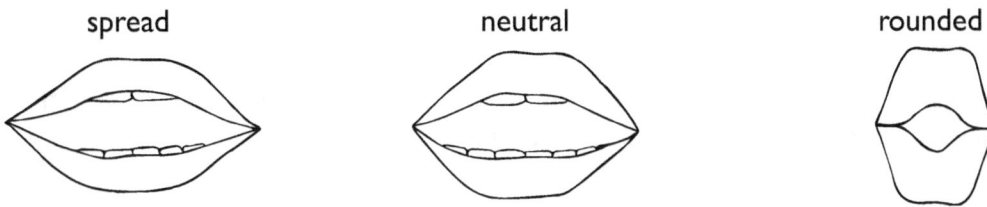

spread   neutral   rounded

Changing the shape of the *lips* for vowel sounds not only impacts on the pronunciation of the word, but also on the tone and quality. For example, try saying the words in each group above but change the shape of the *lips* and you may note a difference in quality.

There is one caveat when exploring the shapes of the lips. To suggest that when speaking in RP the *lips* must always adopt these specific shapes in order to accurately pronounce vowels, might make you feel self-conscious in conversation and might also make you look and feel slightly mannered.

Whilst it's important to notice the differences between your habitual *lip* positions in comparison to the suggested ones to help you more accurately achieve the tone and quality of each vowel sound, consider the suggested shapes for the lips as one part of the pronunciation jigsaw puzzle.

Once you have found the accurate tone and quality of each vowel sound, and practice regularly, the muscle memory of these differences will remain, and you need not focus on them in live communication, as it might be far too distracting and can lead to over-articulation that is unnatural and sounds forced.

before you explore...

> **Tongue – the position and shape of your tongue**

Aside from the shape and position of the *lips*, the shape and position of the *tongue* is perhaps the most influential on the vowel sound. In this book, the various positions of the *tongue* for vowel sounds are described as being *low*, in the *middle* or *high* and being in the *front*, *centre* or *back*.

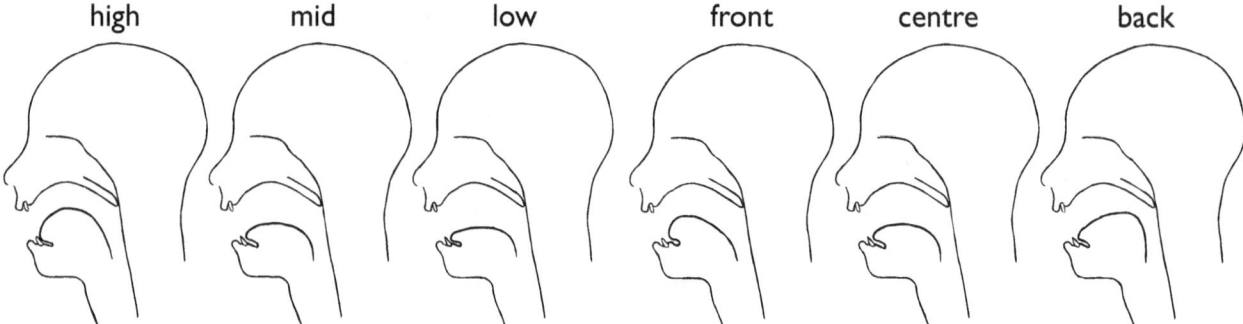

Each of the pages in this section suggests the typical shape and position for the *tongue* for each specific vowel sound, and gives exercises to assist you. Here is a typical phrase used to describe the position of the tongue:

"the *front of the tongue* is *high* in the *front of the mouth*"

So the first part, "the *front of the tongue*...", refers to the part of the *tongue*; "high" refers to the height of the *tongue* in the *mouth*; and "*front of the mouth*" refers to the part of the *mouth* the *tongue* is in. For this reason, it's almost essential to use a mirror to help you see as well as hear and feel the differences. I suggest using a very small torch, or angling yourself towards a light for some vowels, especially for those where the *back of the tongue* is raised and the *lips* are rounded. It should be easier to see the movement of your *tongue* for vowels that use the *front of the tongue* in the *front of the mouth*. When prompted, it might be useful to record yourself saying the words or sentences, to listen back and compare yourself to the audio examples, and then to use the exercises to guide you towards the correct shape and position for the *tongue*.

> **What about the Jaw?**

One challenge with vowel pronunciation in RP is that some vowel sounds (BATH *(p.31)* and STRUT *(p.35)* in particular) require a lot of vertical space in the mouth (space between the *tongue* and *roof of the mouth*). In the absence of being able to get your *tongue* to lie *low* and flat, an easier and quicker way to find this vertical space is to drop the *jaw* down and open. However, the *jaw* is not an articulator – it is essentially too clumsy and can make speech look laboured and forced. Each section has a subsection entitled *How is the ... vowel sound made in an RP accent?* in which the *jaw* is always described as needing to be loose with the *teeth* apart. If you discover that you rely on your *jaw* to articulate certain vowel sounds, you might play this game: repeat the relevant words or exercises but with the tip of your little finger between the *top* and *bottom front teeth*. Avoid biting your little finger, just let it rest gently between the *teeth* as you say the words. This might help you to monitor your *jaw* as well as encourage your *tongue* to do more of the work.

before you explore...

> ## *Lexical Sets*

Just before you explore vowel sounds, consider the difference between learning our first language and a second language. Most speakers tend to acquire their first language (their mother tongue) through imitation, experimentation and repetition. We watch and listen to those around us and copy the sounds they make and the way they make them in relationship to the context in which they are using them. So in this way, pronunciation is learnt aurally (and physically). But a second language tends to be learnt through the written word, which is mostly to do with a sort of intellectual memorisation. Therefore, many non-native speakers use the spelling of a word as a guide to its pronunciation. This might work out for some languages, but because British English is not written phonetically, one vowel sound can be represented by numerous spellings. For this reason, the spelling in British English cannot be trusted for vowel pronunciation. So, as I said before, exploring British English vowel sounds is a lot to do with deprogramming the spelling and focusing on the sounds instead of the letters.

So, the first question might be, 'how do I forget the spelling and pronounce a word accurately?'. Each of the vowel sections helps you to identify your pronunciation habits and gives exercises for how to change. This is the imitation and experimentation part of the process. In addition to this, some speakers find that certain spellings actually encourage them towards accurate pronunciation. Just as an exercise, consider rewriting a word using the spelling that helps. For example: if you find the spelling 'er' helps you to achieve an accurate pronunciation of the NURSE vowel sound (as in 'h<u>er</u>', 'st<u>er</u>n' and 'conc<u>er</u>n' p.21) consider rewriting words like 'w<u>or</u>k', 'h<u>ur</u>t' and 'sh<u>ir</u>t' (also pronounced with the NURSE vowel sound) as 'w<u>er</u>k', 'h<u>er</u>t' and 'sh<u>er</u>t'.

The second question might be, 'how do I know which vowel sound to use?'. The only way to be sure is to check words for their phonetic transcription in a reliable dictionary. Phonetics is a symbol system used to represent the pronunciation of a word. Each of the vowel sections provides you with the relevant phonetic symbol so that you can cross-reference accordingly. You do not need to know phonetics in order to improve your pronunciation but it might serve as a useful guide.

The last question might be 'how do I remember which vowel sound to use?'. Once you are certain which vowel sound to use, you can do what you did when you acquired your first language - practice building it into your muscle memory until it becomes habitual. Which means: repetition, repetition and more repetition. In addition to this, you can then start to create what I call a 'word bank'. Words can be grouped into what are known as *lexical sets* – which is to say that if the vowel in the *primary stressed syllable (book 3 - Intonation)* of a word rhymes with that of another word, they belong in the same group. For example, 'st<u>aff</u>', 'f<u>ar</u>' and 'c<u>al</u>m' are in the same *lexical set* because the main vowel sound in each word rhymes (*lexical sets* were created by phonetician John Wells) Native British English speakers know these groups instinctively, which is why speaking in RP is more about *sound* groups instead of *spelling* groups. I've started you off with a list of fifty or so words in each vowel section and there are more on each of the *practice pages (p.105)*. Expanding these *lexical sets* takes time, awareness and practice. Think of them as metaphoric pronunciation treasure troves: as you collect another word your trove increases and your fluency and accuracy improves. Consider starting a physical or digital *lexical sets* notebook, which you can add to throughout the coming days and weeks.

the Schwa

phonetic symbol - ə

20min

This sound is pronounced in words like:

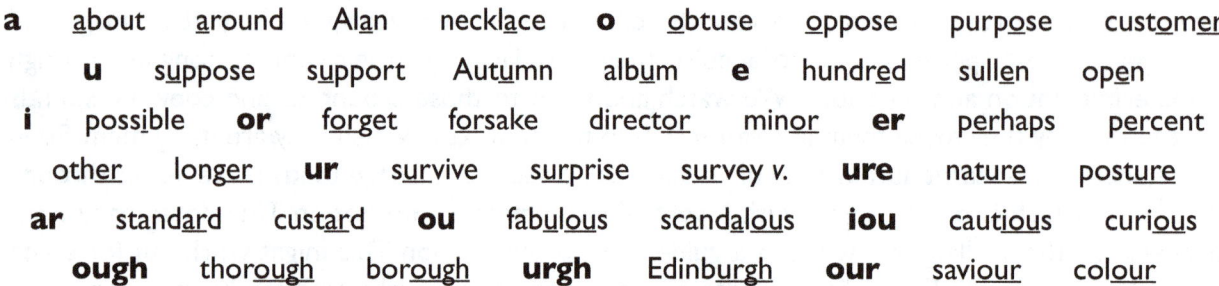

> **How is the SCHWA vowel sound made in an RP accent?**

This vowel sound can be described as the most common and the most neutral in RP. The *tongue tip* is behind the *bottom teeth* and the *middle of the tongue* is in the *middle* of the *centre of the mouth*. The *lips* are *neutral*, the *jaw* is loose and the *teeth* are apart. The SCHWA vowel sound is *short* in duration.

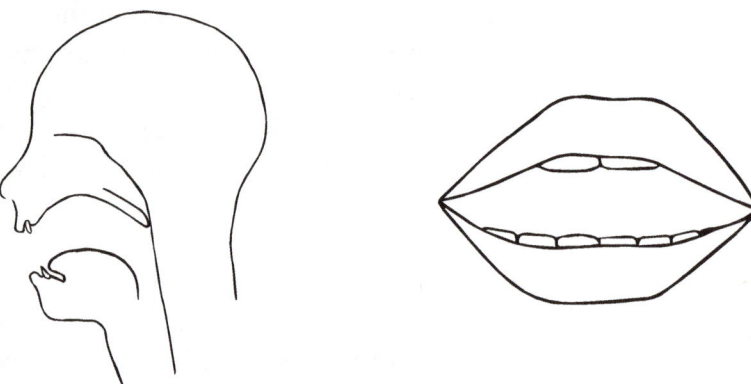

> **Remember this!**

The SCHWA is a vowel sound that has a specific role, which is to represent the vowel in a *weak/unstressed syllable(s)* (book 3 - Intonation) of most polysyllabic words, as in 'tun<u>a</u>', '<u>o</u>ffend' and '<u>a</u>nnounce', or the weak form of a grammatical word (book 3 - Intonation), as in 'th<u>e</u> car', '<u>a</u> cup <u>of</u> tea' and '<u>an</u> apple'. This means that it can spelt in many, many different ways and could be considered as one of the most frequently used vowel sounds in RP. For example, in the word '<u>abandonment</u>', the underlined letters are all pronounced as a SCHWA vowel sound. And the same is true for the underlined 'o', 'a' and 'er' in 'ph<u>o</u>togr<u>a</u>ph<u>er</u>'.

> **What do I do habitually?**

- *Are you pronouncing every written 'r'?*

If you are a *rhotic* speaker (book 2 - Consonants), your habit is to pronounce every written 'r'. The SCHWA vowel sound is often spelt with a written 'r', especially at the end of a word, as in 'oth<u>er</u>', 'weath<u>er</u>', 'mirr<u>or</u>', 'nat<u>ure</u>', 'col<u>our</u>' and 'doct<u>or</u>'. But RP is a *non-rhotic* accent so a written 'r' is only spoken when it is followed by a spoken vowel sound. Listen to the words above, firstly spoken with the R sound and then without, as they should be in RP. If you do this, go to

17

the Schwa

phonetic symbol - ə

- Are you replacing the SCHWA vowel sound with the STRUT or DRESS vowel sound?

Some speakers replace the SCHWA with the STRUT vowel sound *(p.35 - which is made with the middle of the tongue low in the centre of the mouth, and the lips equally as neutral)* or the DRESS vowel sound *(p.78 - which is made with the front of the tongue in the middle of the front of the mouth, and the lips slightly spread).* Listen to the following words, firstly spoken with the STRUT vowel sound, then the DRESS vowel sound, and then with the SCHWA vowel sound, as they should be in RP: 'oth<u>er</u>', 'weath<u>er</u>', 'mirr<u>or</u>', 'nat<u>ure</u>', 'col<u>our</u>' and 'doct<u>or</u>'. If you do this, go to

- Is your pronunciation guided by the spelling?

Many non-native speakers use the spelling of a word as a guide to its pronunciation. But because British English is not written phonetically, one vowel sound can be represented by numerous spellings. For this reason, the spelling in British English cannot be trusted for vowel pronunciation. For example, the SCHWA vowel sound can be represented as the 'er' in 'oth<u>er</u>', the 'or' in 'mirr<u>or</u>', the 'ure' in 'nat<u>ure</u>', the 'our' in 'col<u>our</u>', the 'a' in '<u>a</u>bout', the 'o' in '<u>o</u>btuse', the 'u' in 's<u>u</u>pport', the 'iou' in 'caut<u>iou</u>s' and many, many more. But all these words, despite the variation in spelling, are pronounced with the SCHWA vowel sound.

This tendency to pronounce a word with a vowel sound that you associate with the spelling, means that you might be pronouncing the 'a' in '<u>a</u>bout' with the TRAP vowel sound *(p.57 - as in 't<u>a</u>b')*, the 'o' in '<u>o</u>ppose' with the LOT vowel sound *(p.43 - as in '<u>o</u>pposite')*, the 'u' in 's<u>u</u>pport' with the STRUT vowel sound *(p.35 - as in 's<u>u</u>pper')*, and the 'e' in 'op<u>e</u>n' with the DRESS vowel sound *(p.78 as in 'p<u>e</u>n')*. But again, all these words, despite the variation in spelling, are pronounced with the SCHWA vowel sound. All of this might seem a bit overwhelming, but I have some simple and effective solutions that will help you: go to

> ## How do I change my habit?

 How do I avoid pronouncing a written 'r' that should not be pronounced?

There are some words that end with the SCHWA vowel sound that are not spelt with a written 'r', so it might be helpful to compare them to words that are. In RP, the 'a' in 'tun<u>a</u>' and the 'er' in 'tun<u>er</u>' are both pronounced with a SCHWA vowel sound. When saying, 'tun<u>er</u>', encourage your *tongue tip* to be behind your *bottom front teeth* after the 'n'. This way, the words rhyme with one another. Say the word 'tuna' before each of the following words, encouraging the *tongue tip* to stay down behind the *bottom front teeth* after the final consonant. Listen to the audio to help you imitate the sound accurately and watch your *tongue* in a mirror:

      tun<u>a</u>... oth<u>er</u>   weath<u>er</u>   mirr<u>or</u>   nat<u>ure</u>   col<u>our</u>   doct<u>or</u>   pap<u>er</u>   light<u>er</u>

 How do I find the accurate tongue position for the SCHWA vowel sound?

The SCHWA vowel sound is almost like the sound you might associate with a Neanderthal grunt – a sort of unformed, shapeless, language-less, neutral sound. It is *short* in duration, without any movement in the *lips*, and the *middle of the tongue* is in the *middle of the centre of the mouth*. The position of the *tongue* and *lips* for the SCHWA vowel sound is almost identical to their positions for the NURSE vowel sound *(p.21)*, so it might be helpful to compare them. Look in a mirror as you say 'h<u>er</u>' and 'lov<u>er</u>' (angle yourself towards

the Schwa

phonetic symbol - ə

a light or use a very small torch). It might be helpful to say the vowel sounds on their own after saying the words, in order to see the *tongue* more clearly. For 'h*er*' (the NURSE vowel sound) encourage the *lips* to be *neutral*, the *middle of the tongue* to be in the *middle* of the *centre of the mouth* and the sound to be *long* in duration. For 'lov*er*' (this is the target SCHWA vowel sound) encourage the *middle of the tongue* to be in the *middle* of the *centre of the mouth,* but the sound to be *short* in duration.

NURSE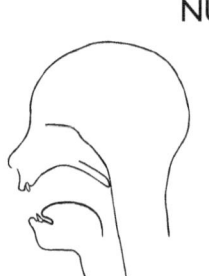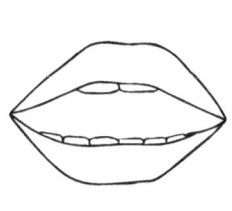

SCHWA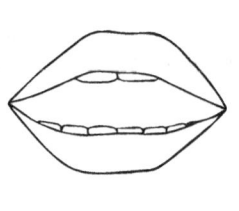

The SCHWA vowel sound in the 'v*er*' of 'lov*er*' should sound exactly the same as the 'v*er*' in the word 'v*er*anda'. Say 'lov*er*' then 'v*er*anda', encouraging the 'v*er*' in both words to sound identical.

Say the word 'h*er*' before each of the following words, encouraging your *lips* and the *middle of your tongue* to remain in the same positions for the SCHWA vowel sounds, which have been underlined. Encourage the sound to be *short* in duration. Listen to the audio to help you imitate the sound accurately:

h*er*... *a*bout neckl*a*ce *o*ppose custo*me*r s*u*pport A*u*tumn alb*u*m

hundr*e*d op*e*n poss*i*ble f*o*rget direct*or* p*er*cent long*er* s*u*rvive

s*ur*vey v. post*ure* stand*ar*d fab*u*lous cau*tious* thor*ough* bor*ough* savi*our*

Here's another game to play: say the SCHWA vowel sound on its own before saying each word, to help you hear whether or not you are pronouncing it accurately and also to give you a reference for how it should sound in the word. Listen to the audio to help you imitate the sound accurately:

*a*round Al*a*n *o*btuse purp*o*se s*u*ppose alb*u*m sull*e*n op*e*n

poss*i*ble f*o*rsake min*or* p*er*haps oth*er* s*ur*prise nat*ure*

cust*ar*d scand*a*lous cur*ious* thor*ough* Edinb*ur*gh col*our*

🔧 *How do I avoid being guided by the spelling?*

Once you have used the exercises above to help you achieve an accurate pronunciation of this vowel sound, go to the *Lexical Sets* subsection *(p.16)* for advice on how to avoid being guided by the spelling.

> Anything else?

The SCHWA vowel sound can also be heard in weak forms of grammatical words, like 'th*e*', 't*o*' and '*a*', which helps to find the rhythm and intonation of RP. This is fully explained in the subsection *The SCHWA in grammatical words (book 3 - Intonation).*

the Schwa

phonetic symbol - ə

🎙 *Practice words and typical spellings for the SCHWA vowel sound*

a about around ahead again ballad Alan necklace banana roundabout India England Nottingham **o** obtuse oppose offend official completely computer communicate consume conductor concern condition melon paddock purpose customer pantomime **u** suppose support suggest circus Autumn album perjury adventurer upon **e** hundred sullen open present *v.* present *n.* begin commitment **i** possible **or** doctor minor forget director forsake mirror author forbid actor sector juror Windsor major raptor manor doctor sailor **er** perhaps percent perceive heather singer other sister teacher brother longer father mower power yesterday eastern mother wonderland **ur** survive surprise survey *v.* **ure** nature posture **ar** burglar tankard custard standard standardise jeopardy calendar **ou** fabulous scandalous cautious ferrous glamorous Bournemouth curious curvaceous vicious marvellous boisterous disastrous gracious anxious **ough** thorough borough Scarborough Loughborough Middlesbrough **urgh** Edinburgh **our** harbour saviour succour colour

> **Bonus Material!**

Great news – there's a FREE online video about the SCHWA on my YouTube channel:

https://www.youtube.com/@ashleyhowardvoicecoach

⏱ 20min n**ur**se

phonetic symbol - 3ː

This sound is pronounced in words like:

er	t<u>er</u>m	det<u>er</u>	prefe<u>rr</u>ed	c<u>er</u>tain	**ur**	h<u>ur</u>t	p<u>ur</u>se	<u>ur</u>ge
	t<u>ur</u>n	p<u>urr</u>	**ir**	sh<u>ir</u>t	b<u>ir</u>d	fi<u>r</u>m	g<u>ir</u>l	**ear**	<u>ear</u>th
s<u>ear</u>ch	h<u>ear</u>d	<u>ear</u>n	**olo**	c<u>olo</u>nel	**or**	w<u>or</u>k	w<u>or</u>th	w<u>or</u>se	w<u>or</u>d
	our	adj<u>our</u>n	c<u>our</u>teous	j<u>our</u>nal	j<u>our</u>ney			

🔊 20

> **How is the NURSE vowel sound made in an RP accent?**

This vowel sound is like a longer version of the SCHWA *(p.17)*. The *tongue tip* is behind the *bottom teeth* and the *middle of the tongue* is in the *middle* of the *centre of the mouth*. The *lips* are *neutral*, the *jaw* is loose and the *teeth* are apart. The NURSE vowel sound is *long* in duration.

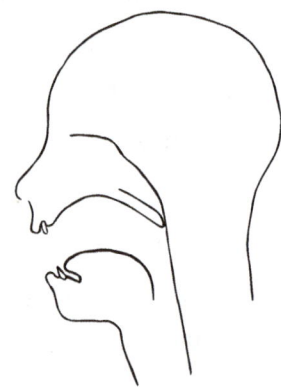
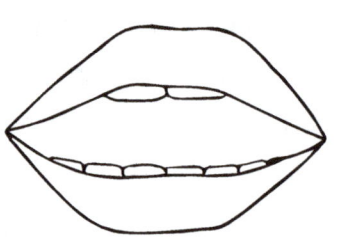

🔊 21

> **What do I do habitually?**

- Are you pronouncing every written 'r'?

If you are a *rhotic* speaker *(book 2 - Consonants)* your habit is to pronounce every written 'r'. The NURSE vowel sound is often spelt with a written 'r', as in 'term', 'hurt', 'shirt', 'earth' 'work' and 'journey'. But RP is a *non-rhotic* accent so a written 'r' is only pronounced when it is followed by a spoken vowel sound. Listen to the words above, firstly spoken with the R sound and then without, as they should be in RP. If you do this, go to 🔧

🔊 22

- Are your lips rounded or spread instead of neutral?

Some speakers have their *tongue* in an accurate position and make the sound *long* in duration, but their *lips* are *rounded* or *spread* instead of *neutral*, which changes the quality/tone of the sound. Listen to the following words, firstly spoken with the *lips rounded*, then *spread*, and then *neutral*, as they should be in RP: 'term', 'hurt', 'shirt', 'earth', 'colonel', 'work' and 'journey'. If you do this, go to 🔧

🔊 23

- Are you pronouncing the NURSE vowel sound too short?

Some speakers have their *tongue* and *lips* in an accurate position but they make the sound *short* in duration, instead of *long*, which impacts on the quality and tone of the sound. Listen to the following words, firstly spoken with the sound *short* in duration and then *long*, as they should be in RP: 'term', 'hurt', 'shirt', 'earth',

🔊 24

nurse

phonetic symbol - 3:

'c<u>o</u>lonel', 'w<u>or</u>k' and 'j<u>our</u>ney'. If you do this, go to 🔧

- Are you replacing the NURSE vowel sound with the THOUGHT vowel sound?

Some speakers replace the NURSE vowel sound with the THOUGHT vowel sound *(p.48)*, especially when it is spelt 'or' as in 'w<u>or</u>k' and 'w<u>or</u>d'. The THOUGHT vowel sound is made with the *back of the tongue* in the *middle* of the *back of the mouth*, the *lips rounded* and the sound equally as *long* in duration. So words like 'w<u>or</u>k' sound more like 'w<u>a</u>lk', and 'w<u>or</u>d' sounds more like 'w<u>ar</u>d'. If you do this, go to 🔧

- Are you replacing the NURSE vowel sound with the DRESS vowel sound?

Some speakers replace the NURSE vowel sound with the DRESS vowel sound *(p.78)*, especially when it is spelt 'e' as in 't<u>e</u>rm' and 'c<u>e</u>rtain'. The DRESS vowel sound is made with the *front of the tongue* in the *middle* of the *front of the mouth*, the *lips* slightly *spread* and the sound *short* in duration. So words like 'b<u>er</u>th' sound more like 'B<u>e</u>th'. Of those that do this, some stretch the DRESS vowel sound and make it *longer*, so 'h<u>er</u>' might sound slightly more like 'h<u>air</u>'. If you do this, go to 🔧

- Are you replacing the NURSE vowel sound with the STRUT vowel sound?

Some speakers replace the NURSE vowel sound with the STRUT vowel sound *(p.35)*, especially when it is spelt 'ur' as in 'h<u>ur</u>t' and '<u>ur</u>ge'. The STRUT vowel sound is made with the *middle of the tongue low* the *centre of the mouth*, the *lips* equally as *neutral* and the sound *short* in duration. So words like 'h<u>ur</u>t' sound more like 'h<u>u</u>t'. Of those that do this, some stretch the STRUT vowel sound and make it *longer*, so 'h<u>ur</u>t' might sound slightly more like 'h<u>ear</u>t'. If you do this, go to 🔧

- Is your pronunciation guided by the spelling?

Many non-native speakers use the spelling of a word as a guide to its pronunciation. But because British English is not written phonetically, one vowel sound can be represented by numerous spellings. For this reason, the spelling in British English cannot be trusted for vowel pronunciation. For example, the NURSE vowel sound can be represented as the 'er' in 'h<u>er</u>', 'ear' in '<u>ear</u>th', the 'ir' in 'sh<u>ir</u>t', the 'or' in 'w<u>or</u>k', the 'our' in 'j<u>our</u>ney', the 'olo' in 'c<u>o</u>lonel', the 'ur' in 'h<u>ur</u>t', and the 'yr' in 'm<u>yr</u>tle'. So, you might mistakenly pronounce the 'ear' in '<u>ear</u>th' as the NEAR vowel sound *(p.74 - as in '<u>ear</u>')*. But all these words, despite the variation in spelling, are pronounced with the NURSE vowel sound.

It is also typical for a speaker to have a certain spelling that they often associate with a vowel sound. For example, many speakers associate the spelling 'er' with the NURSE vowel sound. One might then hope that all words spelt with 'er' would be pronounced as the NURSE vowel sound. Sadly, this is not true, as the 'er' in 'p<u>er</u>haps' should be pronounced as the SCHWA vowel sound *(p.17 - as in 'tun<u>a</u>')*, and in 's<u>er</u>geant' it is pronounced as the BATH vowel sound *(p.31 - as in 'f<u>ar</u>')*. All of this might seem a bit overwhelming, but I have some simple and effective solutions that will help you: go to 🔧

nurse

phonetic symbol - ɜː

> ## How do I change my habit?

🔧 *How do I avoid pronouncing a written 'r' that should not be pronounced?*

Firstly, encourage your *tongue tip* to stay down, touching behind the *bottom front teeth* when you are saying the vowel sound. Secondly, unless the vowel sound is followed by another consonant, encourage the *tongue* to stay completely still throughout, avoiding any movement at the end of the sound. When it is followed by a consonant that needs the *tongue tip*, encourage the *tongue* to move directly to the position for that consonant, and not to pronounce an R sound just before. And lastly, remember that the NURSE vowel sound is made in almost exactly the same way as a SCHWA vowel sound, as in 'tun**a**' *(p.17)*, the only difference being that it is *longer* in duration. Providing that you are accurately pronouncing the SCHWA vowel sound, it might be helpful to say a word like 'tun**a**' before saying the following words, to help you find the accurate *tongue* position. Listen to the audio to help you imitate the sound accurately and watch your *tongue* in a mirror:

tun**a**… h**er**   s**ir**   w**ere**   f**ur**   p**urr**   v**er**b   m**ur**mur   b**ur**n   l**ear**n   wh**ir**l

30

🔧 *How do I encourage my lips to be neutral?*

The only way to guarantee that your *lips* are *neutral* instead of being *spread* or *rounded* is to use a mirror when you practice. Otherwise, you can feel the movement in your *lips* by putting one finger in a vertical line over your *lips* – if your *lips* are rounding your finger will be pushed forwards; and if your *lips* are *neutral* or slightly *spreading* your finger will remain still. Say the following words, either looking in a mirror or with one finger on your *lips*, and encourage them to be *neutral*:

c**er**tain   p**ur**se   h**ur**t   sh**ir**t   s**ear**ch   c**o**lonel   j**our**nal   j**our**ney

31

For words like 'w**or**k' and 'w**or**th', your *lips* should round for the W consonant sound *(book 2 - Consonants)* but then release into *neutral* for the NURSE vowel sound.

32

🔧 *How do I find the accurate tongue position for the NURSE vowel sound?*

The position of the *tongue* and *lips* for the NURSE vowel sound is similar to their positions for the STRUT vowel sound *(p.35)* and DRESS vowel sound *(p.78)*, so it might be helpful to compare them. Look in a mirror as you say 'h**u**t', 'h**ur**t' and 'h**ea**d' (angle yourself towards a light or use a very small torch). It might be helpful to say the vowel sounds on their own after saying the words, in order to see the *tongue* more clearly. For 'h**u**t' (the STRUT vowel sound) encourage the *lips* to be *neutral*, the *middle of the tongue* to be *low* in the *centre of the mouth* and the sound to be *short* in duration. For 'h**ur**t' (this is the target NURSE vowel sound) encourage the *lips* to be equally as *neutral*, the *middle of the tongue* to be in the *middle of the centre of the mouth* and the sound to be *long* in duration. And for 'h**ea**d' (the DRESS vowel sound) encourage the *lips* to be slightly *spread*, the *front of the tongue* to be in the *middle of the front of the mouth* and the sound to be *short* in duration.

33

nurse

phonetic symbol - 3:

STRUT   **NURSE**   DRESS

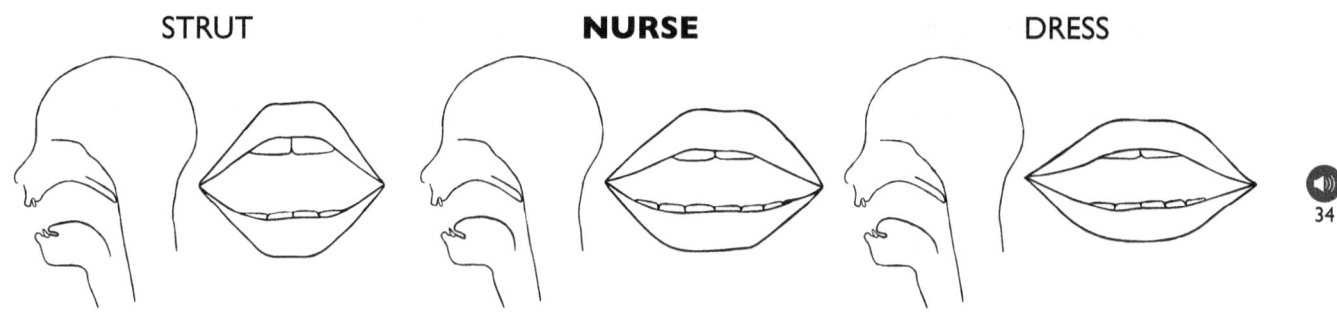

🔊 34

This STRUT, NURSE and DRESS vowel sound sequence can be heard in the following sets of three words. Play with these words and encourage the *middle of your tongue* to remain in between the positions for the STRUT and DRESS vowel sounds. Encourage the *lips* to be *neutral* and the sound to be *long* in duration. Listen to the audio to help you imitate the sound accurately:

       h<u>u</u>t   h<u>ur</u>t   h<u>ea</u>d   c<u>u</u>t   K<u>ur</u>t   K<u>e</u>n   p<u>u</u>tt   p<u>er</u>t   p<u>e</u>t   l<u>u</u>ck   l<u>ur</u>k   l<u>e</u>g

🔊 35

If your habit is to replace the NURSE vowel sound with the DRESS vowel sound, essentially, your *tongue* position is too far *forward*. For this reason, it might be helpful to say words with the THOUGHT vowel sound (which is made with the *tongue* in the *back of the mouth*) before saying words with the NURSE vowel sound, in order to encourage your *tongue* into a more *central* position. For example:

       h<u>oa</u>rd   h<u>ea</u>rd   c<u>or</u>d   K<u>ur</u>t   p<u>or</u>t   p<u>er</u>t   f<u>ou</u>r   f<u>ur</u>   p<u>aw</u>   p<u>urr</u>

🔊 36

Similarly, if your habit is to replace the NURSE vowel sound with the THOUGHT or STRUT vowel sound, then your *tongue* position is too far *back* or too *low*. For this reason, it might be helpful to say words with the DRESS vowel sound (which is made with the *tongue* in the *front of the mouth*) before saying words with the NURSE vowel sound, in order to encourage your *tongue* into a more *central* position. For example:

       h<u>ea</u>d   h<u>ea</u>rd   K<u>e</u>n   K<u>ur</u>t   p<u>e</u>t   p<u>er</u>t   L<u>e</u>n   l<u>ear</u>n   p<u>e</u>ck   p<u>er</u>k

🔊 37

Lastly, here's another game to play: say the NURSE vowel sound on its own before saying each word, to help you hear whether or not you are pronouncing it accurately and also to give you a reference for how it should sound in the word. Listen to the audio to help you imitate the sound accurately:

       er... pref<u>e</u>rred   c<u>er</u>tain   h<u>ur</u>t   p<u>ur</u>se   sh<u>ir</u>t   f<u>ir</u>m   s<u>ear</u>ch

       h<u>ear</u>d   c<u>o</u>lonel   w<u>or</u>k   w<u>or</u>th   j<u>our</u>nal   j<u>our</u>ney

 38

🔧 *How do I avoid being guided by the spelling?*

Once you have used the exercises above to help you achieve an accurate pronunciation of this vowel sound, go to the *Lexical Sets* subsection *(p.16)* for advice on how to avoid being guided by the spelling.

nurse

phonetic symbol - 3:

🎙 *Practice words and typical spellings for the NURSE vowel sound*

er	h<u>er</u>	tw<u>er</u>p	ass<u>er</u>t	j<u>er</u>k	p<u>er</u>ch	b<u>er</u>th	t<u>er</u>se	v<u>er</u>b	em<u>er</u>ge	n<u>er</u>ve
t<u>er</u>m	st<u>er</u>n	det<u>er</u>	pref<u>er</u>red	c<u>er</u>tain	p<u>er</u>son	imm<u>er</u>sion	em<u>er</u>gency			
k<u>er</u>nel	**ur**	n<u>ur</u>ture	us<u>ur</u>p	n<u>ur</u>se	h<u>ur</u>t	ch<u>ur</u>ch	t<u>ur</u>f	p<u>ur</u>se	c<u>ur</u>b	c<u>ur</u>d
<u>ur</u>ge	c<u>ur</u>ve	f<u>ur</u>ze	t<u>ur</u>n	c<u>ur</u>l	sp<u>ur</u>	occ<u>ur</u>red	b<u>ur</u>nt	b<u>ur</u>st	m<u>ur</u>der	
f<u>ur</u>ther	**urr**	p<u>urr</u>	**ir**	v<u>ir</u>tual	sh<u>ir</u>t	<u>ir</u>k	b<u>ir</u>ch	b<u>ir</u>th	b<u>ir</u>d	d<u>ir</u>ge
f<u>ir</u>m	g<u>ir</u>l	st<u>ir</u>red	f<u>ir</u>st	c<u>ir</u>cus	v<u>ir</u>tue	**yr**	m<u>yr</u>rh	m<u>yr</u>tle	B<u>yr</u>ne	
ear	<u>ear</u>th	s<u>ear</u>ch	h<u>ear</u>d	<u>ear</u>n	y<u>ear</u>n	<u>ear</u>l	p<u>ear</u>l	reh<u>ear</u>sal	<u>ear</u>ly	
<u>ear</u>nest	l<u>ear</u>n	**o**	c<u>o</u>lonel	**or**	w<u>or</u>k	w<u>or</u>th	w<u>or</u>se	w<u>or</u>d	w<u>or</u>m	
w<u>or</u>st	w<u>or</u>thy	**our**	sc<u>our</u>ge	adj<u>our</u>n	c<u>our</u>teous	j<u>our</u>nal	j<u>our</u>nalist	j<u>our</u>ney		

🎙 *Practice Sentences for the NURSE vowel sound*

- What a j<u>our</u>ney. I arrived <u>ear</u>ly in B<u>ir</u>mingham! That's a f<u>ir</u>st! Have you h<u>ear</u>d from B<u>er</u>tha?
- I w<u>or</u>ked on Th<u>ur</u>sday to <u>ear</u>n some extra cash. I'm b<u>ur</u>nt out! I'm s<u>ear</u>ching for a different job!
- He is c<u>er</u>tainly p<u>er</u>sonable, but is he det<u>er</u>mined enough? I've h<u>ear</u>d he can get very n<u>er</u>vous.
- The c<u>ir</u>cus was awesome. Our g<u>ir</u>ls loved it! It's w<u>or</u>th coming to. It's f<u>ir</u>st come f<u>ir</u>st s<u>er</u>ved.

Am I pronouncing it accurately?

Get a personalised assessment of every vowel, consonant and aspect of intonation to find out
how well you're doing, exactly what to focus on and what you need to do
to speak in this accent accurately and naturally:

https://www.ashleyhoward.me/pronunciation-evaluation

⏰ 20min

goat
phonetic symbol - əʊ

This sound is pronounced in words like:

| **oa** | s**oa**p | c**oa**t | l**oa**f | r**oa**d | **o_e** | n**o**te | j**o**ke | c**o**de | t**o**ne | **o** | s**o** | n**o** |

d**o**n't   **o**nly   **ow**   **ow**n   kn**ow**   gr**ow**   **ow**e   **ough**   d**ough**   th**ough**

alth**ough**   **o**ther   br**oo**ch   b**eau**   g**au**che   m**au**ve   t**oe**   f**oe**   s**ew**

41

> ### How is the GOAT vowel sound made in an RP accent?

The GOAT vowel sound is a *diphthong* – a combination of two vowel sounds where one slides into the other. The GOAT vowel sound starts as the SCHWA vowel sound *(p.17)* (where the *tongue tip* is behind the *bottom teeth*, the *middle of the tongue* is in the *middle* of the *centre of the mouth*, and the *lips* are *neutral*) which slides into a slightly *shorter* version of the GOOSE vowel sound *(p.90* - where the *tongue tip* stays behind the *bottom teeth,* the *back of the tongue* slides *high* and *backwards* into the *back of the mouth,* and the *lips* round). The *jaw* is loose, the *teeth* are apart, and the sound is *long* in duration.

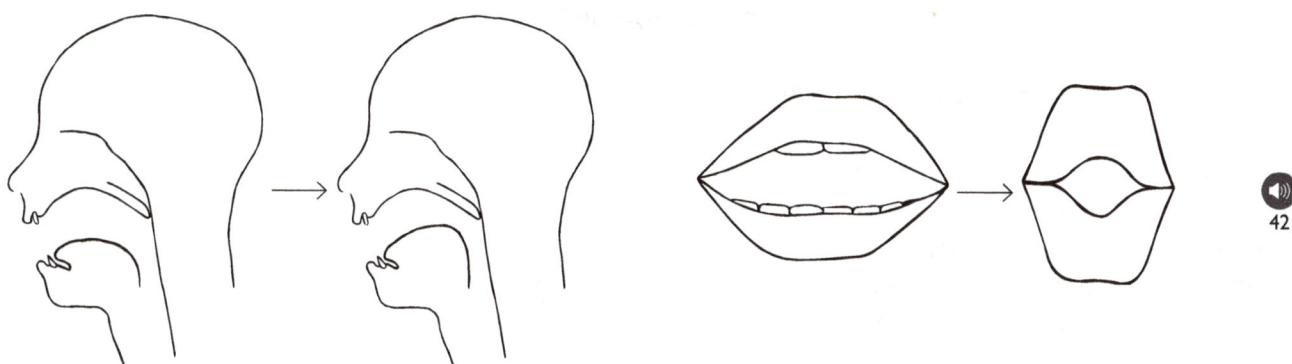

42

> ### What do I do habitually?

- Do your lips remain rounded, neutral or spread throughout the whole diphthong?

Some speakers move their *tongue* through the accurate positions and make the sound *long* in duration, but their *lips* remain *rounded, neutral* or *spread* throughout instead of sliding from *neutral* to *rounded,* which impacts on the quality and tone of the sound. Listen to the following words, firstly spoken with the *lips rounded,* then *neutral,* then *spread,* and then sliding from *neutral* to *rounded,* as they should be in RP: 'soap', 'note', 'so', 'own', 'owe', 'although', 'brooch', 'beau', 'mauve', 'toe' and 'sew'. If you do this, go to

43

- Are you making this diphthong too short or too long in duration?

Some speakers move their *tongue* and *lips* through the accurate positions but they make the *diphthong* too *short* or too *long* in duration, which impacts on the quality and tone of the sound. If you are making the *diphthong* too *long,* either both vowel sounds in the *diphthong* will be too *long,* which will make it sound like two *syllables* instead of one, or one of the vowel sounds in the *diphthong* will be too *long.* Listen to the following words, firstly spoken with the *diphthong* too *short* in duration, then with both vowel sounds too *long,* then with the first vowel sound too *long,* then with the second vowel sound too *long,* and finally as they should be in RP: 'soap', 'note', 'so', 'own', 'owe', 'although', 'brooch', 'beau', 'mauve', 'toe' and 'sew'. If you do this, go to

44

goat

phonetic symbol - əʊ

- Are you replacing the first vowel sound with the THOUGHT vowel sound?

Some speakers replace the first vowel sound (SCHWA) with the THOUGHT vowel sound *(p.48)*, which is made with the *back of the tongue* in the *middle* of the *back of the mouth*, the *lips rounded* and the sound *long* in duration. Listen to the following words, firstly spoken with the THOUGHT vowel sound at the beginning of this *diphthong* and then with the SCHWA vowel sound at the beginning, as they should be in RP: 's<u>oa</u>p', 'n<u>o</u>te', 's<u>o</u>', '<u>ow</u>n', '<u>ow</u>e', 'alth<u>ough</u>', 'br<u>oo</u>ch', 'b<u>eau</u>', 'm<u>au</u>ve', 't<u>oe</u>' and 's<u>ew</u>'. If you think you do this, then go to 🔧

- Are you replacing the first vowel sound with the LOT vowel sound?

Some speakers replace the first vowel sound (SCHWA) with the LOT vowel sound *(p.43)*, which is made with the *back of the tongue low* in the *back of the mouth*, the *lips* slightly *rounded* and the sound *short* in duration. Listen to the following words, firstly spoken with the LOT vowel sound at the beginning of this *diphthong* and then with the SCHWA vowel sound at the beginning, as they should be in RP: 's<u>oa</u>p', 'n<u>o</u>te', 's<u>o</u>', '<u>ow</u>n', '<u>ow</u>e', 'alth<u>ough</u>', 'br<u>oo</u>ch', 'b<u>eau</u>', 'm<u>au</u>ve', 't<u>oe</u>' and 's<u>ew</u>'. If you do this, go to 🔧

- Are you replacing the first vowel sound with the STRUT vowel sound?

Some speakers replace the first vowel sound (SCHWA) with the STRUT vowel sound *(p.35)*, which is made with the *middle of the tongue low* in the *centre of the mouth*, the *lips neutral* and the sound *short* in duration. Listen to the following words, firstly spoken with the STRUT vowel sound at the beginning of this *diphthong* and then with the SCHWA vowel sound at the beginning, as they should be in RP: 's<u>oa</u>p', 'n<u>o</u>te', 's<u>o</u>', '<u>ow</u>n', '<u>ow</u>e', 'alth<u>ough</u>', 'br<u>oo</u>ch', 'b<u>eau</u>', 'm<u>au</u>ve', 't<u>oe</u>' and 's<u>ew</u>'. If you do this, go to 🔧

- Is your pronunciation guided by the spelling?

Many non-native speakers use the spelling of a word as a guide to its pronunciation. But because British English is not written phonetically, one vowel sound can be represented by numerous spellings. For this reason, the spelling in British English cannot be trusted for vowel pronunciation. For example, the GOAT vowel sound can be represented as the 'oo' in 'br<u>oo</u>ch', the 'ou' in 's<u>ou</u>l', the 'oe' in 't<u>oe</u>', the 'ow' in 'kn<u>ow</u>', the 'ough' in 'alth<u>ough</u>', the 'o_e' in 'h<u>o</u>me', the 'oa' in 'r<u>oa</u>d', the 'eau' in 'b<u>eau</u>', the 'ew' in 's<u>ew</u>' and the 'au' in 'm<u>au</u>ve'. So, you might mistakenly pronounce the 'oo' in 'br<u>oo</u>ch' as the GOOSE vowel sound *(p.90 - as in 'f<u>oo</u>d')*. But all these words, despite the variation in spelling, are pronounced with the GOAT vowel sound.

It is also typical for a speaker to have a certain spelling that they often associate with a vowel sound. For example, many speakers associate the spelling 'o' with the GOAT vowel sound. One might then hope that all words spelt with 'o' would be pronounced as the GOAT vowel sound. Sadly, this is not true, as the 'o' in the plural of 'w<u>o</u>men' should be pronounced as the KIT vowel sound *(p.70 - as in '<u>i</u>t')*, in 'd<u>o</u>ne' it is pronounced as the STRUT vowel sound *(p.35 - as in 'c<u>u</u>p')*, in the singular of 'w<u>o</u>men' it is pronounced as the FOOT vowel sound *(p.94 - as in 'p<u>u</u>t')*, in 'st<u>o</u>p' it is pronounced as the LOT vowel sound *(p.43 - as in '<u>o</u>n')*, in '<u>o</u>ffend' it is pronounced as the SCHWA vowel sound *(p.17 - as in 't<u>u</u>na')*, and in 'd<u>o</u>' it is pronounced as the GOOSE vowel sound *(p.90 - as in 'f<u>oo</u>d')*. All of this might seem a bit overwhelming, but I have some simple and effective solutions that will help you: go to 🔧

goat

phonetic symbol - əʊ

> How do I change my habit?

 How do I find the accurate tongue position for the GOAT vowel sound?

Firstly, ensure that you are accurately pronouncing the two component vowel sounds in this *diphthong* by following the exercises in the sections entitled *How do I find the accurate tongue position for the SCHWA vowel sound? (p.18)* and *How do I find the accurate tongue position for the GOOSE vowel sound? (p.88)*.

Once you feel confident with how to make each vowel sound, your *tongue* needs to slide from one into the other to make the *diphthong*. Say each sound on its own, one after the other, with a brief pause between them. Watch your *tongue* and *lips* in a mirror and then take out the pause, sliding them into one another. All *diphthongs* are made with the first vowel slightly more *stressed* than the second. This being said, it is only *slightly* more *stressed* and should be observed with care. And remember that the two vowel sounds in a *diphthong* make a single *syllable*: the *tongue* slides smoothly but swiftly and the sound is *long*, but not too *long*.

Play with the following exercise. It offers you an opportunity to check whether you are accurately pronouncing the first vowel sound in the *diphthong* – the SCHWA (which has been written as 'er' and *rhotic* speakers must remember to avoid pronouncing the written 'r'). Listen to the audio to help you imitate the sound accurately.

| ser... s<u>oa</u>p | ner... n<u>o</u>te | ser... s<u>o</u> | er... <u>ow</u>n | er... <u>ow</u>e | alther... alth<u>ou</u>gh |
| brer... br<u>oo</u>ch | ber... b<u>eau</u> | mer... m<u>au</u>ve | ter... t<u>oe</u> | ser... s<u>ew</u> | |

50

 How do I avoid being guided by the spelling?

Once you have used the exercises above to help you achieve an accurate pronunciation of this vowel sound, go to the *Lexical Sets* subsection *(p.16)* for advice on how to avoid being guided by the spelling.

> Anything Else?

- The difference between GOAT (əʊ) and GOAL (oʊ)

When the GOAT vowel sound is followed by a *dark L (book 2 - Consonants)* - a written L that is followed by a consonant sound or by a pause) most RP speakers pronounce the first vowel sound more like the LOT vowel sound *(p.43 -* as in 'h<u>o</u>t'), instead of the SCHWA vowel sound *(p.17)*. This can be heard in words like 's<u>ou</u>l', '<u>o</u>ld', 'b<u>ow</u>l' and 'h<u>o</u>le'.

51

You may not see these words being transcribed in even the most reliable of dictionaries, but most RP speakers now use this *diphthong* – oʊ. Whilst you may still hear some speakers using the əʊ *diphthong* in these specific types of words, it is considered as a more traditional or historic pronunciation, often associated with older speakers. If you choose to continue using the GOAT instead of GOAL pronunciation for words like these, you will still be clearly understood, and your pronunciation will lie within the RP canon.

goat

phonetic symbol - əʊ

Play with the following exercise. It offers you an opportunity to check whether you are accurately pronouncing the first vowel sound in the *diphthong*. Listen to the audio to help you imitate the sound accurately:

so… s<u>ou</u>l   o… <u>o</u>ld   bo… b<u>ow</u>l   ho… h<u>o</u>le   ro… r<u>o</u>ll   po… p<u>o</u>le   co… c<u>oa</u>l

vo… v<u>o</u>le   po… p<u>ou</u>ltry   co… c<u>o</u>ld   so… s<u>o</u>ld   mo… m<u>ou</u>ld   sho… sh<u>ou</u>lder

52

- The LOWER triphthong: phonetic symbol əʊə

There are five of the eight *diphthongs* that can be extended with a final SCHWA vowel sound *(p.17)*, which turns the *diphthong* into a *triphthong* – a combination of three vowel sounds where one slides into another. The GOAT vowel sound is one such *diphthong*, so words like '<u>lower</u>', 'm<u>ower</u>' and 'G<u>oa</u>' are pronounced with the GOAT vowel sound followed by a SCHWA vowel sound. The *lips* relax back to *neutral* and the *tongue* slides from being in the *back of the mouth* to the *middle* of the *centre of the mouth*.

53

Some RP speakers add a W sound *(book 2 - Consonants)* to link the GOAT vowel sound to the SCHWA vowel sound. This makes words like '<u>lower</u>', 'm<u>ower</u>' and 'G<u>oa</u>' sound like two *syllable* words instead of one. In this version, the *lips round* too much at the end of the *diphthong* and then release quite suddenly into the SCHWA. Other speakers do not add a W sound. Instead, they make the transition of their *lips* from the GOAT vowel sound to the SCHWA vowel sound much more smoothly. This makes the words above sound more like one *syllable*.

54

This variation in pronunciation is in part to do with the evolving nature of accents. And unfortunately these variations are not accounted for in a reliable dictionary. In some ways, this ambiguity could be seen as a frustrating, but another perspective would be to say that is allows for choice, as both are considered correct. Listen to the following words, firstly spoken with the W sound and then without:

l<u>ower</u>   m<u>ower</u>   G<u>oa</u>   N<u>oah</u>   Sam<u>oa</u>   b<u>oa</u>   sl<u>ower</u>   thr<u>ower</u>   bl<u>ower</u>

55

And lastly, many words with these *triphthongs* have a written 'r' in the spelling, which should not be spoken, unless they are followed by a spoken vowel sound *(book 2 - Consonants)*. Encourage your *tongue tip* to remain down, touching the *bottom front teeth* at the end of the *triphthong*.

Practice words and typical spellings for the GOAT vowel sound

oa	s<u>oa</u>p	c<u>oa</u>t	b<u>oa</u>t	<u>oa</u>k	r<u>oa</u>ch	fl<u>oa</u>t	<u>oa</u>f	l<u>oa</u>f	r<u>oa</u>d	m<u>oa</u>t	l<u>oa</u>the
r<u>oa</u>m	l<u>oa</u>n	b<u>oa</u>st	c<u>oa</u>x	**o_e**	n<u>o</u>te	r<u>o</u>pe	j<u>o</u>ke	r<u>o</u>be	c<u>o</u>de	gr<u>ove</u>	
cl<u>o</u>se	r<u>o</u>se	<u>o</u>zone	h<u>o</u>me	t<u>o</u>ne	expl<u>o</u>de	**o**	s<u>o</u>	n<u>o</u>	d<u>o</u>n't	h<u>o</u>st	
<u>o</u>nly	b<u>o</u>th	gr<u>o</u>ss	n<u>o</u>ble	<u>o</u>cean	expl<u>o</u>sion	er<u>o</u>sion	h<u>o</u>ly	r<u>o</u>gue	<u>o</u>ver		
ow	<u>ow</u>n	kn<u>ow</u>	gl<u>ow</u>	gr<u>ow</u>	<u>owe</u>	<u>Ow</u>en	fl<u>ow</u>n	**ough**	d<u>ough</u>		
th<u>ough</u>	alth<u>ough</u>	**other spellings**	br<u>oo</u>ch	b<u>eau</u>	g<u>au</u>che	m<u>au</u>ve	t<u>oe</u>	s<u>ew</u>			

56

29

goat

phonetic symbol - əʊ

🎤 Practice Sentences for the GOAT vowel sound

- Tell <u>O</u>wen that I w<u>o</u>n't be back until late. I'll leave a n<u>o</u>te as well. D<u>o</u>n't forget.
- She <u>ow</u>es me money. I'm g<u>o</u>ing to ph<u>o</u>ne her after work. Her t<u>o</u>ne of voice is s<u>o</u> condescending.
- Do you kn<u>ow</u> Fi<u>o</u>na? She <u>ow</u>ns a gl<u>o</u>bal marketing firm. I'm g<u>o</u>ing <u>o</u>ver tonight - come with me.
- The r<u>oa</u>ds are h<u>o</u>peless. They cl<u>o</u>sed the M25 because a gas main expl<u>o</u>ded! I can't get h<u>o</u>me.

57

bath, palm, start

20min

phonetic symbol - ɑː

This sound is pronounced in words like:

| **a** | st**a**ff | p**a**th | cl**a**ss | gl**a**ss | **ar** | f**ar** | st**ar** | b**ar** | p**ar**t | **al** | h**al**f | c**al**m |
| b**al**m | **al**mond | **er** | s**er**geant | **ear** | h**ear**t | h**ear**th | **are** | | | | | |

 58

> ### How is the BATH vowel sound made in an RP accent?

The *tongue tip* is behind the *bottom teeth* and the *back of the tongue* is *low* in the *back of the mouth*. The *lips* are *neutral*, the *jaw* is loose and the *teeth* are apart. The BATH vowel sound is *long* in duration.

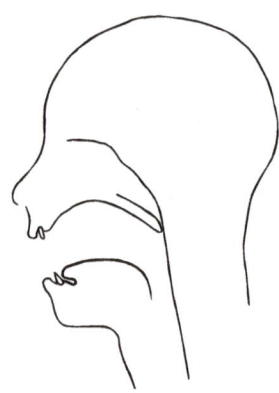 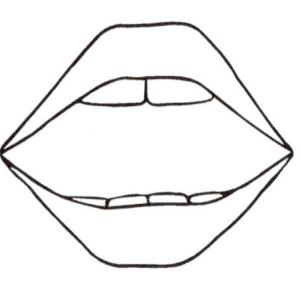

 59

> ### What do I do habitually?

- Are you pronouncing every written 'r'?

If you are a *rhotic* speaker *(book 2 - Consonants)*, your habit is to pronounce every written 'r'. The BATH vowel sound is often spelt with a written 'r', as in 'f**ar**', 'b**ar**', '**are**' and 'h**ear**t'. But RP is a *non-rhotic* accent so a written 'r' is only pronounced when it is followed by a spoken vowel sound. Listen to the words above, firstly spoken with the R sound and then without, as they should be in RP. If you do this, go to 🔧

 60

- Are your lips rounded or spread instead of neutral?

Some speakers have their *tongue* in an accurate position and make the sound *long* in duration, but their *lips* are *spread* or *rounded* instead of *neutral*, which impacts on the quality and tone of the sound. Listen to the following words, firstly spoken with the *lips spread*, then *rounded*, and then *neutral*, as they should be in RP: 'f**ar**', 'b**ar**', 'c**al**m', 'b**al**m', 's**er**geant', 'h**ear**t' and '**are**'. If you do this, go to 🔧

 61

- Are you pronouncing the BATH vowel sound too short?

Some speakers have their *tongue* and *lips* in an accurate position but they make the sound *short* in duration, instead of *long*, which impacts on the quality and tone of the sound. Listen to the following words, firstly spoken with the sound *short* in duration and then *long*, as they should be in RP: 'f**ar**', 'b**ar**', 'c**al**m', 'b**al**m', 's**er**geant', 'h**ear**t' and '**are**'. If you do this, go to 🔧

62

bath, palm, start

phonetic symbol - ɑː

- Are you replacing the BATH vowel sound with the TRAP vowel sound?

Some speakers replace the BATH vowel sound with the TRAP vowel sound *(p.57)*, especially when it is spelt 'a' as in 'st<u>a</u>ff', 'cl<u>a</u>ss', 'gl<u>a</u>ss' and 'p<u>a</u>th'. The TRAP vowel sound is made with the *front of the tongue low* in the *front of the mouth*, the *lips* slight *spread* and the sound *short* in duration. Listen to the words above, firstly spoken with the TRAP vowel sound, then with the BATH vowel sound, as they should be in RP. If you do this, go to 63

- Are you replacing the BATH vowel sound with the STRUT vowel sound?

Some speakers replace the BATH vowel sound with the STRUT vowel sound *(p.35)*, which is made with the *middle of the tongue low* in the *centre of the mouth* and the sound *short* in duration. The *lips* are equally as *neutral* for both vowel sounds. So words like 'c<u>a</u>lm' sound more like 'c<u>o</u>me', 'h<u>a</u>rm' sounds more like 'h<u>u</u>m', 'ps<u>a</u>lm' sounds more like 's<u>u</u>m' and 'c<u>a</u>rt' sounds more like 'c<u>u</u>t'. If you do this, go to 64

- Is your pronunciation guided by the spelling?

Many non-native speakers use the spelling of a word as a guide to its pronunciation. But because British English is not written phonetically, one vowel sound can be represented by numerous spellings. For this reason, the spelling in British English cannot be trusted for vowel pronunciation. For example, the BATH vowel sound can be represented as the 'a' in 'gr<u>a</u>ss', the 'au' in '<u>au</u>nt', the 'al' in 'ps<u>a</u>lm', the 'are' in '<u>are</u>', the 'ear' in 'h<u>ear</u>t' and the 'er' in 's<u>er</u>geant'. So, you might mistakenly pronounce the 'er' in 's<u>er</u>geant' as the NURSE vowel sound *(p.21 - as in 'h<u>er</u>')*. But all these words, despite the variation in spelling, are pronounced with the BATH vowel sound. 65

It is also typical for a speaker to have a certain spelling that they often associate with a vowel sound. For example, many speakers associate the spelling 'ar' with the BATH vowel sound. One might then hope that all words spelt with 'ar' would be pronounced as the BATH vowel sound. Sadly, this is not true, as the 'ar' in 'stand<u>ar</u>d' should be pronounced as the SCHWA vowel sound *(p.17 - as in 't<u>u</u>na')*, in 'tow<u>ar</u>d' it is pronounced as the THOUGHT vowel sound *(p.48 - as in '<u>or</u>')*, and in 'sc<u>ar</u>ce' it is pronounced as the SQUARE vowel sound *(p.86 - as in '<u>air</u>')*. All of this might seem a bit overwhelming, but I have some simple and effective solutions that will help you: go to 66

> How do I change my habit?

 How do I avoid pronouncing a written 'r' that should not be pronounced?

Firstly, encourage your *tongue tip* to stay down, touching the *bottom front teeth* when you are saying the vowel sound. Secondly, unless the vowel sound is followed by another consonant, encourage the *tongue* to stay completely still throughout, avoiding any movement at the end of the sound. When it is followed by a consonant that needs the *tongue tip*, encourage the *tongue* to move directly to the position for that consonant, and not to pronounce an R sound just before. Below are some word pairs. Both words contain the BATH vowel sound, but the first is not spelt with a written 'r'. So it might helpful to use these words to help you find the accurate *tongue* position before saying the words with a written 'r'. Listen to the audio

bath, palm, start

phonetic symbol - ɑː

to help you imitate the sound accurately and watch your *tongue* in a mirror:

L<u>a</u>ma f<u>ar</u>mer p<u>a</u>th p<u>ar</u>t st<u>a</u>ff st<u>ar</u>ve l<u>a</u>st l<u>ar</u>d c<u>a</u>lf c<u>ar</u>ve

🔧 *How do I encourage my lips to be neutral?*

The only way to guarantee that your *lips* are *neutral* instead of *rounding* or *spreading* is to use a mirror when you practice. Otherwise, you can feel the movement in your *lips* by putting one finger in a vertical line over your *lips* – if your *lips* are *rounding* your finger will be pushed forwards; and if your *lips* are *neutral* or slightly *spreading* your finger will remain still. Say the following words, either looking in a mirror or with one finger on your *lips*, and encourage them to be *neutral*:

st<u>a</u>ff p<u>a</u>th cl<u>a</u>ss gl<u>a</u>ss f<u>ar</u> st<u>ar</u> b<u>ar</u> p<u>ar</u>t h<u>a</u>lf c<u>a</u>lm
b<u>a</u>lm <u>a</u>lmond s<u>er</u>geant h<u>ear</u>t h<u>ear</u>th <u>are</u>

🔧 *How do I find the accurate tongue position for the BATH vowel sound?*

The position of the *tongue* and *lips* for the BATH vowel sound is similar to their positions for the STRUT vowel sound *(p.35)* and LOT vowel sound *(p.43)*, so it might be helpful to compare them. Look in a mirror as you say 'hut', 'heart' and 'hot' (angle yourself towards a light or use a very small torch). It might be helpful to say the vowel sounds on their own after saying the words, in order to see the *tongue* more clearly. For 'h<u>u</u>t' (the STRUT vowel sound) encourage the *lips* to be *neutral*, the *middle of the tongue* to be *low* in the *centre of the mouth* and the sound to be *short* in duration. For 'h<u>ear</u>t' (this is the target BATH vowel sound) encourage the *lips* to be equally as *neutral*, the *back of the tongue* to be *low* in the *back of the mouth* and the sound to be *long* in duration. And for 'h<u>o</u>t' (the LOT vowel sound) encourage the *lips* to be slightly *rounded*, the *back of the tongue* to be *low* in the *back of the mouth* and the sound to be *short* in duration.

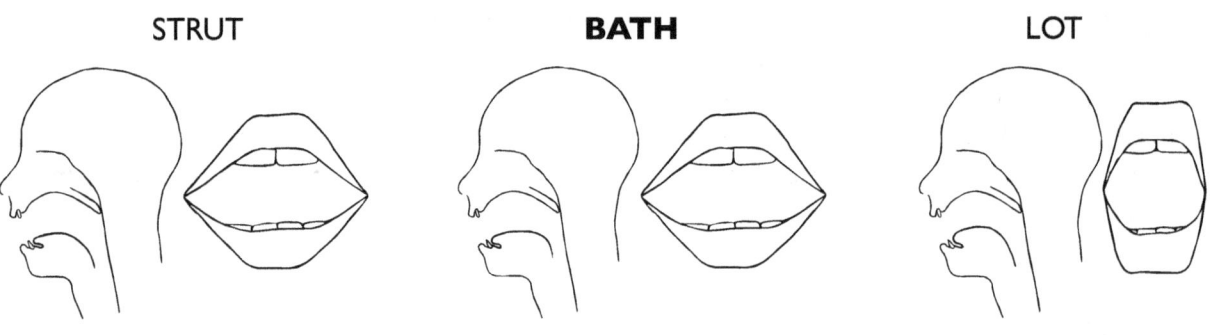

STRUT　　　　　　　　BATH　　　　　　　　LOT

This STRUT, BATH and LOT vowel sound sequence can be heard in the following sets of three words. Play with these words and encourage the *tongue* to remain in between the positions for the STRUT and LOT vowel sounds. Encourage the *lips* to be *neutral* and the sound to be *long* in duration. Listen to the audio to help you imitate the sound accurately:

h<u>u</u>t h<u>ear</u>t h<u>o</u>t c<u>u</u>t c<u>ar</u>t c<u>o</u>t b<u>u</u>m b<u>a</u>lm b<u>o</u>mb l<u>u</u>st l<u>a</u>st l<u>o</u>st

Lastly, here's another game to play: say the BATH vowel sound on its own before saying each word, to help you hear whether or not you are pronouncing it accurately and also to give you a reference for how

bath, palm, start

phonetic symbol - ɑː

it should sound in the word. Listen to the audio to help you imitate the sound accurately:

ah... st<u>a</u>ff   p<u>a</u>th   cl<u>a</u>ss   gl<u>a</u>ss   f<u>ar</u>   st<u>ar</u>   b<u>ar</u>   p<u>ar</u>t   h<u>al</u>f   c<u>al</u>m
b<u>al</u>m   <u>al</u>mond   s<u>er</u>geant   h<u>ear</u>t   h<u>ear</u>th   <u>are</u>

🔧 *How do I avoid being guided by the spelling?*

Once you have used the exercises above to help you achieve an accurate pronunciation of this vowel sound, go to the *Lexical Sets* subsection *(p.16)* for advice on how to avoid being guided by the spelling.

> **Anything Else?**

This is a very minor detail, but occasionally, when the BATH vowel sound is spelt 'a' some RP speakers pronounce the vowel as the TRAP vowel sound *(p.57)*. This only occurs in a handful of words like 'dr<u>a</u>stic', 'm<u>a</u>squerade', 'ex<u>a</u>sperate', 'Gl<u>a</u>sgow' and 'pl<u>a</u>que'. This variation in pronunciation is in part to do with the evolving nature of accents. In some ways, this ambiguity could be seen as frustrating, but another perspective would be to say that is allows for choice, as both are considered correct. The only way to check these variations is to look at the phonetic transcription in a reliable dictionary.

🎤 *Practice words and typical spellings for the BATH vowel sound*

a   st<u>a</u>ff   gir<u>a</u>ffe   p<u>a</u>th   br<u>a</u>ss   cl<u>a</u>ss   gl<u>a</u>ss   gr<u>a</u>ss   p<u>a</u>ss   dr<u>a</u>ft   gr<u>a</u>sp   g<u>a</u>sp
bl<u>a</u>st   c<u>a</u>st   f<u>a</u>st   l<u>a</u>st   p<u>a</u>st   contr<u>a</u>st   v<u>a</u>st   <u>a</u>sk   t<u>a</u>sk   <u>a</u>fter   Sh<u>a</u>ftesbury
m<u>a</u>ster   dis<u>a</u>ster   n<u>a</u>sty   dis<u>a</u>strous   b<u>a</u>sket   d<u>a</u>nce   adv<u>a</u>nce   ch<u>a</u>nce   Fr<u>a</u>nce
gl<u>a</u>nce   ch<u>a</u>nt   pl<u>a</u>nt   adv<u>a</u>ntage   dem<u>a</u>nd   comm<u>a</u>nd   ex<u>a</u>mple   s<u>a</u>mple
<u>a</u>nswer   r<u>a</u>ther   sh<u>a</u>n't   c<u>a</u>n't   Ir<u>a</u>q   mor<u>a</u>le   Ir<u>a</u>n   Sud<u>a</u>n   ban<u>a</u>na   f<u>a</u>ther
br<u>a</u>   B<u>a</u>ch   faç<u>a</u>de   sp<u>a</u>   stacc<u>a</u>to   brav<u>a</u>do   incommunic<u>a</u>do   l<u>a</u>ger
Pakist<u>a</u>n   s<u>a</u>ri   saf<u>a</u>ri   casc<u>a</u>ra   scen<u>a</u>rio   Sah<u>a</u>ra   ti<u>a</u>ra   **ar**   f<u>ar</u>   st<u>ar</u>
b<u>ar</u>   sh<u>ar</u>p   p<u>ar</u>t   b<u>ar</u>k   <u>ar</u>ch   st<u>ar</u>t   sc<u>ar</u>f   f<u>ar</u>ce   h<u>ar</u>sh   g<u>ar</u>b   c<u>ar</u>d
l<u>ar</u>ge   c<u>ar</u>ve   p<u>ar</u>se   f<u>ar</u>m   b<u>ar</u>n   sn<u>ar</u>l   Ch<u>ar</u>les   p<u>ar</u>ty   m<u>ar</u>ket   m<u>ar</u>velous
au   l<u>au</u>gh   <u>au</u>ntie   dr<u>au</u>ght   **al**   c<u>al</u>f   h<u>al</u>f   h<u>al</u>ve   c<u>al</u>m   b<u>al</u>m   ps<u>al</u>m
<u>al</u>mond   **er**   s<u>er</u>geant   **ear**   h<u>ear</u>t   h<u>ear</u>ken   h<u>ear</u>th   **are**   <u>are</u>

🎤 *Practice Sentences for the BATH vowel sound*

- I st<u>ar</u>t work in M<u>ar</u>ch, I've moved into my <u>a</u>partment and Ch<u>ar</u>les has <u>a</u>sked me to marry him!
- You've gr<u>a</u>sped the basics, but the t<u>a</u>sk is <u>a</u>sking for more creativity. The <u>a</u>nswers are adv<u>a</u>nced.
- I played dr<u>au</u>ghts with my <u>au</u>nt Cl<u>a</u>ra, and we l<u>au</u>ghed so h<u>ar</u>d! She's not for the faint-h<u>ear</u>ted!
- <u>Are</u> you ready? Stay c<u>al</u>m and collected! The time will p<u>a</u>ss by so f<u>a</u>st. This is the l<u>a</u>st p<u>ar</u>t!

strut

⏱ 20min

phonetic symbol - ʌ

This sound is pronounced in words like:

    u   c<u>u</u>p   c<u>u</u>t   s<u>u</u>ck   m<u>u</u>ch   **o**   d<u>o</u>ne   c<u>o</u>me   l<u>o</u>ve   m<u>o</u>ther

ou   t<u>ou</u>ch   en<u>ou</u>gh   y<u>ou</u>ng   d<u>ou</u>ble   **oe**   d<u>oe</u>s   **oo**   bl<u>oo</u>d   fl<u>oo</u>d

 76

> How is the STRUT vowel sound made in an RP accent?

The *tongue tip* is behind the *bottom teeth* and the *middle of the tongue* is *low* in the *centre of the mouth*. The *tongue* should look level or slightly lower than the *bottom teeth*. The *lips* are *neutral*, the *jaw* is loose and the *teeth* are apart. The STRUT vowel sound is *short* in duration.

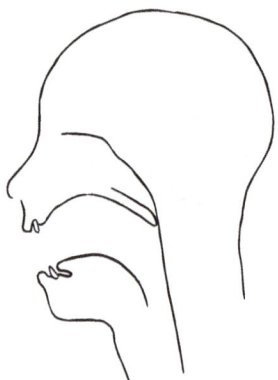 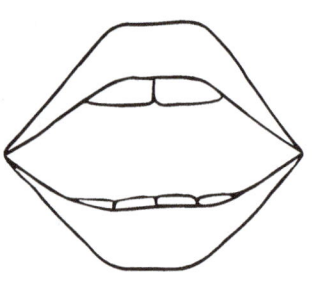

 77

> What do I do habitually?

- Are your lips rounded or slightly spread instead of neutral?

Some speakers have their *tongue* in an accurate position and make the sound *short* in duration, but their *lips* are *rounded* or *spread* instead of *neutral*, which impacts on the quality and tone of the sound. Listen to the following words, firstly spoken with the *lips rounded*, then with the *lips spread*, and then with the *lips neutral*, as they should be in RP: 'c<u>u</u>p', 'c<u>o</u>me', 't<u>ou</u>ch', 'd<u>oe</u>s' and 'bl<u>oo</u>d'. If you do this, go to 🔧

 78

- Are you replacing the STRUT vowel sound with the SCHWA vowel sound?

Some speakers replace the STRUT vowel sound with the SCHWA vowel sound *(p.17)*, which is made with the *middle of the tongue* in the *middle* of the *centre of the mouth*. It isn't straightforward to directly compare words with the SCHWA vowel sound, as it is the sound that tends to represent the *weak syllable* in a word *(book 3 - Intonation)*, and so it can be spelt in many ways. It is the sound that ends words like 'pizz<u>a</u>' and 'tun<u>a</u>'. Listen to the following words, firstly spoken with the SCHWA vowel sound, then with the STRUT vowel sound, as they should be in RP: 'c<u>u</u>p', 'c<u>o</u>me', 't<u>ou</u>ch', 'd<u>oe</u>s' and 'bl<u>oo</u>d'. If you do this, go to 🔧

79

- Are you replacing the STRUT vowel sound with the TRAP vowel sound?

Some speakers replace the STRUT vowel sound with the TRAP vowel sound *(p.57)*, which is made with the *front of the tongue low* in the *front of the mouth*, and the *lips slightly spread*. The sound is equally as *short* in duration. So words like 'l<u>u</u>ck' sound more like 'l<u>a</u>ck', 'c<u>u</u>t' sounds more like 'c<u>a</u>t', 'n<u>u</u>t' sounds more like 'gn<u>a</u>t' and 'h<u>u</u>t' sounds more like 'h<u>a</u>t'. If you do this, go to 🔧

 80

strut

phonetic symbol - ʌ

- Are you replacing the STRUT vowel sound with the LOT vowel sound?

Some speakers replace the STRUT vowel sound with the LOT vowel sound *(p.43 - especially when it is spelt 'o' as in 'c<u>o</u>me' and 'd<u>o</u>ne')* which is made with the *back of the tongue low* of the *back of the mouth*, and the *lips rounded*. Both vowel sounds are equally as *short* in duration. So words like 'n<u>u</u>t' sound more like 'n<u>o</u>t', 'c<u>u</u>t' sounds more like 'c<u>o</u>t', 'g<u>u</u>t' sounds more like 'g<u>o</u>t' and 'm<u>u</u>ck' sounds more like 'm<u>o</u>ck'. If you do this, go to

- Are you replacing the STRUT vowel sound with the BATH vowel sound?

Some speakers replace the STRUT vowel sound with the BATH vowel sound *(p.31)*, which is made with the *back of the tongue low* in the *back of the mouth*, and the sound *longer* in duration. The *lips* are equally as *neutral* for both vowel sounds. So words like 'c<u>u</u>t' sound more like 'c<u>a</u>rt', 'l<u>u</u>ck' sounds more like 'l<u>a</u>rk', and 'p<u>u</u>ck' sounds more like 'p<u>a</u>rk'. If you do this, go to

- Is your pronunciation guided by the spelling?

Many non-native speakers use the spelling of a word as a guide to its pronunciation. But because British English is not written phonetically, one vowel sound can be represented by numerous spellings. For this reason, the spelling in British English cannot be trusted for vowel pronunciation. For example, the STRUT vowel sound can be represented as the 'o' in 'd<u>o</u>ne', the 'ou' in 't<u>ou</u>ch', the 'oe' in 'd<u>oe</u>s', and the 'oo' in 'fl<u>oo</u>d'. So, you might mistakenly pronounce the 'oo' in 'fl<u>oo</u>d' as the GOOSE vowel sound *(p.90 - as in 'f<u>oo</u>d')*, or the 'o' in 'd<u>o</u>ne' as the LOT vowel sound *(p.43 - as in 'h<u>o</u>t')*. But all these words, despite the variation in spelling, are pronounced with the STRUT vowel sound.

It is also typical for a speaker to have a certain spelling that they often associate with a vowel sound. For example, many speakers associate the spelling 'u' with the STRUT vowel sound. One might then hope that all words spelt with 'u' would be pronounced as the STRUT vowel sound. Sadly, this is not true, as the 'u' in 'b<u>u</u>sh' should be pronounced as the FOOT vowel sound *(p.94 - as in 'p<u>u</u>t')*, in 'b<u>u</u>sy' it is pronounced as the KIT vowel sound *(p.70 - as in '<u>i</u>t')*, and in 'h<u>u</u>ge' it is pronounced as a the GOOSE vowel sound *(p.90 - as in 'f<u>oo</u>d')*. All of this might seem a bit overwhelming, but I have some simple and effective solutions that will help you: go to

> *How do I change my habit?*

How do I encourage my lips to be neutral?

The only way to guarantee that your *lips* are *neutral* instead of *rounding* or *spreading* is to use a mirror when you practice. Otherwise, you can feel the movement in your *lips* by putting one finger in a vertical line over your *lips*, which will help you to notice if your *lips* are *rounding* because your finger will be pushed forwards. Say the following words, either looking in a mirror or with one finger on your *lips*, and encourage them to be *neutral*:

        c<u>u</u>p   c<u>u</u>t   s<u>u</u>ck   m<u>u</u>ch   d<u>o</u>ne   c<u>o</u>me   l<u>o</u>ve   m<u>o</u>ther   t<u>ou</u>ch

                en<u>ou</u>gh   y<u>ou</u>ng   d<u>ou</u>ble   d<u>oe</u>s   bl<u>oo</u>d   fl<u>oo</u>d

str<u>u</u>t

phonetic symbol - ʌ

🔧 *How do I find the accurate tongue position for the STRUT vowel sound?*

The position of the *tongue* and *lips* for the STRUT vowel sound is similar to their positions for the BATH vowel sound *(p.31)* and NURSE vowel sound *(p.21)*, so it might be helpful to compare them. Look in a mirror as you say 'h<u>ea</u>rt', 'h<u>u</u>t' and 'h<u>ur</u>t' (angle yourself towards a light or use a very small torch). It might be helpful to say the vowel sounds on their own after saying the words, in order to see the *tongue* more clearly. It might be helpful to say the vowel sounds on their own after saying the words, in order to see the *tongue* more clearly. For 'h<u>ea</u>rt' (the BATH vowel sound) encourage the *lips* to be *neutral*, the *back of the tongue* to be *low* in the *back of the mouth* and the sound to be *long* in duration. For 'h<u>u</u>t' (this is the target STRUT vowel sound) encourage the *lips* to remain *neutral*, but the sound to be *short* in duration, and the *middle of the tongue* to be *low* in the *centre* of the *mouth*. And for 'h<u>ur</u>t' (the NURSE vowel sound) encourage the *lips* to remain *neutral*, but the sound to be *long* in duration, and the *middle of the tongue* to be in the *middle* of the *centre* of the *mouth*.

🔊 86

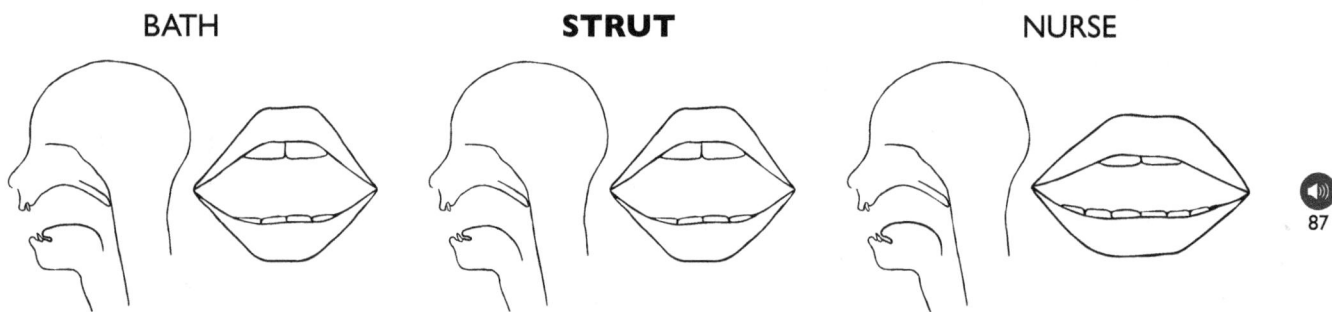

BATH   STRUT   NURSE

🔊 87

This BATH, STRUT and NURSE vowel sound sequence can be heard in the following sets of three words. Play with these words and encourage the *middle of your tongue* to remain in between the positions for the BATH and NURSE vowel sounds. Encourage the *lips* to be *neutral* and the sound to be *short* in duration. Listen to the audio to help you imitate the sound accurately:

    h<u>ea</u>rt h<u>u</u>t h<u>ur</u>t   p<u>a</u>rt p<u>u</u>tt p<u>er</u>t   B<u>a</u>rt b<u>u</u>t B<u>er</u>t   b<u>a</u>rn b<u>u</u>n b<u>ur</u>n

88

If your habit is to replace the STRUT vowel sound with the TRAP or SCHWA vowel sound, essentially, your *tongue* position is too far *forward* or too *high*. For this reason, it might be helpful to say words with the BATH vowel sound (which is made with the *tongue low* in the *back of the mouth*) before saying words with the STRUT vowel sound, in order to encourage your *tongue* into a *lower* and more *central* position. For example:

    h<u>ea</u>rt h<u>u</u>t   p<u>a</u>rt p<u>u</u>tt   B<u>a</u>rt b<u>u</u>t   b<u>a</u>rn b<u>u</u>n   f<u>a</u>rce f<u>u</u>ss   l<u>a</u>st l<u>u</u>st

89

Similarly, if your habit is to replace the STRUT vowel sound with the BATH or LOT vowel sound, then your *tongue* position is too far *back*. For this reason, it might be helpful to say words with the TRAP vowel sound (which is made with the *tongue low* in the *front of the mouth*) before saying words with the STRUT vowel sound, in order to encourage your *tongue* into a more *central* position. For example:

    h<u>a</u>t h<u>u</u>t   p<u>a</u>t p<u>u</u>tt   b<u>a</u>t b<u>u</u>t   b<u>a</u>n b<u>u</u>n   p<u>a</u>ck p<u>u</u>ck   l<u>a</u>ck l<u>u</u>ck

90

strut

phonetic symbol - ʌ

Lastly, here's another game to play: say the STRUT vowel sound on its own before saying each word, to help you hear whether or not you are pronouncing it accurately and also to give you a reference for how it should sound in the word. Listen to the audio to help you imitate the sound accurately:

uh... cup   cut   suck   much   done   come   love   mother   touch
enough   young   double   does   blood   flood

91

How do I avoid being guided by the spelling?

Once you have used the exercises above to help you achieve an accurate pronunciation of this vowel sound, go to the *Lexical Sets* subsection *(p.16)* for advice on how to avoid being guided by the spelling.

Practice words and typical spellings for the STRUT vowel sound

u   cup   cut   suck   much   snuff   fuss   rush   rub   bud   jug   budge
buzz   hum   run   lung   dull   pulse   bulge   punch   lump   hunt   trunk
butter   study   punish   number   mustn't   must   Guthrie   fun   cut   shut
hunter   stuff   Sunday   hurry   **o**   done   come   love   mother
stomach   monk   tongue   onion   money   front   colour   some   something
nothing   wonderful   son   honey   dozen   one   once   London
worry   **ou**   touch   enough   young   double   southern   tough   country
oe   does   **oo**   blood   flood

92

Practice Sentences for the STRUT vowel sound

- I wonder whether I earn enough money to live in London – it's something I'd love to do!
- A double Southern Comfort on a Monday afternoon!? You're either glum or in trouble!
- He's a lovely, wonderful son-in-law, I've nothing bad to say. He's coming to lunch on Sunday.
- She studies hard, she cares for her elderly mother, and she's young – maybe twenty-one.

93

38

p.108

price

phonetic symbol - ɑɪ

This sound is pronounced in words like:

i_e	r**i**pe	wr**i**te	f**i**ve	l**i**ke	**ie**	d**ie**	tr**ie**d	cr**ie**d	**i**	**I**	Fr**i**day	s**i**lent
ch**i**ld	**y**	tr**y**	sh**y**	wh**y**	m**y**	**ye**	d**ye**	r**ye**	**ei**	**ei**der	kal**ei**doscope	
	igh	fl**igh**t	s**igh**	n**igh**t	l**igh**t	**ig**	s**ig**n	ben**ig**n	**eigh**	h**eigh**t		
ui	g**ui**de	disg**ui**se	q**ui**te	**uy**	b**uy**	g**uy**	**other**	**eye**	**ai**sle	ind**i**ct		

> ### How is the PRICE vowel sound made in an RP accent?

The PRICE vowel sound is a *diphthong* – a combination of two vowel sounds where one slides into the other. The PRICE vowel sound starts as a slightly *shorter* version of the BATH vowel sound *(p.31* - where the *tongue tip* is behind the *bottom teeth*, the *back of the tongue* is *low* in the *back of the mouth*, and the *lips* are *neutral*) which slides into a slightly *shorter* version of the FLEECE vowel sound *(p.65* - where the *tongue tip* stays behind the *bottom teeth*, the *front of the tongue* slides *high* and *forwards* into the *front of the mouth* and the *lips* slightly *spread*). The *jaw* is loose, the *teeth* are apart, and the sound is *long* in duration.

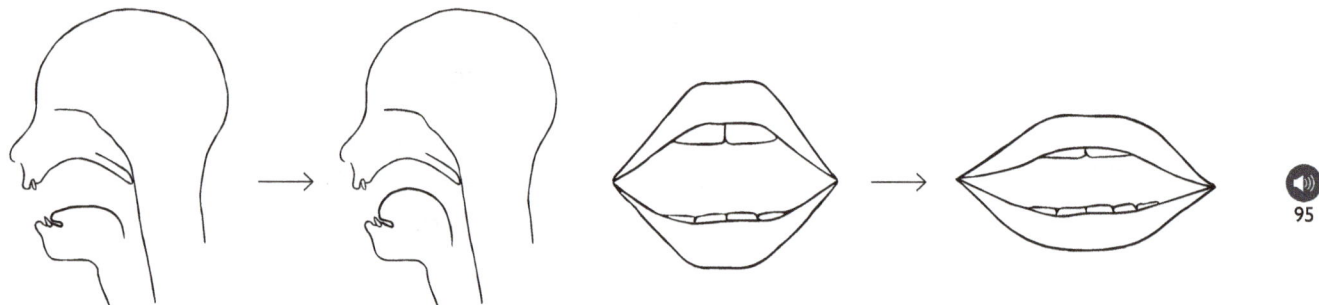

> ### What do I do habitually?

- *Do your lips remain rounded, neutral or spread throughout the whole diphthong?*

Some speakers move their *tongue* through the accurate positions and make the sound *long* in duration, but their *lips* remain *rounded*, *neutral* or *spread* instead of sliding from *neutral* to slightly *spread*, which impacts on the quality and tone of the sound. Listen to the following words, firstly spoken with the *lips rounded*, then *neutral*, then *spread*, and then sliding from *neutral* to slightly *spread*, as they should be in RP: 'ripe', 'tried', 'I', 'try', 'rye', 'height', 'night', 'sign', 'guide', 'buy', 'eye', 'aisle' and 'indict'. If you do this, go to

- *Are you making this diphthong too long or too short in duration?*

Some speakers move their *tongue* and *lips* through the accurate positions but they make the *diphthong* too *short* or too *long* in duration, which impacts on the quality and tone of the sound. If you are making the *diphthong* too *long*, either both vowel sounds in the *diphthong* will be too *long*, which will make it sound like two *syllables* instead of one, or one of the vowel sounds in the *diphthong* will be too *long*. Listen to the following words, firstly spoken with this *diphthong* too *short* in duration, then with both vowel sounds too *long*, then with the first vowel sound too *long*, then with the second vowel sound too *long*, and finally as they should be in RP: 'ripe', 'tried', 'I', 'try', 'rye', 'height', 'night', 'sign', 'guide', 'buy', 'eye', 'aisle' and 'indict'. If you do this, go to 🔧

price

phonetic symbol - ɑɪ

- Are you replacing the first vowel sound with the TRAP vowel sound?

Some speakers replace the first vowel sound (BATH) with the TRAP vowel sound *(p.57)*, which is made with the *front of the tongue low* in the *front of the mouth* and the *lips* slightly *spread*. Listen to the following words, firstly spoken with the TRAP vowel sound at the beginning of this *diphthong* and then with a slightly *shorter* version of the BATH vowel sound at the beginning, as they should be in RP: 'r<u>i</u>pe', 'tr<u>ie</u>d', '<u>I</u>', 'tr<u>y</u>', 'r<u>ye</u>', 'h<u>ei</u>ght', 'n<u>igh</u>t', 's<u>ig</u>n', 'g<u>ui</u>de', 'b<u>uy</u>', '<u>eye</u>', '<u>ai</u>sle' and 'ind<u>i</u>ct'. If you do this, go to

- Are you replacing the first vowel sound with the DRESS vowel sound?

Some speakers replace the first vowel sound (BATH) with the DRESS vowel sound *(p.78)*, which is made with the *front of the tongue* in the *middle* of the *front of the mouth* and the *lips* slightly *spread*. Listen to the following words, firstly spoken with the DRESS vowel sound at the beginning of this *diphthong* and then with a slightly *shorter* version of the BATH vowel sound at the beginning, as they should be in RP: 'r<u>i</u>pe', 'tr<u>ie</u>d', '<u>I</u>', 'tr<u>y</u>', 'r<u>ye</u>', 'h<u>ei</u>ght', 'n<u>igh</u>t'. 's<u>ig</u>n', 'g<u>ui</u>de', 'b<u>uy</u>', '<u>eye</u>', '<u>ai</u>sle' and 'ind<u>i</u>ct'. If you do this, go to

- Are you replacing the first vowel sound with the THOUGHT vowel sound?

Some speakers replace the first vowel sound (BATH) with the THOUGHT vowel sound *(p.48)*, which is made with the *back of the tongue* in the *middle* of the *back of the mouth* and the *lips rounded*. Listen to the following words, firstly spoken with the THOUGHT vowel sound at the beginning of this *diphthong* and then with a slightly *shorter* version of the BATH vowel sound at the beginning, as they should be in RP: 'r<u>i</u>pe', 'tr<u>ie</u>d', '<u>I</u>', 'tr<u>y</u>', 'r<u>ye</u>', 'h<u>ei</u>ght', 'n<u>igh</u>t', 's<u>ig</u>n', 'g<u>ui</u>de', 'b<u>uy</u>', '<u>eye</u>', '<u>ai</u>sle' and 'ind<u>i</u>ct'. If you do this, go to

- Is your pronunciation guided by the spelling?

Many non-native speakers use the spelling of a word as a guide to its pronunciation. But because British English is not written phonetically, one vowel sound can be represented by numerous spellings. For this reason, the spelling in British English cannot be trusted for vowel pronunciation. For example, the PRICE vowel sound can be represented as the '<u>ai</u>' in '<u>ai</u>sle', the 'ei' in 'kal<u>ei</u>doscope', the 'eigh' in 'h<u>eigh</u>t', the 'ie' in 'tr<u>ie</u>d', and the 'y' in 't<u>y</u>pe'. So, you might mistakenly pronounce the 'eigh' in 'h<u>eigh</u>t' as the FACE vowel sound *(p.82 - as in '<u>eigh</u>t')*. But all these words, despite the variation in spelling, are pronounced with the PRICE vowel sound.

It is also typical for a speaker to have a certain spelling that they often associate with a vowel sound. For example, many speakers associate the spelling 'i' with the PRICE vowel sound. One might then hope that all words spelt with 'i' would be pronounced as the PRICE vowel sound. Sadly, this is not true, as the 'i' in 'sh<u>i</u>p' should be pronounced as the KIT vowel sound *(p.70 - as in '<u>i</u>t')*, and in 'pol<u>i</u>ce' it is pronounced as the FLEECE vowel sound *(p.65 - as in 'h<u>e</u>')*. All of this might seem a bit overwhelming, but I have some simple and effective solutions that will help you: go to

price

phonetic symbol - aɪ

> ## How do I change my habit?

 How do I find the accurate tongue position for the PRICE vowel sound?

Firstly, ensure that you are accurately pronouncing the two component vowel sounds in this *diphthong* by following the exercises in the sections entitled *How do I find the accurate tongue position for the BATH vowel sound? (p.31)* and *How do I find the accurate tongue position for the FLEECE vowel sound? (p.64)*.

Once you feel confident with how to make each vowel sound, your *tongue* needs to slide from one into the other to make the *diphthong*. Say each sound on its own, one after the other, with a brief pause between them. Watch your *tongue* and *lips* in a mirror and then take out the pause, sliding them into one another. All *diphthongs* are made with the first vowel slightly more *stressed* than the second. This being said, it is only *slightly* more *stressed* and should be observed with care. And remember that the two vowel sounds in a *diphthong* make a single *syllable*: the *tongue* slides smoothly but swiftly and the sound is *long*, but not too *long*.

Play with the following exercise. It offers you an opportunity to check whether you are accurately pronouncing the first vowel sound in the *diphthong* – BATH. Listen to the audio to help you imitate the sound accurately:

rah... r<u>i</u>pe	trah... tr<u>ie</u>d	trah... tr<u>y</u>	rah... r<u>ye</u>	hah... h<u>eigh</u>t	nah... n<u>igh</u>t
sah... s<u>i</u>gn	gah... g<u>ui</u>ld	bah... b<u>uy</u>	ah... <u>ai</u>sle	indah... ind<u>i</u>ct	

103

 How do I avoid being guided by the spelling?

Once you have used the exercises above to help you achieve an accurate pronunciation of this vowel sound, go to the *Lexical Sets* subsection *(p.16)* for advice on how to avoid being guided by the spelling.

> ## Anything Else?

- The LIAR triphthong: phonemic symbol aɪə

There are five of the eight *diphthongs* that can be extended with a final SCHWA vowel sound, which turns the *diphthong* into a *triphthong* – a combination of three vowel sounds where one slides into another. The PRICE vowel sound is one such *diphthong*, so words like 'l<u>iar</u>', 't<u>ire</u>', 'p<u>yre</u>' and 'br<u>iar</u>' are pronounced with the PRICE vowel sound followed by a SCHWA vowel sound. The *lips* relax back to *neutral* and the *tongue* slides from being in the *back of the mouth* to the *middle* of the *centre of the mouth*.

104

Some RP speakers add a YOD *(book 2 - Consonants)* to link the PRICE vowel sound to the SCHWA vowel sound *(p.17)*. This makes words like 'l<u>iar</u>', 't<u>ire</u>', 'p<u>yre</u>' and 'br<u>iar</u>' sound like two *syllable* words instead of one. In this version, the *tongue* moves quite suddenly into the SCHWA. Other speakers do not add a YOD. Instead, they make the transition of their *tongue* from the PRICE vowel sound to the SCHWA vowel sound much more smoothly. This makes the words above sound more like one *syllable*.

105

This variation in pronunciation is in part to do with the evolving nature of accents. And unfortunately

price

phonetic symbol - aɪ

these variations are not accounted for in a reliable dictionary. In some ways, this ambiguity could be seen as a frustrating, but another perspective would be to say that is allows for choice, as both are considered correct. Listen to the following words, firstly spoken with the YOD and then without:

higher   wire   acquire   prior   attire   dryer   fire   retire   buyer

106

And lastly, many words with these *triphthongs* have a written 'r' in the spelling, which should not be spoken, unless they are followed by a spoken vowel sound *(book 2 - Consonants)*. Encourage your *tongue tip* to remain down, touching the *bottom front teeth* at the end of the *triphthong*.

🎙 *Practice words and typical spellings for the PRICE vowel sound*

i_e	ripe	write	five	drive	like	knife	ice	tribe	side	arrive	writhe
rise	time	fine	kite	mile	**ie**	die	tried	cried	**i**	I	Friday	tiger
silent	violent	liar	science	indict	isle	child	pint	find	ninth	Christ
viscount	bicycle	island	hi	**y**	type	try	shy	sly	hyper	fly	Cyprus
hydrogen	rhyme	sky	hybrid	style	why	my	**ye**	dye	rye	**ei**	eider
kaleidoscope	**igh**	fight	flight	sigh	night	light	sight	high
ig	sign	benign	**eigh**	height	**ui**	beguile	guide	disguise	quite
uy	buy	guy	**other spellings**	eye	aisle	indict

107

🎙 *Practice Sentences for the PRICE vowel sound*

- I'd like to invite you to mine on Friday, would that be alright? We'll eat ice cream all night!
- Why do you keep on lying to me? I hate it! It's childish! I'm almost frightened to know the truth.
- I'm so tired. My eyes are weary. It would be nice to lie down in silence!
- I want to find out why the figures in July were so high, and the kind of clients who were buying.

108

> Bonus Material!

Great news – there's a FREE online video about the PRICE on my YouTube channel:

https://www.youtube.com/@ashleyhowardvoicecoach

lot, cloth

⏱ 20min

phonetic symbol - ɒ

This sound is pronounced in words like:

o	st**o**p	n**o**t	p**o**t	**a**	wh**a**t	qu**a**lity	y**a**cht	**ow**	kn**ow**ledge ackn**ow**ledge
au	**Au**stralia	**Au**stria	**Au**stin	s**au**sage	**ou**	Gl**ou**cester	c**ou**gh	tr**ou**gh	

109

> ### How is the LOT vowel sound made in an RP accent?

The *tongue tip* is behind the *bottom teeth* and the *back of the tongue* is *low* in the *back of the mouth*. The *lips* are slightly *rounded*, the *jaw* is loose and the *teeth* are apart. The LOT vowel sound is *short* in duration.

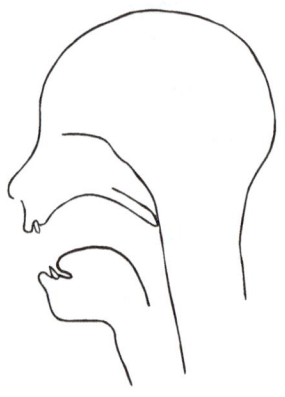 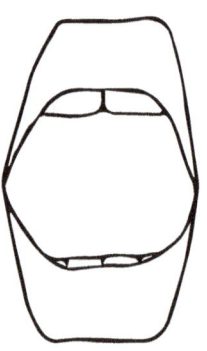

110

> ### What do I do habitually?

- Are your lips spread or neutral instead of rounded?

Some speakers have their *tongue* in an accurate position and make the sound *short* in duration, but their *lips* are *neutral* or *spread* instead of slightly *rounded*, which impacts on the quality and tone of the sound. Listen to the following words, firstly spoken with the *lips spread*, then *neutral*, and then slightly *rounded*, as they should be in RP: 'st**o**p', 'wh**a**t', 'kn**ow**ledge', 's**au**sage' and 'c**ou**gh'. If you do this, go to 🔧

111

- Are you pronouncing the LOT vowel sound too long?

Some speakers have their *tongue* and *lips* in an accurate position but they make the sound *long* in duration, instead of *short*, which impacts on the quality and tone of the sound. Listen to the following words, firstly spoken with the sound *long* in duration and then *short*, as they should be in RP: 'st**o**p', 'wh**a**t', 'kn**ow**ledge', 's**au**sage' and 'c**ou**gh'. If you do this, go to 🔧

112

- Are you replacing the LOT vowel sound with the THOUGHT vowel sound?

Some speakers replace the LOT vowel sound with the THOUGHT vowel sound *(p.48)*, which is made with the *back of the tongue* slightly *higher* in the *back of the mouth*, the sound *long* in duration and the *lips* are slightly more *rounded*. So words like 'st**o**ck' sound more like 'st**a**lk', and 'r**o**d' sounds more like 'r**oa**red'. If you do this, go to 🔧

113

lot, cloth

phonetic symbol - ɒ

- Are you replacing the LOT vowel sound with the BATH vowel sound?

Some speakers replace the LOT vowel sound with the BATH vowel sound *(p.31)*, which is made with the *back of the tongue low* in the *back of the mouth*. The *lips* are *neutral* and the sound is *long* in duration. So words like 'st<u>o</u>ck' sound more like 'st<u>ar</u>k', and 'l<u>o</u>ck' sounds more like 'l<u>ar</u>k'. If you do this, go to 🔧
114

- Are you replacing the LOT vowel sound with the STRUT vowel sound?

Some speakers replace the LOT vowel sound with the STRUT vowel sound *(p.35)*, which is made with the *middle of the tongue low* in the *middle of the mouth*. The *lips* are *neutral* and the sound is equally as *short* in duration. So words like 'st<u>o</u>ck' sound more like 'st<u>u</u>ck' and 'l<u>o</u>ck' sounds more like 'l<u>u</u>ck'. If you do this, go to 🔧
115

- Are you replacing the LOT vowel sound with the GOAT vowel sound?

Some speakers replace the LOT vowel sound with the GOAT vowel sound *(p.26)*, which is a *diphthong* – a combination of two vowel sounds where one slides into the other. The GOAT vowel sound starts with the *middle of the tongue* in the *middle of the centre of the mouth* and the *lips neutral* and then the *tongue* slides upwards and backwards *high* into the *back of the mouth* and the *lips round*. The sound is *long* in duration. So words like 'st<u>o</u>ck' sound more like 'st<u>o</u>ke', 'c<u>o</u>t' sounds more like 'c<u>oa</u>t', 'cl<u>o</u>ck' sounds more like 'cl<u>oa</u>k' and 's<u>o</u>ck' sounds more like 's<u>oa</u>k'. If you do this, go to 🔧
116

- Are you replacing the LOT vowel sound with the TRAP vowel sound?

Some speakers replace the LOT vowel sound with the TRAP vowel sound *(p.57)*, which is made with the *front of the tongue low* in the *front of the mouth*. The *lips* are slightly *spread* and the sound is also as *short* in length. So words like 'r<u>o</u>t' sound more like 'r<u>a</u>t', and 'l<u>o</u>ck' sounds more like 'l<u>a</u>ck'. If you do this, go to 🔧
117

- Is your pronunciation guided by the spelling?

Many non-native speakers use the spelling of a word as a guide to its pronunciation. But because British English is not written phonetically, one vowel sound can be represented by numerous spellings. For this reason, the spelling in British English cannot be trusted for vowel pronunciation. For example, the LOT vowel sound can be represented as the 'a' in 'wh<u>a</u>t', the 'au' in '<u>Au</u>stralia', the 'ow' in 'kn<u>ow</u>ledge', and the 'ou' in 'c<u>ou</u>gh'. So, you might mistakenly pronounce the 'a' in 'wh<u>a</u>t' as the TRAP vowel sound *(p.57 - as in 'p<u>a</u>t')*. But all these words, despite the variation in spelling, are pronounced with the LOT vowel sound.
118

It's quite typical to have a certain spelling associated with a vowel sound. For example, many speakers associate the spelling 'o' with the LOT vowel sound. One might then hope that all words spelt with 'o' would be pronounced as the LOT vowel sound. Sadly, this is not true, as the 'o' in the singular of 'w<u>o</u>man' should be pronounced as the FOOT vowel sound *(p.94 - as in 'sh<u>ou</u>ld')*, in 'd<u>o</u>ne' it is pronounced as the STRUT vowel sound *(p.35 - as in 'h<u>u</u>t')*, in the plural of 'w<u>o</u>men' it is pronounced as the KIT vowel sound *(p.70 - as in '<u>i</u>t')*, in '<u>o</u>ffend' it is pronounced as the SCHWA vowel sound *(p.17 - as in 'tun<u>a</u>')*, in 'd<u>o</u>' it is pronounced as the GOOSE vowel sound *(p.90 - as in 'f<u>oo</u>d')*, and in 'n<u>o</u>' it is pronounced as the GOAT vowel sound *(p.26 - as in 'l<u>ow</u>')*. All of this might seem a bit overwhelming, but I have some simple and effective solutions that will help you: go to 🔧
119

lot, cloth

phonetic symbol - ɒ

> ## How do I change my habit?

🔧 *How do I encourage my lips to be rounded?*

The only way to guarantee that your *lips* are *rounded* accurately instead of being *neutral* or *spread* is to use a mirror when you practice. Otherwise, you can feel the movement in your *lips* by putting one finger in a vertical line over your *lips* – if your *lips* are *rounding* your finger will be pushed forwards; and if your *lips* are *neutral* or slightly *spreading* your finger will remain still. Say the following words, either looking in a mirror or with one finger on your *lips*, and encourage them to be *rounded* accurately:

stop   not   pot   sock   what   swan   quality   yacht   knowledge
acknowledge   Australia   Austria   Austin   sausage   Gloucester   cough   trough

120

🔧 *How do I find the accurate tongue position for the LOT vowel sound?*

The position of the *tongue* and *lips* for the LOT vowel sound is similar to their positions for the BATH vowel sound *(p.31)* and THOUGHT vowel sound *(p.48)*, so it might be helpful to compare them. Look in a mirror as you say 'heart', 'hot' and 'hoard' (angle yourself towards a light or use a very small torch - although you might still struggle to see the *back of the tongue* because the *lips* need to be *rounded* when saying these vowel sounds). It might be helpful to say the vowel sounds on their own after saying the words, in order to see the *tongue* more clearly. For 'heart' (the BATH vowel sound) encourage the *lips* to be *neutral*, the *back of the tongue* to be *low* in the *back of the mouth* and the sound to be *long* in duration. For 'hot' (this is the target LOT vowel sound) encourage the *lips* to be slightly *rounded*, the sound to be *short* in duration, and the *back of the tongue* to be only slightly *higher* in the *back of the mouth*. And for 'hoard' (the THOUGHT vowel sound) encourage the *lips* to be more *rounded*, the *back of the tongue* to be slightly *higher* still in the *back of the mouth* and the sound to be *long* in duration.

121

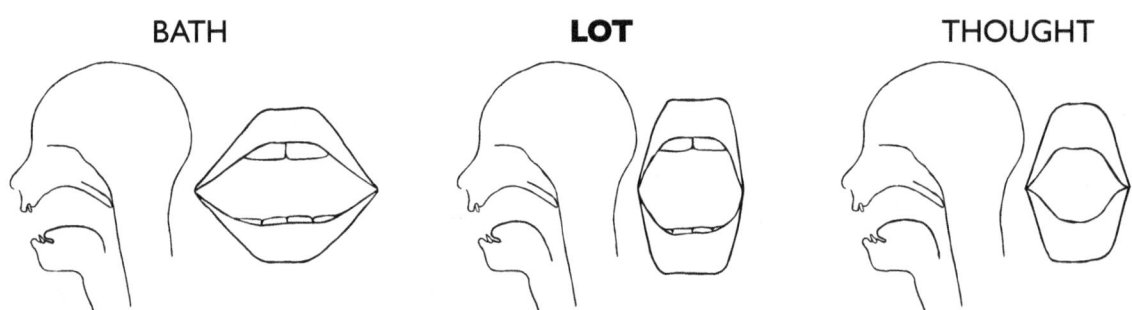

BATH   LOT   THOUGHT

122

This BATH, LOT and THOUGHT vowel sound sequence can be heard in the following sets of three words. Play with these words and encourage the *front of your tongue* to remain in between the positions for the BATH and THOUGHT vowel sounds. Encourage the *lips* to be slightly *rounded* and the sound to be *long* in duration. Listen to the audio to help you imitate the sound accurately:

stark   stock   stalk   lark   lock   lawn   shark   shock   short   card   cod   cord

123

If your habit is to replace the LOT vowel sound with the THOUGHT vowel sound, essentially, your *tongue* position is too *high*. For this reason, it might be helpful to say words with the BATH vowel sound (which is made with the *tongue lower* in the *back of the mouth*) before saying words with the LOT vowel sound, in

lot, cloth

phonetic symbol - ɒ

order to encourage your *tongue* into a *lower* position. For example:

st**a**rk st**o**ck   l**a**rk l**o**ck   sh**a**rk sh**o**ck   c**a**rd c**o**d   h**ea**rt h**o**t   p**a**rt p**o**t

Similarly, if your habit is to replace the LOT vowel sound with the BATH, STRUT or TRAP vowel sound, then your *tongue* position is too *low* or too far *forward*. For this reason, it might be helpful to say words with the THOUGHT vowel sound (which is made with the *tongue* in the slightly *higher* in the *back of the mouth*) before saying words with the LOT vowel sound, in order to encourage your *tongue higher* and further *back*. For example:

st**a**lk st**o**ck   l**aw**n l**o**ck   sh**or**t sh**o**ck   c**or**d c**o**d   h**oa**rd h**o**t   p**or**t p**o**t

Lastly, here's another game to play: say the LOT vowel sound on its own before saying each word, to help you hear whether or not you are pronouncing it accurately and also to give you a reference for how it should sound in the word. Listen to the audio to help you imitate the sound accurately:

st**o**p   n**o**t   p**o**t   s**o**ck   wh**a**t   sw**a**n   qu**a**lity   y**a**cht   kn**ow**ledge
ackn**ow**ledge   A**u**stralia   A**u**stria   A**u**stin   s**au**sage   Gl**ou**cester   c**ou**gh   tr**ou**gh

🔧 *How do I avoid being guided by the spelling?*

Once you have used the exercises above to help you achieve an accurate pronunciation of this vowel sound, go to the *Lexical Sets* subsection *(p.16)* for advice on how to avoid being guided by the spelling.

🎤 ***Practice words and typical spellings for the LOT vowel sound***

o   st**o**p   n**o**t   p**o**t   s**o**ck   n**o**tch   G**o**th   r**o**b   **o**dd   c**o**g   d**o**dge
T**o**m   c**o**n   d**o**ll   s**o**lve   r**o**mp   f**o**nt   c**o**pse   b**o**x   pr**o**fit   p**o**ssible
pr**o**verb   b**o**ther   r**o**sin   h**o**nest   p**o**nder   **o**ff   br**o**th   fr**o**th   cr**o**ss   acr**o**ss
l**o**ss   fl**o**ss   t**o**ss   d**o**ss   s**o**ft   cr**o**ft   l**o**st   **o**ft   c**o**st   fr**o**st   **o**ften
s**o**ften   l**o**fty   g**o**ne   m**o**th   b**o**ss   gl**o**ss   j**o**ss   m**o**ss   R**o**ss   l**o**ng   str**o**ng
wr**o**ng   g**o**ng   s**o**ng   t**o**ngs   thr**o**ng   c**o**ffee   c**o**ffer   c**o**ffin   **o**ffer
office   **o**fficer   gl**o**ssy   f**o**ster   B**o**ston   **o**rigin   **O**regon   **o**ratory   **o**rator
orange   a**u**thority   b**o**rrow   categ**o**rical   c**o**rrelate   c**o**roner   c**o**ral   fl**o**rid
Fl**o**rida   fl**o**rist   hist**o**ric   h**o**rrid   h**o**rrible   maj**o**rity   h**o**rrify   h**o**rror
metaph**o**ric   M**o**rris   m**o**ral   p**o**rridge   rhet**o**rical   s**o**rrel   s**o**rrow
tom**o**rrow   s**o**rry   **a**   wh**a**t   sw**a**n   qu**a**lity   y**a**cht   w**a**sp   w**a**tch   squ**a**bble
w**a**ffle   qu**a**rrel   qu**a**ntity   qu**a**rry   w**a**rrant   w**a**rren   w**a**rrior   w**a**sh   w**a**nted
ow   kn**ow**ledge   ackn**ow**ledge   **au**   A**u**stralia   A**u**stria   A**u**stin   s**au**sage
L**au**rence   l**au**rel   **ou**   Gl**ou**cester   c**ou**gh   tr**ou**gh

lot, cloth

phonetic symbol - ɒ

🎙 *Practice Sentences for the LOT vowel sound*

- Wh<u>a</u>t are you doing tom<u>o</u>rrow? Are you at the <u>o</u>ffice? Is it p<u>o</u>ssible to dr<u>o</u>p L<u>o</u>lly <u>o</u>ff at the fl<u>o</u>rist?
- My b<u>o</u>ss is <u>o</u>n H<u>o</u>liday until Monday. She's g<u>o</u>ne to Gl<u>ou</u>cester with R<u>o</u>b. I'm completely sw<u>a</u>mped!
- Is your p<u>o</u>rridge h<u>o</u>t enough Sc<u>o</u>tt? I've also made some w<u>a</u>ffles, with <u>o</u>range c<u>o</u>mp<u>o</u>te. C<u>o</u>ffee?
- You always wear <u>o</u>dd s<u>o</u>cks! What's wr<u>o</u>ng with you? Do you n<u>o</u>t st<u>o</u>p to look?

128

Am I pronouncing it accurately?

Get a personalised assessment of every vowel, consonant and aspect of intonation to find out
how well you're doing, exactly what to focus on and what you need to do
to speak in this accent accurately and naturally:

https://www.ashleyhoward.me/pronunciation-evaluation

⏱ 20min

th<u>ou</u>ght, n<u>or</u>th, f<u>or</u>ce

phonetic symbol - ɔː

This sound is pronounced in words like:

au	s<u>au</u>ce	c<u>au</u>se	P<u>au</u>l	<u>au</u>tumn	**aw**	cr<u>aw</u>l	s<u>aw</u>n	y<u>aw</u>n	l<u>aw</u>
ar	tow<u>ar</u>d	w<u>ar</u>	qu<u>ar</u>ter	w<u>ar</u>d	**a**	w<u>a</u>ter	<u>a</u>ll	f<u>a</u>ll	sm<u>a</u>ll
augh	t<u>augh</u>t	c<u>augh</u>t	n<u>augh</u>ty	d<u>augh</u>ter	**al**	ch<u>al</u>k	t<u>al</u>k	w<u>al</u>k	st<u>al</u>k
ough	br<u>ough</u>t	f<u>ough</u>t	s<u>ough</u>t	th<u>ough</u>t	**oa**	br<u>oa</u>d	h<u>oa</u>ry	**oar**	h<u>oar</u>se
b<u>oa</u>rd	h<u>oa</u>rd	b<u>oa</u>rder	**our**	y<u>our</u>	m<u>our</u>n	c<u>our</u>se	c<u>our</u>t	**or**	<u>or</u>
sh<u>or</u>t	Ge<u>or</u>ge	sp<u>or</u>t	**ore**	m<u>ore</u>	s<u>ore</u>	bef<u>ore</u>	expl<u>ore</u>		

129

> ## How is the THOUGHT vowel sound made in an RP accent?

The *tongue tip* is behind the *bottom teeth* and the *back of the tongue* is *in the middle* of the *back of the mouth*. The *lips* are *rounded*, the *jaw* is loose and the *teeth* are apart. The THOUGHT vowel sound is *long* in duration.

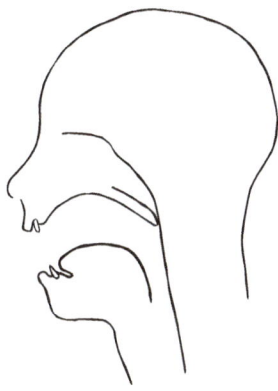
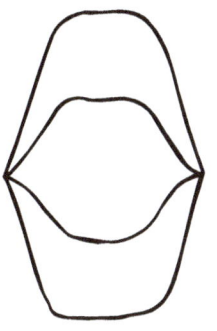

130

> ## What do I do habitually?

- Are you pronouncing every written 'r'?

If you are a *rhotic speaker (book 2 - Consonants)*, your habit is to pronounce every written 'r'. The THOUGHT vowel sound is often spelt with a written 'r', as in 'w<u>ar</u>d', 'b<u>oa</u>rd', 'y<u>our</u>', '<u>or</u>' and 'm<u>ore</u>'. But RP is a *non-rhotic* accent so a written 'r' is only spoken when it is followed by a spoken vowel sound. Listen to the words above, firstly spoken with the R sound and then without, as they should be in RP. If you do this, go to

131

- Are your lips spread or neutral instead of rounded?

Some speakers have their *tongue* in an accurate position and make the sound *long* in duration, but their *lips* are *neutral*, *spread* or too *rounded*, which impacts on the quality and tone of the sound. Listen to the following words, firstly spoken with the *lips neutral*, then *spread*, then too *rounded*, and then slightly *rounded*, as they should be in RP: 's<u>au</u>ce', 'l<u>aw</u>', 'w<u>ar</u>', '<u>a</u>ll', 't<u>augh</u>t', 't<u>al</u>k', 'br<u>oa</u>d', 'b<u>oa</u>rd', 'y<u>our</u>', '<u>or</u>' and 'm<u>ore</u>'. If you do this, go to

132

thought, north, force

phonetic symbol - ɔː

- Are you pronouncing the THOUGHT vowel sound too short?

Some speakers have their *tongue* and *lips* in an accurate position but they make the sound *short* in duration, instead of *long*, which impacts on the quality and tone of the sound. Listen to the following words, firstly spoken with the sound *short* in duration and then *long*, as they should be in RP: 'sauce', 'law', 'war', 'all', 'taught', 'talk', 'broad', 'board', 'your', 'or' and 'more'. If you do this, go to 🔧

133

- Are you replacing the THOUGHT vowel sound with the LOT vowel sound?

Some speakers replace the THOUGHT vowel sound with the LOT vowel sound *(p.43)* which is made with the *back of the tongue low* in the *back of the mouth*, the *lips* slightly less *rounded* and the sound *short* in duration. So words like 'caught' sound more like 'cot', and 'short' sounds more like 'shot'. If you do this, go to 🔧

134

- Are you replacing the THOUGHT vowel sound with the BATH vowel sound?

Some speakers replace the THOUGHT vowel sound with the BATH vowel sound *(p.31)*, which is made with the *back of the tongue low* in the *back of the mouth*. The *lips* are *neutral* and the sound is equally as *long* in duration. So words like 'caught' sound more like 'cart', and 'port' sounds more like 'part'. If you do this, go to 🔧

135

- Are you replacing the THOUGHT vowel sound with the STRUT vowel sound?

Some speakers replace the THOUGHT vowel sound with the STRUT vowel sound *(p.35)*, which is made with the *middle of the tongue low* in the *centre of the mouth*. The *lips* are *neutral* and the sound is *short* in duration. So words like 'caught' sound more like 'cut', and 'bought' sounds more like 'but'. If you do this, go to 🔧

136

- Is your pronunciation guided by the spelling?

Many non-native speakers use the spelling of a word as a guide to its pronunciation. But because British English is not written phonetically, one vowel sound can be represented by numerous spellings. For this reason, the spelling in British English cannot be trusted for vowel pronunciation. For example, the THOUGHT vowel sound can be represented as the 'a' in 'all', the 'au' in 'sauce', the 'ar' in 'toward', the 'aw' in 'yawn', the 'augh' in 'caught', the 'al' in 'talk', the 'ough' in 'bought', the 'our' in 'course', the 'oa' in 'broad', the 'oar' in 'board' and the 'ore' in 'more'. So, you might mistakenly pronounce the 'ough' in 'bought' as the GOAT vowel sound *(p.26 - as in 'although')*. But all these words, despite the variation in spelling, are pronounced with the THOUGHT vowel sound.

137

It is also typical for a speaker to have a certain spelling that they often associate with a vowel sound. For example, many speakers associate the spelling 'or' with the THOUGHT vowel sound. One might then hope that all words spelt with 'or' would be pronounced as the THOUGHT vowel sound. Sadly, this is not true, as the 'or' in 'forget' should be pronounced as the SCHWA vowel sound *(p.17 - as in 'tuna')*, and in 'work' it is pronounced as the NURSE vowel sound *(p.21 - as in 'her')*. All of this might seem a bit overwhelming, but I have some simple and effective solutions that will help you: go to 🔧

138

thought, north, force

phonetic symbol - ɔː

> How do I change my habit?

How do I avoid pronouncing a written 'r' that should not be pronounced?

There are a number of words pronounced with the THOUGHT vowel sound which are called *homophones* – words pronounced the same but spelt differently with different meanings, for example 's<u>aw</u>' and 's<u>ore</u>'. Many come in pairs, one with a written 'r' and one without, so it might be helpful to compare them. When saying 's<u>aw</u>', encourage your *tongue tip* to be behind your *bottom front teeth* after the 's' – so the *tongue tip* moves from it's position for the 's' down behind the *bottom front teeth* without touching anything along the way. When saying 's<u>ore</u>', encourage the *tongue tip* to do exactly the same thing. This way, the words rhyme with one another, as they should in RP. Play with the following pairs of words, and encourage the *tongue tip* to stay down behind the *bottom front teeth* during the THOUGHT vowel sound in both words. Listen to the audio to help you imitate the sound accurately and watch your tongue in a mirror:

s<u>aw</u>   s<u>ore</u>   p<u>aw</u>   p<u>oor</u>   r<u>aw</u>   r<u>oar</u>   <u>awe</u>   <u>or</u>   l<u>aw</u>   l<u>ore</u>   c<u>augh</u>t   c<u>our</u>t

How do I encourage my lips to be rounded?

The only way to guarantee that your *lips* are *rounded* accurately instead of being *neutral, spread* or too *rounded* is to use a mirror when you practice. Otherwise, you can feel the movement in your *lips* by putting one finger in a vertical line over your *lips* – if your *lips* are *rounding* your finger will be pushed forwards; and if your *lips* are *neutral* or slightly *spreading* your finger will remain still. If your lips are too *rounded*, they will be pushed slightly further forward than for the THOUGHT vowel sound. Say the following words, either looking in a mirror or with one finger on your *lips*, and encourage them to be *rounded* accurately:

s<u>au</u>ce   c<u>au</u>se   y<u>aw</u>n   l<u>aw</u>   t<u>owar</u>d   w<u>ar</u>d   w<u>a</u>ter   <u>a</u>ll   t<u>augh</u>t   c<u>augh</u>t   t<u>a</u>lk

w<u>a</u>lk   br<u>oa</u>d   b<u>oar</u>d   h<u>oar</u>d   y<u>our</u>   c<u>our</u>se   c<u>our</u>t   <u>or</u>   sh<u>or</u>t   m<u>ore</u>

How do I find the accurate tongue position for the THOUGHT vowel sound?

The position of the *tongue* and *lips* for the THOUGHT vowel sound is similar to their positions for the LOT vowel sound *(p.43)* and FOOT vowel sound *(p.94)*, so it might be helpful to compare them. Look in a mirror as you say 'h<u>o</u>t', 'h<u>oar</u>d' and 'h<u>oo</u>d' (angle yourself towards a light or use a very small torch – although you might still struggle to see the *back of the tongue* because the *lips* need to be *rounded* when saying these vowel sounds).

It might be helpful to say the vowel sounds on their own after saying the words, in order to see the *tongue* more clearly. For 'h<u>o</u>t' (the LOT vowel sound) encourage the *lips* to be slightly *rounded*, the *back of the tongue* to be *low* in the *back of the mouth,* and the sound to be *short* in duration. For 'h<u>oar</u>d' (this is the target THOUGHT vowel sound) encourage the *lips* to be more *rounded*, the *back of the tongue* to in the *middle* of the *back of the mouth*, and the sound to be *long* in duration. And for 'h<u>oo</u>d' (the FOOT vowel sound) encourage the *lips* to be more *rounded*, the *back of the tongue* to be slightly *higher* still in the *back of the mouth* and the sound to be *long* in duration.

thought, north, force

phonetic symbol - ɔː

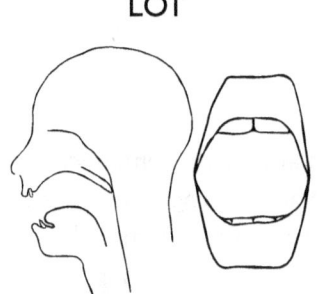
LOT

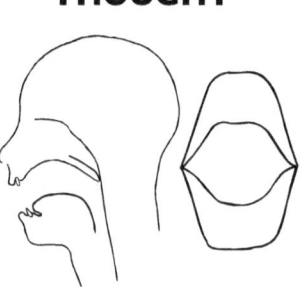
THOUGHT

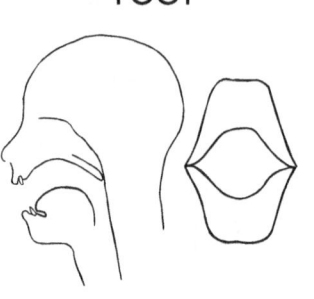
FOOT

143

This LOT, THOUGHT and FOOT vowel sound sequence can be heard in the following sets of three words. Play with these words and encourage the *back of your tongue* to remain in between the positions for the LOT and FOOT vowel sounds. Encourage the *lips* to be *rounded* and the sound to be *long* in duration. Listen to the audio to help you imitate the sound accurately:

c<u>o</u>t   c<u>au</u>ght   c<u>oo</u>k   sh<u>o</u>ck   sh<u>or</u>t   sh<u>oo</u>k   t<u>o</u>p   t<u>a</u>lk   t<u>oo</u>k   wh<u>a</u>t   w<u>ar</u>d   w<u>oo</u>d

144

If your habit is to replace the THOUGHT vowel sound with the LOT, BATH or STRUT vowel sound, essentially, your *tongue* position is too *low*. For this reason, it might be helpful to say words with the FOOT vowel sound (which is made with the *tongue* slightly *higher*) before saying words with the THOUGHT vowel sound, in order to encourage your *tongue* into a *higher* position. For example:

c<u>oo</u>k   c<u>au</u>ght   sh<u>oo</u>k   sh<u>or</u>t   t<u>oo</u>k   t<u>a</u>lk   w<u>oo</u>d   w<u>ar</u>d   h<u>oo</u>d   h<u>oar</u>d   t<u>oo</u>k   t<u>a</u>lk

145

Lastly, here's another game to play: say the THOUGHT vowel sound on its own before saying each word, to help you hear whether or not you are pronouncing it accurately and also to give you a reference for how it should sound in the word. Listen to the audio to help you imitate the sound accurately:

s<u>au</u>ce   c<u>au</u>se   y<u>aw</u>n   l<u>aw</u>   tow<u>ar</u>d   w<u>ar</u>d   w<u>a</u>ter   <u>a</u>ll   t<u>au</u>ght   c<u>au</u>ght   t<u>a</u>lk
w<u>a</u>lk   br<u>oa</u>d   b<u>oar</u>d   h<u>oar</u>d   y<u>our</u>   c<u>our</u>se   c<u>our</u>t   <u>or</u>   sh<u>or</u>t   m<u>ore</u>

146

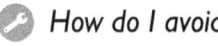 *How do I avoid being guided by the spelling?*

Once you have used the exercises above to help you achieve an accurate pronunciation of this vowel sound, go to the *Lexical Sets* subsection *(p.16)* for advice on how to avoid being guided by the spelling.

> Anything Else?

This is a very minor detail, but sometimes, when the THOUGHT vowel sound is followed by a dark L (*book 2 - Consonants*) - a written 'l' that is followed by a consonant sound or by a pause) some RP speakers pronounce the vowel as the THOUGHT vowel sound and some pronounce it with the LOT vowel sound *(p.43)*.

This can be heard in words like 'halt', 'salt', 'malt' and occasionally in words like 'false', 'alter', 'also', 'alderman', 'walrus', 'fault', 'vault' (on the audio they are spoken firstly with the THOUGHT vowel sound and then with the LOT vowel sound). This variation is indicated in most reliable pronunciation dictionaries for words

147

thought, north, force

phonetic symbol - ɔː

such as 'h<u>al</u>t', 's<u>al</u>t' and 'm<u>al</u>t', but not for others. As I said, this is a very minor detail and would add further specificity to your pronunciation, but if you were to continue to pronounce the THOUGHT vowel sound in words like these, you will still be clearly understood and your pronunciation will lie within the RP canon.

Practice words and typical spellings for the THOUGHT vowel sound

au	s<u>au</u>ce	c<u>au</u>se	P<u>au</u>l	<u>au</u>tumn	c<u>au</u>tion	<u>au</u>thor	L<u>au</u>ra	**aw**	g<u>aw</u>p
	h<u>aw</u>k	cr<u>aw</u>l	s<u>aw</u>n	y<u>aw</u>n	j<u>aw</u>	l<u>aw</u>	s<u>aw</u>	dr<u>aw</u>	<u>aw</u>e	p<u>aw</u>
ar	tow<u>ar</u>d	w<u>ar</u>	qu<u>ar</u>t	qu<u>ar</u>ter	qu<u>ar</u>tz	sw<u>ar</u>d	sw<u>ar</u>m	sw<u>ar</u>thy	w<u>ar</u>ble
w<u>ar</u>d	w<u>ar</u>den	w<u>ar</u>drobe	w<u>ar</u>lock	w<u>ar</u>m	w<u>ar</u>mth	w<u>ar</u>p	W<u>ar</u>saw	w<u>ar</u>t
a	w<u>a</u>ter	<u>a</u>ll	f<u>a</u>ll	sm<u>a</u>ll	w<u>a</u>ll	app<u>a</u>ll	inst<u>a</u>ll	b<u>a</u>ld	t<u>a</u>ll	**augh**	t<u>augh</u>t
c<u>augh</u>t	n<u>augh</u>ty	d<u>augh</u>ter	n<u>augh</u>t	**ough**	<u>ough</u>t	b<u>ough</u>t	wr<u>ough</u>t	br<u>ough</u>t
f<u>ough</u>t	s<u>ough</u>t	th<u>ough</u>t	**al**	ch<u>al</u>k	t<u>al</u>k	w<u>al</u>k	st<u>al</u>k	c<u>al</u>k	**oa**	br<u>oa</u>d
h<u>oa</u>ry	**oar**	h<u>oar</u>se	b<u>oar</u>d	h<u>oar</u>d	b<u>oar</u>der	**our**	y<u>our</u>	m<u>our</u>n	c<u>our</u>se
c<u>our</u>t	f<u>our</u>th	c<u>our</u>se	res<u>our</u>ce	s<u>our</u>ce	c<u>our</u>tier	p<u>our</u>	**or**	<u>or</u>	sh<u>or</u>t
Ge<u>or</u>ge	sp<u>or</u>t	f<u>or</u>m	b<u>or</u>n	f<u>or</u>tunate	imp<u>or</u>tant	sh<u>or</u>ten	<u>or</u>der	<u>or</u>dinary
<u>or</u>ganise	n<u>or</u>mal	f<u>or</u>ward	rep<u>or</u>t	supp<u>or</u>t	aff<u>or</u>d	sw<u>or</u>d	t<u>or</u>n
ore	m<u>ore</u>	s<u>ore</u>	bef<u>ore</u>	expl<u>ore</u>	ign<u>ore</u>	m<u>ore</u>	sc<u>ore</u>	sn<u>ore</u>	st<u>ore</u>

Practice Sentences for the THOUGHT vowel sound

- I th<u>ough</u>t that we <u>a</u>ll agreed – the t<u>a</u>llest first and the sh<u>or</u>test last? The <u>or</u>der is imp<u>or</u>tant!
- I b<u>ough</u>t a w<u>ar</u>m jumper in <u>au</u>tumn and I'm wearing it in <u>Au</u>gust!? It's app<u>a</u>lling! I'm b<u>ore</u>d of it!
- It's f<u>or</u>tunate that I was w<u>al</u>king behind you. You would have f<u>a</u>llen and broken your j<u>aw</u>!
- Bef<u>ore</u> we t<u>al</u>k, I impl<u>ore</u> you not to mention P<u>au</u>l. It's too <u>aw</u>kward. L<u>au</u>ra? Are you <u>a</u>lright?

choice

20min

phonetic symbol - ɔɪ

This sound is pronounced in words like:

oy b<u>oy</u> t<u>oy</u> ann<u>oy</u> empl<u>oy</u> **oi** n<u>oi</u>se ch<u>oi</u>ce rej<u>oi</u>ce c<u>oi</u>n j<u>oi</u>n

150

> *How is the CHOICE vowel sound made in an RP accent?*

The CHOICE vowel sound is a *diphthong* – a combination of two vowel sounds where one slides into the other. The CHOICE vowel sound starts as the THOUGHT vowel sound (*p.48* - where the *tongue tip* is behind the *bottom teeth*, the *back of the tongue* is in the *middle* of the *back of the mouth*, and the *lips* are *rounded*) which slides into a slightly *shorter* version of the FLEECE vowel sound (*p.65* - where the *tongue tip* stays behind the *bottom teeth*, the *front of the tongue* slides *high* and *forwards* into the *front of the mouth* and the *lips* slightly *spread*). The *jaw* is loose, the *teeth* are apart, and the sound is *long* in duration.

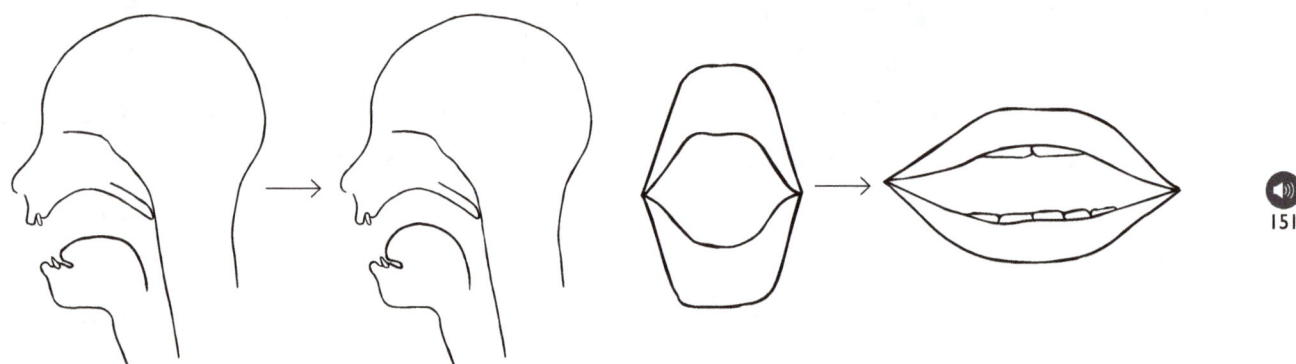
151

> *What do I do habitually?*

- Do your lips remain rounded, neutral or spread throughout the whole diphthong?

Some speakers move their *tongue* through the accurate positions and make the sound *long* in duration, but their *lips* remain *rounded*, *neutral* or *spread* throughout instead of sliding from *rounded* to slightly *spread*, which impacts on the quality and tone of the sound. Listen to the following words, firstly spoken with the *lips rounded*, then *neutral*, then *spread*, and then sliding from *rounded* to slightly *spread*, as they should be in RP: 'b<u>oy</u>', 't<u>oy</u>', 'ann<u>oy</u>', 'empl<u>oy</u>', 'n<u>oi</u>se', 'ch<u>oi</u>ce', 'rej<u>oi</u>ce', 'c<u>oi</u>n' and 'j<u>oi</u>n'. If you do this, go to

152

- Are you making this diphthong too long or too short in duration?

Some speakers move their *tongue* and *lips* through the accurate positions but they make the *diphthong* too *short* or too *long* in duration, which impacts on the quality and tone of the sound. If you are making the *diphthong* too *long*, either both vowel sounds in the *diphthong* will be too *long*, which will make it sound like two *syllables* instead of one, or one of the vowel sounds in the *diphthong* will be too *long*. Listen to the following words, firstly spoken with the *diphthong* too *short* in duration, then with both vowel sounds too *long*, then with the first vowel sound too *long*, then with the second vowel sound too *long*, and finally as they should be in RP: 'b<u>oy</u>', 't<u>oy</u>', 'ann<u>oy</u>', 'empl<u>oy</u>', 'n<u>oi</u>se', 'ch<u>oi</u>ce', 'rej<u>oi</u>ce', 'c<u>oi</u>n' and 'j<u>oi</u>n'. If you do this, go to

153

choice

phonetic symbol - ɔɪ

- Are you replacing the first vowel sound with the LOT vowel sound?

Some speakers replace the first vowel sound (THOUGHT) with the LOT vowel sound *(p.43)*, which is made with the *back of the tongue low* in the *back of the mouth* and the *lips* slightly less *rounded*. Listen to the following words, firstly spoken with the LOT vowel sound at the beginning of this *diphthong* and then with the THOUGHT vowel sound at the beginning, as they should be in RP: 'b<u>oy</u>', 't<u>oy</u>', 'ann<u>oy</u>', 'empl<u>oy</u>', 'n<u>oi</u>se', 'ch<u>oi</u>ce', 'rej<u>oi</u>ce', 'c<u>oi</u>n' and 'j<u>oi</u>n'. If you do this, go to

- Are you replacing the first vowel sound with the STRUT vowel sound?

Some speakers replace the first vowel sound (THOUGHT) with the STRUT vowel sound *(p.35)*, which is made with the *middle of the tongue low* in the *centre of the mouth* and the *lips neutral*. Listen to the following words, firstly spoken with the STRUT vowel sound at the beginning of this *diphthong* and then with the THOUGHT vowel sound at the beginning, as they should be in RP: 'b<u>oy</u>', 't<u>oy</u>', 'ann<u>oy</u>', 'empl<u>oy</u>', 'n<u>oi</u>se', 'ch<u>oi</u>ce', 'rej<u>oi</u>ce', 'c<u>oi</u>n' and 'j<u>oi</u>n'. If you do this, go to

- Are you replacing the CHOICE vowel sound with the THOUGHT vowel sound?

Some speakers replace the CHOICE vowel sound with the THOUGHT vowel sound *(p.48)*. The THOUGHT vowel sound is made with the *back of the tongue* in the *middle* of the *back of the mouth*, the *lips rounded* and the sound *long* in duration. Listen to the following words, spoken firstly only with a THOUGHT vowel sound, and then the CHOICE vowel sound, as they should be in RP: 'b<u>oy</u>', 't<u>oy</u>', 'ann<u>oy</u>', 'empl<u>oy</u>', 'n<u>oi</u>se', 'ch<u>oi</u>ce', 'rej<u>oi</u>ce', 'c<u>oi</u>n' and 'j<u>oi</u>n'. If you do this, go to

- Is your pronunciation guided by the spelling?

Many non-native speakers use the spelling of a word as a guide to its pronunciation. But because British English is not written phonetically, one vowel sound can be represented by numerous spellings. For this reason, the spelling in British English cannot be trusted for vowel pronunciation. However, unlike almost all other vowel sounds, the CHOICE vowel sound tends only to be represented by the letters 'oi' and 'oy', and thankfully, no other vowel sound tends to use this spelling. This means that when you see the spelling 'oi' or 'oy' we can say almost certainly that you should use the CHOICE vowel sound.

There are a few exceptions: in 'mem<u>oir</u>' it is a weak syllable, and is pronounced with the BATH vowel sound *(p.31)*, preceded by a W sound; in 'ch<u>oir</u>', it is the LIAR *triphthong (p.39)*; and in 'c<u>oi</u>ncide' and 'g<u>oi</u>ng' they are separated into two syllables, pronounced as the GOAT vowel sound *(p.26)* followed by the KIT vowel sound *(p.70)*. If you confuse the pronunciation words like these, go to

> ### How do I change my habit?

 How do I find the accurate tongue position for the CHOICE vowel sound?

Firstly, ensure that you are accurately pronouncing the two component vowel sounds in this *diphthong* by following the exercises in the sections entitled *How do I find the accurate tongue position for the THOUGHT vowel sound? (p.47)* and *How do I find the accurate tongue position for the FLEECE vowel sound? (p.64)*.

choice

phonetic symbol - ɔɪ

Once you feel confident with how to make each vowel sound, your *tongue* needs to slide from one into the other to make the *diphthong*. Say each sound on its own, one after the other, with a brief pause between them. Watch your *tongue* and *lips* in a mirror and then take out the pause, sliding them into one another. All *diphthongs* are made with the first vowel slightly more *stressed* than the second. This being said, it is only *slightly* more *stressed* and should be observed with care. And remember that the two vowel sounds in a *diphthong* make a single *syllable*: the *tongue* slides smoothly but swiftly and the sound is *long*, but not too *long*.

Play with the following exercise. It offers you an opportunity to check whether you are accurately pronouncing the first vowel sound in the *diphthong* – THOUGHT (which has been written as 'or' and *rhotic* speakers must remember to avoid pronouncing the written 'r'). Listen to the audio to help you imitate the sound accurately:

158

    bor... b<u>oy</u>   tor... t<u>oy</u>   annor... ann<u>oy</u>   emplor... empl<u>oy</u>   nor... n<u>oi</u>se

    chor... ch<u>oi</u>ce   rejor... rej<u>oi</u>ce   cor... c<u>oi</u>n   jor... j<u>oi</u>n

🔧 *How do I avoid being guided by the spelling?*

Once you have used the exercises above to help you achieve an accurate pronunciation of this vowel sound, go to the *Lexical Sets* subsection *(p.16)* for advice on how to avoid being guided by the spelling.

> Anything Else?

- The LAWYER triphthong: phonetic symbol ɔɪə

There are five of the eight *diphthongs* that can be extended with a final SCHWA vowel sound, which turns the *diphthong* into a *triphthong* – a combination of three vowel sounds where one slides into another. The CHOICE vowel sound is one such *diphthong*, so words like 'l<u>awyer</u>', 's<u>oya</u>' and 'empl<u>oyer</u>', 'paran<u>oia</u>', 'l<u>oyal</u>' and 'r<u>oyal</u>' are pronounced with the CHOICE vowel sound followed by a SCHWA vowel sound. The *lips* relax back to *neutral* and the *tongue* slides from being in the *back of the mouth* to the *middle* of the *centre of the mouth*.

159

Some RP speakers add a YOD *(book 2 - Consonants)* to link the CHOICE vowel sound to the SCHWA vowel sound. This makes words like 'l<u>awyer</u>', 's<u>oya</u>' and 'empl<u>oyer</u>' sound like two *syllable* words instead of one. In this version, the *tongue* moves quite suddenly into the SCHWA. Other speakers do not add a YOD. Instead, they make the transition of their *tongue* from the CHOICE vowel sound to the SCHWA vowel sound much more smoothly. This makes the words above sound more like one *syllable*.

160

This variation in pronunciation is in part to do with the evolving nature of accents. And unfortunately these variations are not accounted for in a reliable dictionary. In some ways, this ambiguity could be seen as a frustrating, but another perspective would be to say that is allows for choice, as both are considered correct. Listen to the following words, firstly spoken with the YOD and then without:

    l<u>awyer</u>   s<u>oya</u>   empl<u>oyer</u>   r<u>oyal</u>   l<u>oyal</u>   paran<u>oia</u>

161

choice

phonetic symbol - ɔɪ

And lastly, many words with these *triphthongs* have a written 'r' in the spelling, which should not be spoken, unless they are followed by a spoken vowel sound *(book 2 - Consonants)*. Encourage your *tongue tip* to remain down, touching the *bottom front teeth* at the end of the *triphthong*.

Practice words and typical spellings for the CHOICE vowel sound

| **oy** | b<u>oy</u> | t<u>oy</u> | j<u>oy</u> | ann<u>oy</u> | <u>oy</u>ster | c<u>oy</u> | bu<u>oy</u> | empl<u>oy</u> | **oi** | n<u>oi</u>se | v<u>oi</u>ce |

ch<u>oi</u>ce rej<u>oi</u>ce v<u>oi</u>d m<u>oi</u>st c<u>oi</u>n j<u>oi</u>n <u>oi</u>l b<u>oi</u>l s<u>oi</u>l sp<u>oi</u>l t<u>oi</u>l

p<u>oi</u>son <u>oi</u>ntment gr<u>oi</u>n l<u>oi</u>ter h<u>oi</u>st j<u>oi</u>st n<u>oi</u>sy expl<u>oi</u>ted all<u>oy</u>

162

Practice Sentences for the CHOICE vowel sound

- You ann<u>oy</u>ed me yesterday. You were so b<u>oi</u>sterous and n<u>oi</u>sy that you sp<u>oi</u>led the atmosphere.
- The p<u>oi</u>nt of j<u>oi</u>ning the march is to b<u>oy</u>cott the organisation and use your v<u>oi</u>ce.
- He was overj<u>oy</u>ed! He enj<u>oy</u>ed every second. The t<u>oy</u>s were perfect! He was b<u>uoy</u>ant all day!
- Her empl<u>oy</u>er destr<u>oy</u>ed all of her confidence by breaking its l<u>oy</u>alty – it's embr<u>oi</u>led in scandal!

163

⏱ 20min

trap

phonetic symbol - æ

This sound is pronounced in words like:

a   p**a**ttern   m**a**tch   c**a**sh   m**a**d   st**a**ndard   h**a**m   m**a**n   underst**a**nd   h**a**ng   sh**a**ll   m**a**tter   h**a**nd   th**a**nk   **a**ngry   t**a**x   c**a**rriage   c**a**ncel   s**a**nd   l**a**ck   s**a**ck 164

r**a**ck   l**a**nd   g**a**p   sl**a**m   **ai**   pl**ai**d   **ua**   g**ua**rantee

> **How is the TRAP vowel sound made in an RP accent?**

The *tongue tip* is behind the *bottom teeth* and the *front of the tongue* is *low* in the *front of the mouth*. The *lips* are slightly *spread*, the *jaw* is loose and the *teeth* are apart. The TRAP vowel sound is *short* in duration.

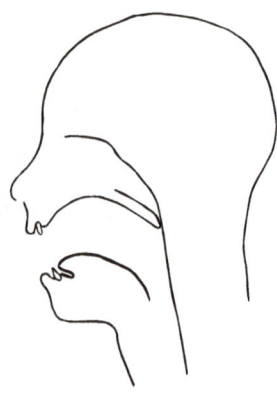
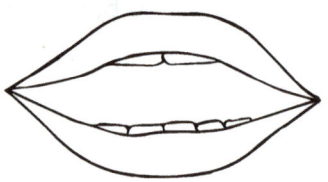
165

> **What do I do habitually?**

- Are your *lips rounded* or *neutral* instead of *slightly spread*?

Some speakers have their *tongue* in an accurate position and make the sound *short* in duration, but their *lips* are *rounded* instead of slightly *spread*, which impacts on the quality and tone of the sound. Listen to the following words, firstly spoken with the *lips rounded* and then with the *lips* slightly *spread*, as they should be in RP: 'p**a**ttern', 'c**a**sh', 'c**a**ncel', 'pl**ai**d' and 'g**ua**rantee'. If you do this, go to 🔧 166

- Are you pronouncing the TRAP vowel sound *too long*?

Some speakers have their *tongue* and *lips* in an accurate position but they make the sound *long* in duration, instead of *short*, which impacts on the quality and tone of the sound. Listen to the following words, firstly spoken with the sound *long* in duration and then *short*, as they should be in RP: 'p**a**ttern', 'c**a**sh', 'm**a**tter', 't**a**x' and 'g**ua**rantee'. If you do this, go to 🔧 167

- Are you *replacing* the TRAP vowel sound with the DRESS vowel sound?

Some speakers replace the TRAP vowel sound with the DRESS vowel sound *(p.78)*, which is made with the *front of the tongue* very slightly *higher* in the *front of the mouth*. The *lips* are equally as *spread* for both vowel sounds and they are equally as *short* in duration. So words like 'm**a**n' sound more like 'm**e**n', and 's**a**nd' sounds more like 's**e**nd'. If you do this, go to 🔧 168

tr**a**p

phonetic symbol - æ

- Are you replacing the TRAP vowel sound with the BATH vowel sound?

Some speakers replace the TRAP vowel sound with the BATH vowel sound *(p.31)*, which is made with the *back of the tongue low* in the *back of the mouth*, the sound is *longer* in duration and the *lips* are *neutral*. So words like 'c**a**t' sound more like 'c**a**rt', and 'b**a**n' sounds more like 'b**a**rn'. If you do this, go to 169

- Are you replacing the TRAP vowel sound with the STRUT vowel sound?

Some speakers replace the TRAP vowel sound with the STRUT vowel sound *(p.35)*, which is made with the *middle of the tongue low* in the *centre of the mouth*. The *lips* are equally as *spread* for both vowel sounds and they are equally as *short* in duration. So words like 'c**a**t' sound more like 'c**u**t', and 'f**a**n' sounds more like 'f**u**n'. If you do this, go to 170

- Is your pronunciation guided by the spelling?

Many non-native speakers use the spelling of a word as a guide to its pronunciation. But because British English is not written phonetically, one vowel sound can be represented by numerous spellings. For this reason, the spelling in British English cannot be trusted for vowel pronunciation. For example, the TRAP vowel sound can be represented as the '**ai**' in 'pl**ai**d' and the '**ua**' in 'g**ua**rantee'. So, you might mistakenly pronounce the 'ai' in 'pl**ai**d' as the FACE vowel sound *(p.82 - as in 'w**ai**t')*. But all these words, despite the variation in spelling, are pronounced with the TRAP vowel sound. 171

It is also typical for a speaker to have a certain spelling that they often associate with a vowel sound. For example, many speakers associate the spelling 'a' with the TRAP vowel sound. One might then hope that all words spelt with 'a' would be pronounced as the TRAP vowel sound. Sadly, this is not true, as the 'a' in '**a**ny' should be pronounced as the DRESS vowel sound *(p.78 - as in 'th**e**n')*, in 'w**a**tch' it is pronounced as the LOT vowel sound *(p.43 - as in 'h**o**t')*, in '**a**ll' it is pronounced as the THOUGHT vowel sound *(p.48 - as in 'n**or**th')*, in 'gr**a**ss' it is pronounced as the BATH vowel sound *(p.31 - as in '**ar**t')*, in 'st**a**tion' it is pronounced as the FACE vowel sound *(p.82 - as in 'w**ei**gh')*, and in 'v**a**rious' it is pronounced as the SQUARE vowel sound *(p.86 - as in '**air**')*. All of this might seem a bit overwhelming, but I have some simple and effective solutions that will help you: go to 172

> How do I change my habit?

How do I encourage my lips to be slightly spread?

The only way to guarantee that you are slightly *spreading* your *lips* accurately instead of *rounding* them is to use a mirror when you practice. Otherwise, you can feel the movement in your *lips* by putting one finger in a vertical line over your *lips* – if your *lips* are *rounding* your finger will be pushed forwards; and if your *lips* are *neutral* or slightly *spreading* your finger will remain still. Say the following words, either looking in a mirror or with one finger on your *lips*, and encourage them to be slightly *spread* accurately:

p**a**ttern   m**a**tch   c**a**sh   m**a**d   st**a**ndard   h**a**m   m**a**n   underst**a**nd   h**a**ng

sh**a**ll   m**a**tter   h**a**nd   th**a**nk   **a**ngry   t**a**x   c**a**rriage   c**a**ncel   pl**ai**d   g**ua**rantee

 173

trap

phonetic symbol - æ

🔧 *How do I find the accurate tongue position for the TRAP vowel sound?*

The position of the *tongue* and *lips* for the TRAP vowel sound is similar to their positions for the NURSE vowel sound *(p.21)* and DRESS vowel sound *(p.78)*, so it might be helpful to compare them. Look in a mirror as you say 'h<u>ear</u>d', 'h<u>a</u>d' and 'h<u>ea</u>d' (angle yourself towards a light or use a very small torch). It might be helpful to say the vowel sounds on their own after saying the words, in order to see the *tongue* more clearly. For 'h<u>ear</u>d' (the NURSE vowel sound) encourage the *lips* to be *neutral*, the *middle of the tongue* to be in the *middle* of the *centre of the mouth* and the sound to be *long* in duration. For 'h<u>a</u>d' (this is the target TRAP vowel sound) encourage the *lips* to be slightly *spread*, the sound to be *short* in duration and the *front of the tongue* to be *low* in the *front of the mouth,* just visible over the *bottom front teeth*. And for 'h<u>ea</u>d' (the DRESS vowel sound) encourage the *lips* to be equally as *spread*, and the sound to be equally as *short* in duration but the *front of the tongue* to be very slightly *higher* in the *front of the mouth*.

🔊 174

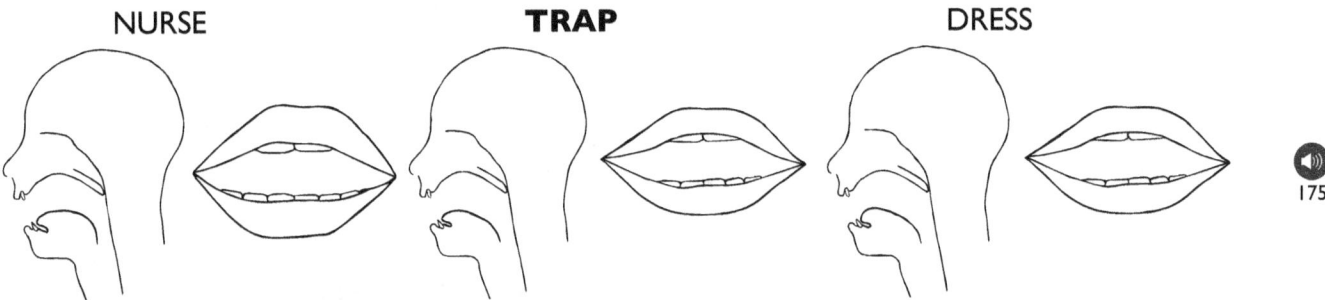

NURSE   TRAP   DRESS

🔊 175

This NURSE, TRAP and DRESS vowel sound sequence can be heard in the following sets of three words. Play with these words and encourage the *front of your tongue* to remain *low* in the *front of the mouth*, somewhat between the NURSE and DRESS vowel sounds. Encourage the *lips* to be slightly *spread* and the sound to be *short* in duration. Listen to the audio to help you imitate the sound accurately:

     p<u>er</u>t   p<u>a</u>t   p<u>e</u>t   f<u>er</u>n   f<u>a</u>n   f<u>e</u>n   b<u>ur</u>n   b<u>a</u>n   B<u>e</u>n   p<u>er</u>k   p<u>a</u>ck   p<u>e</u>ck

🔊 176

If your habit is to replace the TRAP vowel sound with the DRESS vowel sound, essentially, your *tongue* position is too *high*. For this reason, it might be helpful to say words with the STRUT vowel sound (which is made with the *tongue lower*) before saying words with the TRAP vowel sound, in order to encourage your *tongue* into a *lower* position. For example:

     p<u>u</u>tt   p<u>a</u>t   f<u>u</u>n   f<u>a</u>n   b<u>u</u>n   b<u>a</u>n   p<u>u</u>ck   p<u>a</u>ck   t<u>u</u>g   t<u>a</u>g   r<u>u</u>g   r<u>a</u>g

🔊 177

Similarly, if your habit is to replace the TRAP vowel sound with the BATH or STRUT vowel sound, then your *tongue* position is too *low*. For this reason, it might be helpful to say words with the DRESS vowel sound (which is made with the *tongue higher*) before saying words with the TRAP vowel sound, in order to encourage your *tongue* into a *higher* position. For example:

     p<u>e</u>t   p<u>a</u>t   f<u>e</u>n   f<u>a</u>n   B<u>e</u>n   b<u>a</u>n   p<u>e</u>ck   p<u>a</u>ck   sl<u>e</u>pt   sl<u>a</u>pped   wr<u>e</u>ck   r<u>a</u>ck

🔊 178

trap

phonetic symbol - æ

Lastly, here's another game to play: say the TRAP vowel sound on its own before saying each word, to help you hear whether or not you are pronouncing it accurately and also to give you a reference for how it should sound in the word. Listen to the audio to help you imitate the sound accurately:

a... p<u>a</u>ttern   m<u>a</u>tch   c<u>a</u>sh   m<u>a</u>d   st<u>a</u>ndard   h<u>a</u>m   m<u>a</u>n   underst<u>a</u>nd   h<u>a</u>ng

sh<u>a</u>ll   m<u>a</u>tter   h<u>a</u>nd   th<u>a</u>nk   <u>a</u>ngry   t<u>a</u>x   c<u>a</u>rriage   c<u>a</u>ncel   pl<u>ai</u>d   g<u>ua</u>rantee

How do I avoid being guided by the spelling?

Once you have used the exercises above to help you achieve an accurate pronunciation of this vowel sound, go to the *Lexical Sets* subsection *(p.16)* for advice on how to avoid being guided by the spelling.

> Anything Else?

This is a very minor detail, but when the TRAP vowel sound precedes some *voiced* consonants – especially, (but not consistently) the N sound *(book 2 - Consonants)* – it is slightly *longer* in duration. This can be heard in words like 'th<u>a</u>n', '<u>a</u>nd', 'c<u>a</u>nvas', 'exp<u>a</u>nsion', 'f<u>a</u>mily', 'l<u>a</u>nd', 'm<u>a</u>n', '<u>a</u>nt', 'b<u>a</u>g', 'b<u>a</u>nd', 'fl<u>a</u>g' 'h<u>a</u>nd', 'b<u>a</u>d', 's<u>a</u>d', 'm<u>a</u>d', 'r<u>a</u>g', 'b<u>a</u>dge', 'beg<u>a</u>n', 'st<u>a</u>ndard', 'h<u>a</u>m', 'underst<u>a</u>nd', 'c<u>a</u>ndle', 'l<u>a</u>mb', 'm<u>a</u>ndatory', 'c<u>a</u>ncel' and 'p<u>a</u>nda'. This is not indicated in pronunciation dictionaries as it only occurs in a handful of words, namely the ones above. As I said, this is a very minor detail and would add further specificity to your pronunciation, but if you were to continue to pronounce the TRAP vowel sound in words like these as *short* in duration, you will still be clearly understood and your pronunciation will lie within the RP canon.

Practice words and typical spellings for the TRAP vowel sound

a   t<u>a</u>p   c<u>a</u>t   b<u>a</u>tch   p<u>a</u>ttern   f<u>a</u>t   g<u>a</u>ff   mathem<u>a</u>tics   m<u>a</u>ss   m<u>a</u>tch

d<u>a</u>sh   c<u>a</u>sh   m<u>a</u>d   r<u>a</u>g   b<u>a</u>dge   beg<u>a</u>n   st<u>a</u>ndard   h<u>a</u>ve   j<u>a</u>zz   h<u>a</u>m   m<u>a</u>n

underst<u>a</u>nd   h<u>a</u>ng   m<u>a</u>gic   c<u>a</u>ndle   sh<u>a</u>ll   sc<u>a</u>lp   l<u>a</u>mb   <u>a</u>nt   m<u>a</u>tter   h<u>a</u>nd

th<u>a</u>nk   <u>a</u>ngry   l<u>a</u>pse   t<u>a</u>x   <u>a</u>rrow   c<u>a</u>rriage   m<u>a</u>ndatory   b<u>a</u>nner   <u>a</u>bbey   t<u>a</u>ssel

c<u>a</u>ncel   p<u>a</u>nda   pl<u>a</u>stic   el<u>a</u>stic   gymn<u>a</u>stic   enthusi<u>a</u>stic   m<u>a</u>sculine   bl<u>a</u>sphemy

m<u>a</u>sturbate   circumst<u>a</u>ntial   intr<u>a</u>nsigent   subst<u>a</u>ntial   tr<u>a</u>nsit   tr<u>a</u>nsport   tr<u>a</u>nsfer

tr<u>a</u>nsform   tr<u>a</u>nsitory   tr<u>a</u>nsient   <u>a</u>lto   Cleop<u>a</u>tra   **ai**   pl<u>ai</u>d   **ua**   g<u>ua</u>rantee

Practice Sentences for the TRAP vowel sound

- I h<u>a</u>ven't h<u>a</u>d any time to rel<u>a</u>x – it's been m<u>a</u>nic! H<u>a</u>ndling the f<u>a</u>mily well is a m<u>a</u>ssive ch<u>a</u>llenge!
- He's a h<u>a</u>ppily m<u>a</u>rried m<u>a</u>n who m<u>a</u>nages a tr<u>a</u>nsport company but he f<u>a</u>ncies himself <u>a</u>s an <u>a</u>ctor
- I was h<u>a</u>nging around after the m<u>a</u>tch when S<u>a</u>m called: he's d<u>a</u>maged his b<u>a</u>ck in an <u>a</u>ccident!
- H<u>a</u>ve you got the m<u>a</u>p and your thermal h<u>a</u>t? What about the bl<u>a</u>ck ruks<u>a</u>ck? Language J<u>a</u>ck!

mouth

phonetic symbol - aʊ

⏱ 20min

This sound is pronounced in words like:

ou <u>ou</u>t   d<u>ou</u>bt   c<u>ou</u>ncil   h<u>ou</u>se   **ow**   br<u>ow</u>se   d<u>ow</u>n   all<u>ow</u>   t<u>ow</u>n

ough   b<u>ough</u>   pl<u>ough</u>   d<u>ough</u>ty   **other**   MacCl<u>eo</u>d

183

> ### How is the MOUTH vowel sound made in an RP accent?

The MOUTH vowel sound is a *diphthong* – a combination of two vowel sounds where one slides into the other. The MOUTH vowel sound starts as the TRAP vowel sound (*p.57 - where the tongue tip is behind the bottom teeth, the front of the tongue is low in the front of the mouth, and the lips are slightly spread*) which slides into a slightly *shorter* version of the GOOSE vowel sound (*p.90 - where the tongue tip stays behind the bottom teeth, the back of the tongue slides high and backwards into the back of the mouth, and the lips round*). The *jaw* is loose, the *teeth* are apart, and the sound is *long* in duration.

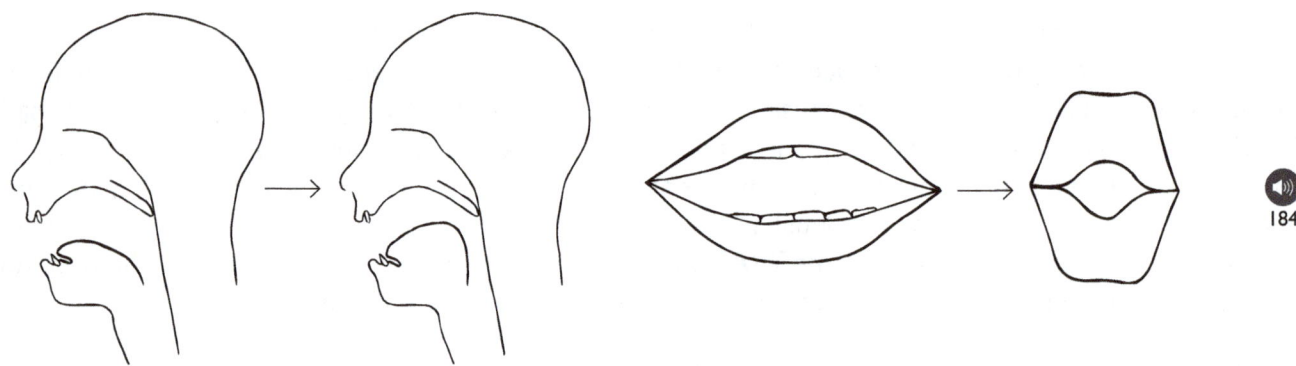
184

> ### What do I do habitually?

- *Do your lips remain rounded, neutral or spread throughout the whole diphthong?*

Some speakers move their *tongue* through the accurate positions and make the sound *long* in duration, but their *lips* remain *rounded, neutral* or *spread* throughout instead of sliding from slightly *spread* to *rounded*, which impacts on the quality and tone of the sound. Listen to the following words, firstly spoken with the *lips rounded*, then *neutral*, then *spread,* and then sliding from slightly *spread* to *rounded*, as they should be in RP: '<u>ou</u>t', 't<u>ow</u>n', 'pl<u>ough</u>' and 'MacCl<u>eo</u>d'. If you do this, go to

185

- *Are you making this diphthong too long or too short in duration?*

Some speakers move their *tongue* and *lips* through the accurate positions but they make the *diphthong* too *short* or too *long* in duration, which impacts on the quality and tone of the sound. If you are making the *diphthong* too *long*, either both vowel sounds in the *diphthong* will be too *long*, which will make it sound like two *syllables* instead of one, or one of the vowel sounds in the *diphthong* will be too *long*. Listen to the following words, firstly spoken with the *diphthong* too *short* in duration, then with both vowel sounds too *long*, then with the first vowel sound too *long*, then with the second vowel sound too *long*, and finally as they should be in RP: '<u>ou</u>t', 't<u>ow</u>n', 'pl<u>ough</u>' and 'MacCl<u>eo</u>d'. If you do this, go to

186

mouth

phonetic symbol - aʊ

- Are you replacing the first vowel sound with the LOT vowel sound?

Some speakers replace the first vowel sound (TRAP) with the LOT vowel sound *(p.43)*, which is made with the *back of the tongue low* in the *back of the mouth*, the *lips* slightly *rounded* and the sound *short* in duration. Listen to the following words, firstly spoken with the LOT vowel sound at the beginning of this *diphthong* and then with the TRAP vowel sound at the beginning, as they should be in RP: 'out', 'town', 'plough' and 'MacCleod'. If you do this, go to 🔧

- Are you replacing the first vowel sound with the STRUT vowel sound?

Some speakers replace the first vowel sound (TRAP) with the STRUT vowel sound *(p.35)*, which is made with the *middle of the tongue low* in the *centre of the mouth*, the *lips neutral* and the sound *short* in duration. Listen to the following words, firstly spoken with the STRUT vowel sound at the beginning of this *diphthong* and then with the TRAP vowel sound at the beginning, as they should be in RP: 'out', 'town', 'plough' and 'MacCleod'. If you do this, go to 🔧

- Are you replacing the first vowel sound with the FOOT vowel sound?

Some speakers replace the first vowel sound (TRAP) with the FOOT vowel sound *(p.94)*, which is made with the *back of the tongue high* in the *back of the mouth*, the *lips rounded* and the sound *short* in duration. Listen to the following words, firstly spoken with the FOOT vowel sound at the beginning of this *diphthong* and then with the TRAP vowel sound at the beginning, as they should be in RP: 'out', 'town', 'plough' and 'MacCleod'. If you do this, go to 🔧

- Is your pronunciation guided by the spelling?

Many non-native speakers use the spelling of a word as a guide to its pronunciation. But because British English is not written phonetically, one vowel sound can be represented by numerous spellings. For this reason, the spelling in British English cannot be trusted for vowel pronunciation. For example, the MOUTH vowel sound can be represented as the 'ow' in 'down', the 'ough' in 'plough' and the 'eo' in 'MacCleod'. So, you might mistakenly pronounce the 'ough' in 'plough' as the GOAT vowel sound *(p.26 - as in 'although')*. But all these words, despite the variation in spelling, are pronounced with the MOUTH vowel sound.

It is also typical for a speaker to have a certain spelling that they often associate with a vowel sound. For example, many speakers associate the spelling 'ou' with the MOUTH vowel sound. One might then hope that all words spelt with 'ou' would be pronounced as the MOUTH vowel sound. Sadly, this is not true, as the 'ou' in 'touch' should be pronounced as the STRUT vowel sound *(p.35 - as in 'cup')*, in 'could' it is pronounced as the FOOT vowel sound *(p.94 - as in 'put')*, in 'cough' it is pronounced as the LOT vowel sound *(p.43 - as in 'hot')*, in 'gracious' it is pronounced as the SCHWA vowel sound *(p.17 - as in 'tuna')*, in 'group' it is pronounced as the GOOSE vowel sound *(p.90 - as in 'food')*, and in 'soul' it is pronounced as the GOAL version of the GOAT vowel sound *(p.27 - as in 'hole')*. All of this might seem a bit overwhelming, but I have some simple and effective solutions that will help you: go to 🔧

m<u>ou</u>th

phonetic symbol - aʊ

> How do I change my habit?

How do I find the accurate tongue position for the MOUTH vowel sound?

Firstly, ensure that you are accurately pronouncing the two component vowel sounds in this *diphthong* by following the exercises in the sections entitled *How do I find the accurate tongue position for the TRAP vowel sound? (p.56)* and *How do I find the accurate tongue position for the GOOSE vowel sound? (p.88).*

Once you feel confident with how to make each vowel sound, your *tongue* needs to slide from one into the other to make the *diphthong*. Say each sound on its own, one after the other, with a brief pause between them. Watch your *tongue* and *lips* in a mirror and then take out the pause, sliding them into one another. All *diphthongs* are made with the first vowel slightly more *stressed* than the second. This being said, it is only *slightly* more *stressed* and should be observed with care. And remember that the two vowel sounds in a *diphthong* make a single *syllable*: the *tongue* slides smoothly but swiftly and the sound is *long*, but not too *long*.

Play with the following exercise. It offers you an opportunity to check whether you are accurately pronouncing the first vowel sound in the *diphthong* – TRAP. Listen to the audio to help you imitate the sound accurately:

a... <u>ou</u>t ta... t<u>ow</u>n pla... pl<u>ough</u> MacCla... MacCl<u>eo</u>d

192

How do I avoid being guided by the spelling?

Once you have used the exercises above to help you achieve an accurate pronunciation of this vowel sound, go to the *Lexical Sets* subsection *(p.16)* for advice on how to avoid being guided by the spelling.

> Anything Else?

- The HOUR triphthong: phonetic symbol aʊə

There are five of the eight *diphthongs* that can be extended with a final SCHWA vowel sound, which turns the *diphthong* into a *triphthong* – a combination of three vowel sounds where one slides into another. The MOUTH vowel sound is one such *diphthong*, so words like 'h<u>our</u>', '<u>our</u>', 't<u>ower</u>' and 's<u>our</u>' are pronounced with the MOUTH vowel sound followed by a SCHWA vowel sound. The *lips* relax back to *neutral* and the *tongue* slides from being in the *back of the mouth* to the *middle* of the *centre of the mouth*.
193

Some RP speakers add a W *(book 2 - Consonants)* to link the MOUTH vowel sound to the SCHWA vowel sound. This makes words like 'h<u>our</u>', '<u>our</u>', 't<u>ower</u>' and 's<u>our</u>' sound like two *syllable* words instead of one. In this version, the *lips round* too much at the end of the *diphthong* and then release quite suddenly into the SCHWA. Other speakers do not add a W. Instead, they make the transition of their *lips* from the MOUTH vowel sound to the SCHWA vowel sound much more smoothly. This makes the words above sound more like one *syllable*.
194

This variation in pronunciation is in part to do with the evolving nature of accents. And unfortunately these variations are not accounted for in a reliable dictionary. In some ways, this ambiguity could be seen

mouth

phonetic symbol - aʊ

as a frustrating, but another perspective would be to say that is allows for choice, as both are considered correct. Listen to the following words, firstly spoken with the W and then without:

fl<u>ou</u>r   s<u>ou</u>r   fl<u>ower</u>   c<u>ow</u>ard   p<u>ow</u>er   t<u>ow</u>er   c<u>ow</u>er   sh<u>ow</u>er   h<u>ou</u>r

195

And lastly, many words with these *triphthongs* have a written 'r' in the spelling, which should not be spoken, unless they are followed by a spoken vowel sound. Encourage your *tongue tip* to remain down, touching the *bottom front teeth* at the end of the *triphthong*.

🎤 *Practice words and typical spellings for the MOUTH vowel sound*

ou	<u>ou</u>t	p<u>ou</u>ch	d<u>ou</u>bt	s<u>ou</u>th	h<u>ou</u>se	sh<u>ou</u>t	l<u>ou</u>d	g<u>ou</u>ge	m<u>ou</u>th *v.*
	r<u>ou</u>se	n<u>ou</u>n	f<u>ou</u>l	th<u>ou</u>	c<u>ou</u>nt	r<u>ou</u>nd	pron<u>ou</u>nce	<u>ou</u>st	tr<u>ou</u>sers
	m<u>ou</u>ntain	pr<u>ou</u>d	c<u>ou</u>ncil	b<u>ou</u>ndary	ar<u>ou</u>nd	b<u>ou</u>nce	**ow**	cr<u>ow</u>d	br<u>ow</u>se
<u>ow</u>l	d<u>ow</u>n	c<u>ow</u>	all<u>ow</u>	d<u>ow</u>ry	fr<u>ow</u>n	t<u>ow</u>el	p<u>ow</u>der	t<u>ow</u>n	br<u>ow</u>n
ough	b<u>ough</u>	pl<u>ough</u>	d<u>ough</u>ty	**other spellings**	MacCl<u>eo</u>d				

196

🎤 *Practice Sentences for the MOUTH vowel sound*

- Go left <u>ou</u>t of my h<u>ou</u>se, ar<u>ou</u>nd the r<u>ou</u>ndab<u>ou</u>t towards t<u>ow</u>n and d<u>ow</u>n towards the c<u>ou</u>ncil.
- It was such a l<u>ou</u>d s<u>ou</u>nd - the cr<u>ow</u>d were ast<u>ou</u>nded. There must have been a th<u>ou</u>sand or so.
- The am<u>ou</u>nt of f<u>ou</u>l language they all<u>ow</u>ed is <u>ou</u>trageous. I lost c<u>ou</u>nt! And they were so pr<u>ou</u>d!
- I fell from the b<u>ough</u> of that tree, split my br<u>ow</u>n tr<u>ou</u>sers and g<u>ou</u>ged my leg on the gr<u>ou</u>nd.

197

> Bonus Material!

Great news – there's a FREE online video about the MOUTH on my YouTube channel:

https://www.youtube.com/@ashleyhowardvoicecoach

⏱ 20min

fleece

phonetic symbol - iː

This sound is pronounced in words like:

ee	m<u>ee</u>t	t<u>ee</u>th	ch<u>ee</u>se	s<u>ee</u>	marqu<u>ee</u>	**e**	m<u>e</u>	b<u>e</u>	<u>e</u>ven	th<u>e</u>se
ie	bel<u>ie</u>f	br<u>ie</u>f	p<u>ie</u>ce	bel<u>ie</u>ve	**ei**	c<u>ei</u>ling	dec<u>ei</u>ve	rec<u>ei</u>ve	s<u>ei</u>ze	
ey	k<u>ey</u>	mon<u>ey</u>	**y**	happ<u>y</u>	worr<u>y</u>	sorr<u>y</u>	hurr<u>y</u>	**eo**	p<u>eo</u>ple	Ph<u>oe</u>nix
subp<u>oe</u>na	f<u>oe</u>tus	**ea**	<u>ea</u>ch	m<u>ea</u>t	sp<u>ea</u>k	t<u>ea</u>ch	**ae**	C<u>ae</u>sar	an<u>ae</u>mic	
<u>Ae</u>sop	**i**	pol<u>i</u>ce	un<u>i</u>que	mach<u>i</u>ne	v<u>i</u>sa	**ay**	Qu<u>ay</u>			

198

> **How is the FLEECE vowel sound made in an RP accent?**

The *tongue tip* is behind the *bottom teeth* and the *front of the tongue* is *high* in the *front of the mouth*. The *lips* are slightly *spread*, the *jaw* is loose and the *teeth* are apart. The FLEECE vowel sound is *long* in duration. Compared to all other vowel sounds, the *front of the tongue* is most *high* and *forwards* for the FLEECE vowel sound.

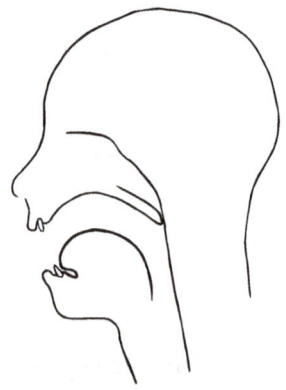
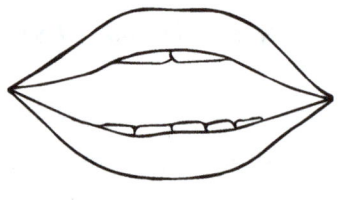

199

> **What do I do habitually?**

- Are your lips rounded or neutral instead of slightly spread?

Some speakers have their *tongue* in an accurate position and make the sound *long* in duration, but their *lips* are *rounded* or *neutral* instead of slightly *spread*, which impacts on the quality and tone of the sound. Listen to the following words, firstly spoken with the *lips rounded*, then *neutral* and then slightly *spread*, as they should be in RP: 'm<u>ee</u>t', 'm<u>e</u>', 'bel<u>ie</u>f', 'c<u>ei</u>ling', 'mon<u>ey</u>', 'p<u>eo</u>ple', 'subp<u>oe</u>na', '<u>ea</u>ch', 'an<u>ae</u>mic', 'pol<u>i</u>ce' and 'Qu<u>ay</u>'. If you do this, go to 🔧

200

- Are you pronouncing the FLEECE vowel sound too short?

Some speakers have their *tongue* and *lips* in an accurate position but they make the sound *short* in duration, instead of *long*, which impacts on the quality and tone of the sound. Listen to the following words, firstly spoken with the sound *short* in duration and then *long*, as they should be in RP: 'm<u>ee</u>t', 'm<u>e</u>', 'bel<u>ie</u>f', 'c<u>ei</u>ling', 'mon<u>ey</u>', 'p<u>eo</u>ple', 'subp<u>oe</u>na', '<u>ea</u>ch', 'an<u>ae</u>mic', 'pol<u>i</u>ce' and 'Qu<u>ay</u>'. If you do this, go to 🔧

201

fleece

phonetic symbol - iː

- Are you replacing the FLEECE vowel sound with the KIT vowel sound?

Some speakers replace the FLEECE vowel sound with the KIT vowel sound *(p.70)*, which is made with the *front of the tongue* slightly *lower* in the *front of the mouth*, and sound *short* in duration. The *lips* are equally as *spread* for both vowel sounds. So words like 's<u>ee</u>n' sound more like 's<u>i</u>n', and 'h<u>ea</u>t' sounds more like 'h<u>i</u>t'. If you do this, go to 202

- Are you replacing the FLEECE vowel sound with the DRESS vowel sound?

Some speakers replace the FLEECE vowel sound with the DRESS vowel sound *(p.78)*, which is made with the *front of the tongue* in the *middle* of the *front of the mouth*, and the sound is *short* in duration. The *lips* are equally as *spread* for both vowel sounds. So words like 'p<u>ea</u>k' sound more like 'p<u>e</u>ck', and 'b<u>ee</u>n' sounds more like 'B<u>e</u>n'. If you do this, go to 203

- Are you adding a SCHWA vowel sound before the FLEECE vowel sound?

Some speakers add a SCHWA vowel sound *(p.17)*, as in 'tun<u>a</u>', just before the FLEECE vowel sound, so the *middle of the tongue* starts in the *middle* of the *centre of the mouth* before sliding up and forwards. Listen to the following words, firstly spoken with a SCHWA vowel sound before the FLEECE vowel sound, and then just with the FLEECE vowel sound, as they should be in RP: 'm<u>ee</u>t', 'm<u>e</u>', 'bel<u>ie</u>f', 'c<u>ei</u>ling', 'mon<u>ey</u>', 'p<u>eo</u>ple', 'subp<u>oe</u>na', '<u>ea</u>ch', 'an<u>ae</u>mic', 'pol<u>i</u>ce' and 'Qu<u>ay</u>'. If you do this, go to 204

- Is your tongue too high?

Some speakers make the FLEECE vowel sound with their *tongue* too *high* in the *front of the mouth*. It is still clearly the FLEECE vowel sound and is not misunderstood as another vowel sound but it has a different quality and tone. Listen to the following words, firstly spoken with the *tongue* too *high*, and then with the *tongue* slightly *lower* and more relaxed, as they should be in RP: 'm<u>ee</u>t', 'm<u>e</u>', 'bel<u>ie</u>f', 'c<u>ei</u>ling', 'mon<u>ey</u>', 'p<u>eo</u>ple', 'subp<u>oe</u>na', '<u>ea</u>ch', 'an<u>ae</u>mic', 'pol<u>i</u>ce' and 'Qu<u>ay</u>'. If you do this, go to 205

- Is your pronunciation guided by the spelling?

Many non-native speakers use the spelling of a word as a guide to its pronunciation. But because British English is not written phonetically, one vowel sound can be represented by numerous spellings. For this reason, the spelling in British English cannot be trusted for vowel pronunciation. For example, the FLEECE vowel sound can be represented as the '<u>ae</u>' in 'an<u>ae</u>mic', the 'ay' in 'qu<u>ay</u>', the 'e' in 'th<u>e</u>se', the 'ea' in 'm<u>ea</u>t', the 'eo' in 'p<u>eo</u>ple', the 'ei' in 'rec<u>ei</u>ve', the 'ey' in 'k<u>ey</u>', the 'i_e' in 'pol<u>i</u>ce' and the 'ie' in 'br<u>ie</u>f'. So, you might mistakenly pronounce the 'ea' in 'm<u>ea</u>t' as the FACE vowel sound *(p.82 - as in 'great')*. But all these words, despite the variation in spelling, are pronounced with the FLEECE vowel sound. 206

It is also typical for a speaker to have a certain spelling that they often associate with a vowel sound. For example, many speakers associate the spelling 'ee' with the FLEECE vowel sound. And thankfully, this spelling is a good guide to when to use this vowel sound, except that in '<u>ee</u>rie' it should be pronounced as the NEAR vowel sound *(p.74 - as in 'ear')*. All of this might seem a bit overwhelming, but I have some simple and effective solutions that will help you: go to 207

fleece

phonetic symbol - iː

> ***How do I change my habit?***

How do I encourage my lips to be slightly spread?

The only way to guarantee that you are slightly *spreading* your *lips* accurately instead of them being *rounded* or *neutral* is to use a mirror when you practice. Otherwise, you can feel the movement in your *lips* by putting one finger in a vertical line over your *lips* – if your *lips* are *rounding* your finger will be pushed forwards; and if your *lips* are *neutral* or slightly *spreading* your finger will remain still. Say the following words, either looking in a mirror or with one finger on your *lips*, and encourage them to be slightly *spread* accurately:

m<u>ee</u>t   s<u>ee</u>   m<u>e</u>   b<u>e</u>   bel<u>ie</u>f   br<u>ie</u>f   dec<u>ei</u>ve   rec<u>ei</u>ve   k<u>ey</u>   mon<u>ey</u>

happ<u>y</u>   sorr<u>y</u>   p<u>eo</u>ple   Ph<u>oe</u>nix   subp<u>oe</u>na   <u>ea</u>ch   m<u>ea</u>t   C<u>ae</u>sar

an<u>ae</u>mic   pol<u>i</u>ce   v<u>i</u>sa   Qu<u>ay</u>

208

How do I find the accurate tongue position for the FLEECE vowel sound?

The position of the *tongue* and *lips* for the FLEECE vowel sound is similar to their positions for the DRESS vowel sound *(p.78)* and KIT vowel sound *(p.70)*, so it might be helpful to compare them. Look in a mirror as you say 'h<u>ea</u>d', 'h<u>i</u>d' and 'h<u>ee</u>d' (angle yourself towards a light or use a very small torch). It might be helpful to say the vowel sounds on their own after saying the words, in order to see the *tongue* more clearly. In all of these vowel sounds the *lips* are slightly *spread*. For 'h<u>ea</u>d' (the DRESS vowel sound) encourage the *front of the tongue* to be in the *middle* of the *front of the mouth* and the sound to be *short* in duration. For 'h<u>i</u>d' (the KIT vowel sound) encourage the sound to be equally as *short* in duration, but the *front of the tongue* to be slightly *higher* in the *front of the mouth*. And for 'h<u>ee</u>d' (this is the target FLEECE vowel sound) encourage the *front of the tongue* to be slightly *higher* still in the *front of the mouth* and the sound to be *long* in duration.

209

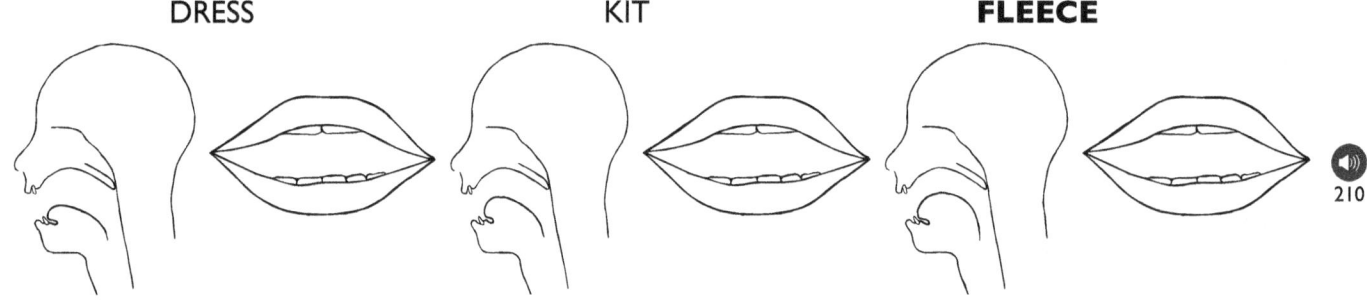

210

This DRESS, KIT and FLEECE vowel sound sequence can be heard in the following sets of three words. Play with these groups of three words, and encourage the *front of your tongue* to be in the *highest* position for the final word. Encourage the *lips* to be slightly *spread* and the sound to be *long* in duration. Listen to the audio to help you imitate the sound accurately:

p<u>e</u>t   p<u>i</u>t   p<u>ea</u>t   s<u>e</u>t   s<u>i</u>t   s<u>ea</u>t   n<u>e</u>t   n<u>i</u>t   n<u>ea</u>t   b<u>e</u>t   b<u>i</u>t   b<u>ea</u>t   b<u>e</u>d   b<u>i</u>d   b<u>ea</u>d

211

Here's another game to play that might be helpful (especially if you discovered that you were adding a

fleece

phonetic symbol - iː

SCHWA vowel sound before the FLEECE vowel sound): say the FLEECE vowel sound on its own before saying each word, to help you hear whether or not you are pronouncing it accurately and also to give you a reference for how it should sound in the word. Listen to the audio to help you imitate the sound accurately:

ee... m_ee_t   s_ee_   m_e_   b_e_   bel_ie_f   br_ie_f   dec_ei_ve   rec_ei_ve   k_ey_   mon_ey_

happ_y_   sorr_y_   p_eo_ple   Ph_oe_nix   subp_oe_na   _ea_ch   m_ea_t   C_ae_sar

an_ae_mic   pol_i_ce   v_i_sa   Qu_ay_

212

If you discovered that you were making the FLEECE vowel sound with your *tongue* was too *high* you might play with replacing the FLEECE vowel sound with the KIT vowel sound *(p.70 - which is made with the tongue lower)*. So say 'h_ea_t' then 'h_i_t', paying attention to the feeling of the *tongue* being lower for 'h_i_t'. Then say 'h_ea_t' again, encouraging your *tongue* not to move too much away from its position for 'h_i_t'. Listen to the audio to help you imitate the sound accurately:

213

p_i_t   p_ea_t   s_i_t   s_ea_t   n_i_t   n_ea_t   b_i_t   b_ea_t   b_i_d   b_ea_d   l_i_tter   l_i_tre   f_i_t   f_ee_t

214

🔧 *How do I avoid being guided by the spelling?*

Once you have used the exercises above to help you achieve an accurate pronunciation of this vowel sound, go to the *Lexical Sets* subsection *(p.16)* for advice on how to avoid being guided by the spelling.

> Anything Else?

This is a very minor detail, but when the FLEECE vowel sound is spelt 'y' at the end of a word, it is very slightly *shorter* in duration, as in 'happ_y_', 'sorr_y_', 'worr_y_', 'hurr_y_' and 'carr_y_'. In some reliable dictionaries, this can be seen in the phonetic transcription as iː without the dots – i. Avoid it being too *short* in duration, or else it will sound like the KIT vowel sound *(p.70)*. Listen to the words above, firstly spoken with the sound *long* in duration and then slightly *shorter*, as they should be in RP.

215

🎤 ***Practice words and typical spellings for the FLEECE vowel sound***

ee   cr_ee_p   m_ee_t   s_ee_k   b_ee_ch   r_ee_f   t_ee_th   s_ee_d   sl_ee_ve   s_ee_the

ch_ee_se   s_ee_m   gr_ee_n   f_ee_l   s_ee_   tr_ee_   agr_ee_   n_ee_dle   f_ee_der   sw_ee_ten

e   gr_e_be   th_e_se   P_e_ter   _e_ven   b_e_   m_e_   m_e_tre   _e_qual   d_e_cent   l_e_gal

p_e_nal   compl_e_te   sc_e_ne   sh_e_   h_e_   w_e_   **ie**   shr_ie_k   bel_ie_f   br_ie_f   p_ie_ce

bel_ie_ve   gr_ie_ve   f_ie_ld   **ei**   c_ei_ling   K_ei_th   Sh_ei_la   dec_ei_ve   rec_ei_ve   s_ei_ze

ey   k_ey_   mon_ey_   **y**   happ_y_   worr_y_   marr_y_   sorr_y_   hurr_y_   **eo**   p_eo_ple

oe   Ph_oe_nix   subp_oe_na   f_oe_tus   **ea**   r_ea_p   _ea_ch   m_ea_t   sp_ea_k   t_ea_ch

l_ea_f   ben_ea_th   s_ea_   p_ea_ce   l_ea_sh   l_ea_d   l_ea_gue   l_ea_ve   p_ea_   br_ea_the

pl_ea_se   t_ea_m   m_ea_n   d_ea_l   s_ea_   t_ea_   f_ea_ts   r_ea_son   w_ea_sel   _ea_sy   _Ea_ster

ae   C_ae_sar   an_ae_mic   _Ae_sop   **i**   pol_i_ce   un_i_que   mach_i_ne   prest_i_ge   el_i_te

mosqu_i_to   cas_i_no   v_i_sa   tr_i_o   sk_i_   ch_i_c   **ay**   Qu_ay_

216

68

fleece

phonetic symbol - iː

🎙 **Practice Sentences for the FLEECE vowel sound**

- The p<u>eo</u>ple are <u>ea</u>sy going, the str<u>ee</u>ts are cl<u>ea</u>n, the <u>e</u>venings are p<u>ea</u>ceful – it's a dr<u>ea</u>m!
- Hurr<u>y</u> up! W<u>e</u> have to m<u>ee</u>t L<u>ee</u> on Oxford Str<u>ee</u>t at thr<u>ee</u> o'clock. Pl<u>ea</u>se! H<u>e</u> will l<u>ea</u>ve!
- Have you rec<u>ei</u>ved the l<u>ea</u>gue tables yet? What r<u>ea</u>son did they give? <u>E</u>ven K<u>ei</u>th has s<u>ee</u>n them!
- Have a s<u>ea</u>t. Would you like a cup of t<u>ea</u>? Coff<u>ee</u>? Whisk<u>ey</u>? I make a m<u>ea</u>n margar<u>i</u>ta!?

217

Am I pronouncing it accurately?

Get a personalised assessment of every vowel, consonant and aspect of intonation to find out how well you're doing, exactly what to focus on and what you need to do to speak in this accent accurately and naturally:

https://www.ashleyhoward.me/pronunciation-evaluation

🕐 20min

kit

phonetic symbol - **I**

This sound is pronounced in words like:

i	h<u>i</u>m	b<u>i</u>t	w<u>i</u>th	st<u>i</u>ff	**y**	m<u>y</u>th	s<u>y</u>mbol	rh<u>y</u>thm	Fl<u>y</u>nn	**e**	pr<u>e</u>tty

E<u>n</u>gland   E<u>n</u>glish   **ui**   b<u>ui</u>ld   g<u>ui</u>lt   bisc<u>ui</u>t   **a**   dam<u>a</u>ge   man<u>a</u>ge   salv<u>a</u>ge

vill<u>a</u>ge   **o**   w<u>o</u>men *pl.*   **ie**   s<u>ie</u>ve   **u**   b<u>u</u>sy   b<u>u</u>siness

ai   capt<u>ai</u>n   mount<u>ai</u>n   fount<u>ai</u>n

218

> ## How is the KIT vowel sound made in an RP accent?

The *tongue tip* is behind the *bottom teeth* and the *front of the tongue* is *high* in the *front of the mouth*. The *lips* are slightly *spread*, the *jaw* is loose and the *teeth* are apart. The KIT vowel sound is *short* in duration.

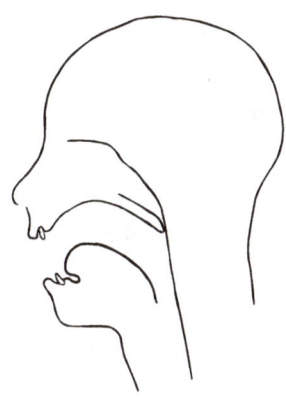 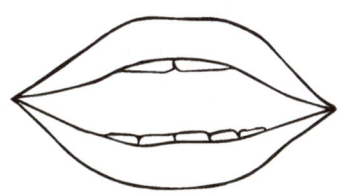

219

> ## What do I do habitually?

- Are your lips rounded or neutral instead of slightly spread?

Some speakers have their *tongue* in an accurate position and make the sound *short* in duration, but their *lips* are *rounded* instead of slightly *spread*, which impacts on the quality and tone of the sound. Listen to the following words, firstly spoken with the *lips rounded* and then with the *lips* slightly *spread*, as they should be in RP: 'sh<u>i</u>p', 's<u>y</u>mbol', 'pr<u>e</u>tty', 'E<u>n</u>glish', 'b<u>ui</u>ld', 'dam<u>a</u>ge', 'w<u>o</u>men', 's<u>ie</u>ve', 'b<u>u</u>sy' and 'b<u>u</u>siness'. If you do this, go to 🔧

220

- Are you pronouncing the KIT vowel sound too long?

Some speakers have their *tongue* and *lips* in an accurate position but they make the sound *long* in duration, instead of *short*, which impacts on the quality and tone of the sound. Listen to the following words, firstly spoken with the sound *long* in duration and then *short*, as they should be in RP: 'sh<u>i</u>p', 's<u>y</u>mbol', 'pr<u>e</u>tty', 'E<u>n</u>glish', 'b<u>ui</u>ld', 'dam<u>a</u>ge', 'w<u>o</u>men', 's<u>ie</u>ve', 'b<u>u</u>sy' and 'b<u>u</u>siness'. If you do this, go to 🔧

221

- Are you replacing the KIT vowel sound with the FLEECE vowel sound?

Some speakers replace the KIT vowel sound with the FLEECE vowel sound *(p.65)*, which is made with the *front of the tongue* very slightly *higher* in the *front of the mouth*, and the sound *longer* in duration. The *lips* are

kit

phonetic symbol - **I**

equally as *spread* for both vowel sounds. So words like 'p<u>i</u>t' sound more like 'P<u>e</u>te', 'h<u>i</u>t' sounds more like 'h<u>ea</u>t', '<u>i</u>t' sounds more like '<u>ea</u>t' and '<u>i</u>s' sounds more like '<u>ea</u>se'. If you do this, go to

- Are you replacing the KIT vowel sound with the DRESS vowel sound?

Some speakers replace the KIT vowel sound with the DRESS vowel sound *(p.78)*, which is made with the *front of the tongue* very slightly *lower* in the *front of the mouth*. The *lips* are equally as *spread* for both vowel sounds and they are equally as *short* in duration. So words like 'p<u>i</u>t' sound more like 'p<u>e</u>t', 'sl<u>i</u>pped' sounds more like 'sl<u>e</u>pt', 'f<u>i</u>ll' sounds more like 'f<u>e</u>ll' and 'J<u>i</u>ll' sounds more like 'g<u>e</u>l'. If you do this, go to

- Is your pronunciation guided by the spelling?

Many non-native speakers use the spelling of a word as a guide to its pronunciation. But because British English is not written phonetically, one vowel sound can be represented by numerous spellings. For this reason, the spelling in British English cannot be trusted for vowel pronunciation. For example, the KIT vowel sound can be represented as the 'y' in 's<u>y</u>mbol', the 'e' in '<u>E</u>ngland', the 'ui' in 'b<u>ui</u>ld', the 'a' in 'vill<u>a</u>ge', the 'o' in the plural 'w<u>o</u>men', the 'ie' in 's<u>ie</u>ve', the 'u' in 'b<u>u</u>sy' and the 'ai' in 'capt<u>ai</u>n'. So, you might mistakenly pronounce the 'e' in 'England' as the DRESS vowel sound *(p.78 - as in '<u>e</u>nd')*, or the 'a' in 'village' as the FACE vowel sound *(p.82 - as in '<u>a</u>ge')*. But all these words, despite the variation in spelling, are pronounced with the KIT vowel sound.

It is also typical for a speaker to have a certain spelling that they often associate with a vowel sound. For example, many speakers associate the spelling 'i' with the KIT vowel sound. One might then hope that all words spelt with 'i' would be pronounced as the KIT vowel sound. Sadly, this is not true, as the 'i' in 'pol<u>i</u>ce' should be pronounced as the longer FLEECE vowel sound *(p.65 - as in 's<u>ee</u>n')*, and in '<u>i</u>ce' it is pronounced as the PRICE vowel sound *(p.39 - as in '<u>eye</u>')*. All of this might seem a bit overwhelming, but I have some simple and effective solutions that will help you: go to

> **> How do I change my habit?**

🔧 *How do I encourage my lips to be slightly spread?*

The only way to guarantee that you are slightly *spreading* your *lips* accurately instead of *rounding* them is to use a mirror when you practice. Otherwise, you can feel the movement in your *lips* by putting one finger in a vertical line over your *lips* – if your *lips* are *rounding* your finger will be pushed forwards; and if your *lips* are *neutral* or slightly *spreading* your finger will remain still. Say the following words, either looking in a mirror or with one finger on your *lips*, and encourage them to be slightly *spread* accurately:

    sh<u>i</u>p   b<u>i</u>t   m<u>y</u>th   s<u>y</u>mbol   pr<u>e</u>tty   <u>E</u>ngland   b<u>ui</u>ld   g<u>ui</u>lt   dam<u>a</u>ge   man<u>a</u>ge

    w<u>o</u>men *pl.*   s<u>ie</u>ve   b<u>u</u>sy   b<u>u</u>siness   mount<u>ai</u>n   fount<u>ai</u>n

 How do I find the accurate tongue position for the KIT vowel sound?

The position of the *tongue* and *lips* for the KIT vowel sound is similar to their positions for the DRESS vowel sound *(p.78)* and FLEECE vowel sound *(p.65)*, so it might be helpful to compare them. Look in a

kit

phonetic symbol - **I**

mirror as you say 'head', 'hid' and 'heed' (angle yourself towards a light or use a very small torch). It might be helpful to say the vowel sounds on their own after saying the words, in order to see the *tongue* more clearly. For 'head' (the DRESS vowel sound) encourage the *lips* to be slightly *spread*, the *front of the tongue* to be in the *middle* of the *front of the mouth* and the sound to be *short* in duration. For 'hid' (this is the target KIT vowel sound) encourage the *lips* to be just as *spread*, the sound to be just as *short* in duration, but the *front of the tongue* to be very slightly *higher* in the front of the *mouth*. And for 'heed' (the FLEECE vowel sound) encourage the *lips* to be just as *spread*, but the *front of the tongue* to be slightly *higher* still in the *front of the mouth* and the sound to be *longer* in duration.

227

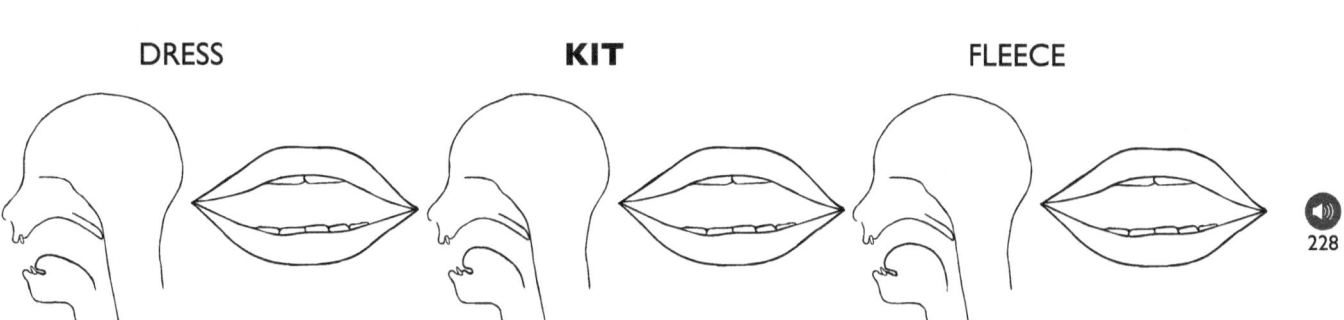

228

This DRESS, KIT and FLEECE vowel sound sequence can be heard in the following sets of three words. Play with these words and encourage the *front of your tongue* to remain in between the positions for the DRESS and FLEECE vowel sounds. Encourage the *lips* to be slightly *spread* and the sound to be *short* in duration. Listen to the audio to help you imitate the sound accurately:

      p<u>e</u>t p<u>i</u>t p<u>ea</u>t   L<u>e</u>n L<u>y</u>nn l<u>ea</u>n   B<u>e</u>n b<u>i</u>n b<u>ea</u>n   wh<u>e</u>n w<u>i</u>n w<u>ea</u>n

229

If your habit is to replace the KIT vowel sound with the FLEECE vowel sound, essentially, your *tongue* position is too *high* and *forward*. For this reason, it might be helpful to say words with the DRESS vowel sound (which is made with the *tongue* slightly *lower*) before saying words with the KIT vowel sound, in order to encourage your *tongue* into a *lower* position. For example:

      p<u>e</u>t p<u>i</u>t   L<u>e</u>n L<u>y</u>nn   B<u>e</u>n b<u>i</u>n   wh<u>e</u>n w<u>i</u>n   h<u>e</u>m h<u>i</u>m   sl<u>e</u>pt sl<u>i</u>pped

230

Similarly, if your habit is to replace the KIT vowel sound with the DRESS vowel sound, then your *tongue* position is too *low*. For this reason, it might be helpful to say words with the FLEECE vowel sound (which is made with the *tongue* slightly *higher*) before saying words with the KIT vowel sound, in order to encourage your *tongue* into a *higher* position. For example:

      p<u>ea</u>t p<u>i</u>t   l<u>ea</u>n L<u>y</u>nn   b<u>ea</u>n b<u>i</u>n   w<u>ea</u>n w<u>i</u>n   sl<u>ee</u>p sl<u>i</u>p   w<u>ee</u>p wh<u>i</u>p

231

Lastly, here's another game to play: say the KIT vowel sound on its own before saying each word, to help you hear whether or not you are pronouncing it accurately and also to give you a reference for how it should sound in the word. Listen to the audio to help you imitate the sound accurately:

      i... h<u>i</u>m b<u>i</u>t w<u>i</u>th m<u>y</u>th s<u>y</u>mbol pr<u>e</u>tty <u>E</u>ngland <u>E</u>nglish b<u>ui</u>ld

      g<u>ui</u>lt dam<u>a</u>ge man<u>a</u>ge vill<u>a</u>ge w<u>o</u>men *pl.* s<u>ie</u>ve b<u>u</u>sy b<u>u</u>siness mount<u>ai</u>n

232

kit

phonetic symbol - **I**

🔧 *How do I avoid being guided by the spelling?*

Once you have used the exercises above to help you achieve an accurate pronunciation of this vowel sound, go to the *Lexical Sets* subsection *(p.16)* for advice on how to avoid being guided by the spelling.

🎤 *Practice words and typical spellings for the KIT vowel sound*

i	ship	bit	sick	stiff	pith	this	wish	rib	kid	dig	bridge	give
	his	dim	skin	sing	fill	milk	limp	hint	drink	lift	list	plinth
	mix	slither	vision	spirit	dinner	silly	winter	sister	service	**y**	myth
	symbol	rhythm	Flynn	gym	**e**	pretty	England	English	women *(pl)*
ui	build	guilt	biscuit	**a(ge)**	damage	manage	salvage	village	baggage
	cabbage	**o**	women *pl.*	**ie**	sieve	**u**	busy	business	**ai**	captain
				mountain	fountain

🎤 *Practice Sentences for the KIT vowel sound*

- The women in the film are interesting mythical characters but he gave them such dismal narrative.
- Is Kim going to inquire about the missing data? It's incredible that Philip is still working here!
- If we go to the gym, will you consider coming to swim with me? It's really intimidating!
- The mountains are enormous; the people are fascinating; and the cottage is beautiful!

🕐 20min

near

phonetic symbol - ɪə

This sound is pronounced in words like:

eer	b<u>eer</u>	d<u>eer</u>	ch<u>eer</u>	car<u>eer</u>	**ere**	h<u>ere</u>	m<u>ere</u>	sinc<u>ere</u>	interf<u>ere</u>
ier	p<u>ier</u>	f<u>ier</u>ce	cash<u>ier</u>	p<u>ier</u>ce	**eir**	w<u>eir</u>d	w<u>eir</u>	**ear**	f<u>ear</u> <u>ear</u>
n<u>ear</u>	app<u>ear</u>	**e**	s<u>e</u>rious	myst<u>e</u>rious	p<u>e</u>riod	h<u>e</u>ro	**ee**	<u>ee</u>rie	p<u>ee</u>rage
	ea	r<u>ea</u>l	id<u>ea</u>	r<u>ea</u>lly	Europ<u>ea</u>n	**eu**	Mus<u>eu</u>m	Coloss<u>eu</u>m	
		other	diarrh<u>oea</u>	Mad<u>ei</u>ra					

🔊 235

> ***How is the NEAR vowel sound made in an RP accent?***

The NEAR vowel sound is a *diphthong* – a combination of two vowel sounds where one slides into the other. The NEAR vowel sound starts as the KIT vowel sound *(p.70 - where the tongue tip is behind the bottom teeth, the front of the tongue is high in the front of the mouth, and the lips are slightly spread)* which slides into the SCHWA vowel sound *(p.17 - where the tongue tip stays behind the bottom teeth, the lips release back to neutral and the middle of the tongue slides back into the middle of the centre of the mouth)*. The *jaw* is loose, the *teeth* are apart, and the sound is *long* in duration.

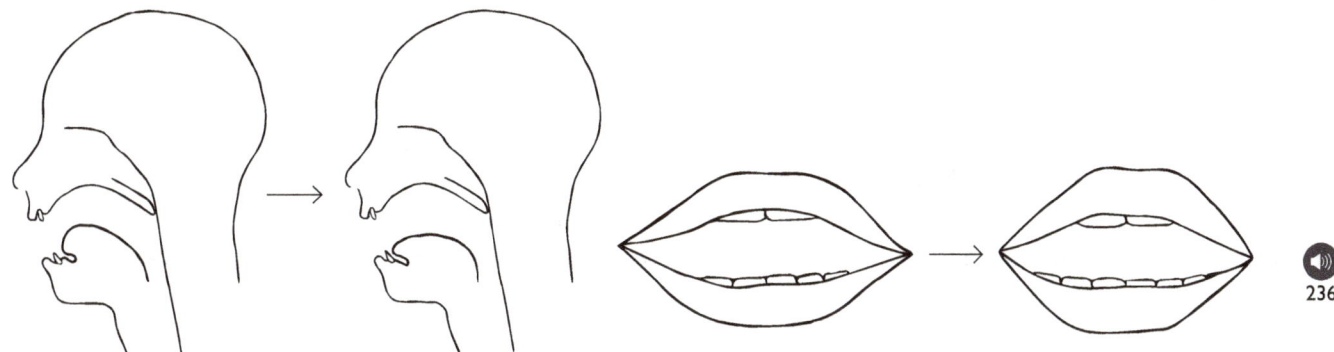

🔊 236

> ***What do I do habitually?***

- Are you pronouncing every written 'r'?

If you are a *rhotic* speaker *(book 2 - Consonants)*, your habit is to pronounce every written 'r'. The NEAR vowel sound is often spelt with a written 'r' as in 'app<u>ear</u>', 'sinc<u>ere</u>', 'b<u>eer</u>', 'h<u>ere</u>', 'p<u>ier</u>', 'w<u>eir</u>' and 'f<u>ear</u>'. But RP is a *non-rhotic* accent so a written 'r' is only pronounced when it is followed by a spoken vowel sound. Listen to the words above, firstly spoken with the R sound and then without, as they should be in RP. If you do this, go to

🔊 237

- Do your lips remain rounded, neutral or spread throughout the whole diphthong?

Some speakers move their *tongue* through the accurate positions and make the sound *long* in duration, but their *lips* remain *rounded*, *neutral* or *spread* throughout instead of sliding from being slightly *spread* to *neutral*, which impacts on the quality and tone of the sound. Listen to the following words, firstly spoken with the *lips rounded*, then *neutral*, then *spread*, and then sliding from being slightly *spread* to *neutral*, as they should be in RP: 'b<u>eer</u>', 'h<u>ere</u>', 'p<u>ier</u>', 'w<u>eir</u>', 'f<u>ear</u>', 's<u>e</u>rious', '<u>ee</u>rie', 'id<u>ea</u>' and 'mus<u>eu</u>m'. If you do this, go to

🔊 238

74

near

phonetic symbol - ɪə

- Are you making this diphthong too long or too short in duration?

Some speakers move their *tongue* and *lips* through the accurate positions but they make the *diphthong* too *short* or too *long* in duration, which impacts on the quality and tone of the sound. If you are making the *diphthong* too *long*, either both vowel sounds in the *diphthong* will be too *long*, which will make it sound like two *syllables* instead of one, or one of the vowel sounds in the *diphthong* will be too *long*. Listen to the following words, firstly spoken with the *diphthong* too *short* in duration, then with both vowel sounds too *long*, then with the first vowel sound too *long*, then with the second vowel sound too *long*, and finally as they should be in RP: 'b<u>eer</u>', 'h<u>ere</u>', 'p<u>ier</u>', 'w<u>eir</u>', 'f<u>ear</u>', 's<u>erious</u>', '<u>ee</u>rie', 'id<u>ea</u>' and 'mus<u>eu</u>m'. If you do this, go to 🔧

- Are you replacing the first vowel sound with the DRESS vowel sound?

Some speakers replace the first vowel sound (KIT) with the DRESS vowel sound *(p.78)*, which is made with the *front of the tongue* slightly *lower* in the *front of the mouth*. The *lips* are equally as *spread* for both vowel sounds. Listen to the following words, firstly spoken with the DRESS vowel sound at the beginning of this *diphthong* and then with the KIT vowel sound at the beginning, as they should be in RP: 'b<u>eer</u>', 'h<u>ere</u>', 'p<u>ier</u>', 'w<u>eir</u>', 'f<u>ear</u>', 's<u>erious</u>', '<u>ee</u>rie', 'id<u>ea</u>'. If you do this, go to 🔧

- Are you replacing the first vowel sound with the FLEECE vowel sound?

Some speakers replace the first vowel sound (KIT) with the FLEECE vowel sound *(p.65)*, which is made with the *front of the tongue* slightly *higher* in the *front of the mouth*. The *lips* are equally as *spread* for both vowel sounds. Listen to the following words, firstly spoken with the FLEECE vowel sound at the beginning of this *diphthong* and then with the KIT vowel sound at the beginning, as they should be in RP: 'b<u>eer</u>', 'h<u>ere</u>', 'p<u>ier</u>', 'w<u>eir</u>', 'f<u>ear</u>', 's<u>erious</u>', '<u>ee</u>rie', 'id<u>ea</u>' and 'mus<u>eu</u>m'. If you do this, go to 🔧

- Are you replacing the second vowel sound with the STRUT or DRESS vowel sound?

Some speakers replace the final vowel sound (SCHWA) with the STRUT vowel sound *(p.35)* – which is made with the *middle of the tongue low* in the *centre of the mouth* and the *lips* equally as *neutral* – or with the DRESS vowel sound *(p.78)* – which is made with the *front of the tongue* in the *middle* of the *front of the mouth* and the *lips* slightly *spread*. Listen to the following words, firstly spoken with the STRUT vowel sound as the final vowel sound of this *diphthong*, then with the DRESS vowel sound as the final vowel sound, and then with the SCHWA vowel sound as the vowel sound, as they should be in RP: 'b<u>eer</u>', 'h<u>ere</u>', 'p<u>ier</u>', 'w<u>eir</u>', 'f<u>ear</u>', and 'id<u>ea</u>'. If you do this, go to 🔧

- Are you only pronouncing the KIT vowel sound and making it too long in duration?

Some speakers only say the KIT vowel sound *(p.70 -* which is made with the *front of the tongue high* in the *front of the mouth* and the *lips* slightly *spread)* but they also make the sound *long* in duration. Listen to the following words, firstly spoken with a lengthened KIT vowel sound and then with the NEAR vowel sound, as they should be in RP: 'b<u>eer</u>', 'h<u>ere</u>', 'p<u>ier</u>', 'w<u>eir</u>', 'f<u>ear</u>' and 'id<u>ea</u>'. If you do this, go to 🔧

near

phonetic symbol - ɪə

- Is your pronunciation guided by the spelling?

Many non-native speakers use the spelling of a word as a guide to its pronunciation. But because British English is not written phonetically, one vowel sound can be represented by numerous spellings. For this reason, the spelling in British English cannot be trusted for vowel pronunciation. For example, the NEAR vowel sound can be represented as the 'e' in 's<u>e</u>rious', the 'ee' in '<u>ee</u>rie', the 'eer' in 'b<u>eer</u>', the 'ere' in 'h<u>ere</u>', the 'ear' in 'n<u>ear</u>', the 'ei' in 'mad<u>ei</u>ra', the 'eir' in 'w<u>eir</u>d', the 'ie' in 'f<u>ie</u>rce', and the 'eoa' in 'diarrh<u>eoa</u>'. So, you might mistakenly pronounce the 'ear' in 'n<u>ear</u>' as the NURSE vowel sound (p.21 - as in '<u>ear</u>th'). But all these words, despite the variation in spelling, are pronounced with the NEAR vowel sound.

It is also typical for a speaker to have a certain spelling that they often associate with a vowel sound. For example, many speakers associate the spelling 'ea' with the NEAR vowel sound. One might then hope that all words spelt with 'ea' would be pronounced as the NEAR vowel sound. Sadly, this is not true, as the 'ea' in 'thr<u>ea</u>t' is pronounced as the DRESS vowel sound (p.78 - as in 'l<u>e</u>t'), in 'serg<u>ea</u>nt' it is pronounced as the SCHWA vowel sound (p.17 - as in 'tun<u>a</u>'), in 'gr<u>ea</u>t' it is pronounced as the FACE vowel sound (p.82 - as in 'd<u>ay</u>'), and in 'm<u>ea</u>t' it is pronounced as the FLEECE vowel sound (p.65 - as in 'h<u>e</u>'). All of this might seem a bit overwhelming, but I have some simple and effective solutions that will help you: go to

> How do I change my habit?

How do I avoid pronouncing a written 'r' that should not be pronounced?

Firstly, encourage your *tongue tip* to stay down, touching the *bottom front teeth* when you are saying the vowel sound. Secondly, unless the vowel sound is followed by another consonant, encourage the *tongue* to stay completely still throughout, avoiding any movement at the end of the sound. When it is followed by a consonant that needs the *tongue*, encourage the *tongue* to move directly to the position for whatever consonant it needs to make, and not to pronounce an R sound just before.

Here is an exercise to help you avoid the R sound. Say the word 'mus<u>eu</u>m' without the final 'm' to help you hear the NEAR vowel sound without an R sound. Say this version of the word before each of the other words to help you find the accurate *tongue* position without a R sound. Listen to the audio to help you imitate the sound accurately and watch your *tongue* in a mirror:

musea… app<u>ear</u>   sinc<u>ere</u>   b<u>eer</u>   h<u>ere</u>   p<u>ier</u>   w<u>eir</u>   f<u>ear</u>

How do I find the accurate tongue position for the NEAR vowel sound?

Firstly, ensure that you are accurately pronouncing the two component vowel sounds in this *diphthong* by following the exercises in the sections entitled *How do I find the accurate tongue position for the KIT vowel sound?* (p.77) and *How do I find the accurate tongue position for the SCHWA vowel sound?* (p.18).

Once you feel confident with how to make each vowel sound, your *tongue* needs to slide from one into the other to make the *diphthong*. Say each sound on its own, one after the other, with a brief pause between them. Watch your *tongue* and *lips* in a mirror and then take out the pause, sliding them into one another. All *diphthongs* are made with the first vowel slightly more *stressed* than the second. This being said, it is only *slightly* more *stressed* and should be observed with care. And remember that the two vowel sounds in

near

phonetic symbol - ɪə

a *diphthong* make a single *syllable*: the *tongue* slides smoothly but swiftly and the sound is *long*, but not too *long*. Play with the following exercise. It offers you an opportunity to check whether you are accurately pronouncing the first vowel sound in the *diphthong* - KIT. Listen to the audio to help you imitate the sound accurately:

bi...	b<u>ee</u>r	hi...	h<u>ere</u>	pi...	p<u>ier</u>	wi...	w<u>eir</u>	fi...	f<u>ear</u>
si...	s<u>e</u>rious	i...	<u>ee</u>rie	idi...	id<u>ea</u>	musi...	mus<u>eu</u>m		

247

🔑 How do I avoid being guided by the spelling?

Once you have used the exercises above to help you achieve an accurate pronunciation of this vowel sound, go to the *Lexical Sets* subsection *(p.16)* for advice on how to avoid being guided by the spelling.

🎤 **Practice words and typical spellings for the NEAR vowel sound**

eer	b<u>ee</u>r	d<u>ee</u>r	ch<u>ee</u>r	car<u>ee</u>r	m<u>ee</u>rkat	**ere**	h<u>ere</u>	m<u>ere</u>	sinc<u>ere</u>
interf<u>ere</u>	**ier**	b<u>ier</u>	p<u>ier</u>	fi<u>er</u>ce	cash<u>ier</u>	p<u>ier</u>ce	**eir**	w<u>eir</u>d	w<u>eir</u>
ear	f<u>ear</u>	<u>ear</u>	t<u>ear</u>ful	app<u>ear</u>	y<u>ear</u>ling	b<u>ear</u>d	n<u>ear</u>	sp<u>ear</u>	cl<u>ear</u>
e	s<u>e</u>rious	myst<u>e</u>rious	p<u>e</u>riod	s<u>e</u>rum	sup<u>e</u>rior	diphth<u>e</u>ria	h<u>e</u>ro		
ee	<u>ee</u>rie	p<u>ee</u>rage	**ea**	dr<u>ea</u>ry	id<u>ea</u>	r<u>ea</u>lly	Ko<u>rea</u>	Europ<u>ea</u>n	Jacob<u>ea</u>n
	Crim<u>ea</u>n	r<u>ea</u>l	id<u>ea</u>l	th<u>ea</u>tre	**eu**	Mus<u>eu</u>m	Coloss<u>eu</u>m		
	other spellings		diarrh<u>oea</u>	Ma<u>dei</u>ra	th<u>eo</u>ry				

248

🎤 **Practice Sentences for the NEAR vowel sound**

- I'm r<u>ea</u>lly f<u>ear</u>ful of going n<u>ear</u> the edge. I'm s<u>e</u>rious! It's not w<u>eir</u>d! Look – r<u>ea</u>l t<u>ear</u>s!
- I began my car<u>eer</u> in th<u>ea</u>tre the same y<u>ear</u> that you started at that dr<u>ea</u>ry Mus<u>eu</u>m.
- I'm being sinc<u>ere</u>! Get your <u>ear</u>s p<u>ier</u>ced and I'll buy you a b<u>ee</u>r and we'll have chips on the p<u>ier</u>.
- Come h<u>ere</u>! Look at those d<u>ee</u>r! These woods are so myst<u>e</u>rious. They're quite <u>ee</u>rie.

249

> **Bonus Material!**

Great news – there's a FREE online video about the NEAR on my YouTube channel:

https://www.youtube.com/@ashleyhowardvoicecoach

p.117

⏱ 20min

dr<u>e</u>ss

phonetic symbol - **e**

This sound is pronounced in words like:

e	dr<u>e</u>ss	W<u>e</u>dnesday	st<u>e</u>p	y<u>e</u>s	**ea**	thr<u>ea</u>t	sw<u>ea</u>t	spr<u>ea</u>d	d<u>ea</u>f
eo	l<u>eo</u>pard	L<u>eo</u>nard	**ie**	fr<u>ie</u>nd	**ai**	s<u>ai</u>d	ag<u>ai</u>n		
a	<u>a</u>ny	m<u>a</u>ny	s<u>ay</u>s	**u**	b<u>u</u>ry				

250

> **How is the DRESS vowel sound made in an RP accent?**

The *tongue tip* is behind the *bottom teeth* and the *front of the tongue* is in the *middle* of the *front of the mouth*. The *lips* are slightly *spread*, the *jaw* is loose and the *teeth* are apart. The DRESS vowel sound is *short* in duration.

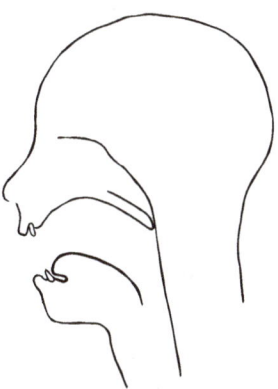 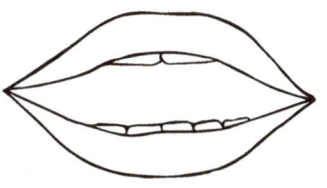

251

> **What do I do habitually?**

- Are your lips rounded or neutral instead of slightly spread?

Some speakers have their *tongue* in an accurate position and make the sound *short* in duration, but their *lips* are *rounded* instead of slightly *spread*, which impacts on the quality and tone of the sound. Listen to the following words, firstly spoken with the *lips rounded* and then with the *lips* slightly *spread*, as they should be in RP: 'dr<u>e</u>ss', 'thr<u>ea</u>t', 'l<u>eo</u>pard', 'fr<u>ie</u>nd', 's<u>ai</u>d', '<u>a</u>ny', 'b<u>u</u>ry' and 's<u>ay</u>s'. If you do this, go to 🔧

252

- Are you pronouncing the DRESS vowel sound too long?

Some speakers have their *tongue* and *lips* in an accurate position but they make the sound *long* in duration, instead of *short*, which impacts on the quality and tone of the sound. Listen to the following words, firstly spoken with the sound *long* in duration and then *short*, as they should be in RP: 'dr<u>e</u>ss', 'v<u>e</u>ry', 'f<u>e</u>rry', 'thr<u>ea</u>t', 'l<u>eo</u>pard', 'fr<u>ie</u>nd', 's<u>ai</u>d', '<u>a</u>ny', 'b<u>u</u>ry' and 's<u>ay</u>s'. If you do this, go to 🔧

253

- Are you replacing the DRESS vowel sound with the KIT vowel sound?

Some speakers replace the DRESS vowel sound with the KIT vowel sound *(p.70)*, which is made with the *front of the tongue* slightly *higher* in the *front of the mouth*. The *lips* are equally as *spread* for both vowel sounds and they are equally as *short* in duration. So words like 'p<u>e</u>t' sound more like 'p<u>i</u>t', 'l<u>e</u>t' sounds more like 'l<u>i</u>t', 'b<u>e</u>t' sounds more like 'b<u>i</u>t' and 's<u>e</u>ll' sounds more like 's<u>i</u>ll'. If you do this, go to 🔧

254

dress

phonetic symbol - **e**

- Are you replacing the DRESS vowel sound with the TRAP vowel sound?

Some speakers replace the DRESS vowel sound with the TRAP vowel sound *(p.57)*, which is made with the *front of the tongue low* in the *front of the mouth*. The *lips* are equally as *spread* for both vowel sounds and they are equally as *short* in duration. So words like 'pet' sound more like 'pat', 'slept' sounds more like 'slapped', 'met' sounds more like 'mat' and 'Ben' sounds more like 'ban'. If you do this, go to

- Is your pronunciation guided by the spelling?

Many non-native speakers use the spelling of a word as a guide to its pronunciation. But because British English is not written phonetically, one vowel sound can be represented by numerous spellings. For this reason, the spelling in British English cannot be trusted for vowel pronunciation. For example, the DRESS vowel sound can be represented as the 'ea' in 'thr<u>ea</u>t', the 'eo' in 'l<u>eo</u>pard', the 'ie' in 'fr<u>ie</u>nds', the 'ai' in 's<u>ai</u>d', the 'a' in '<u>a</u>ny', the 'u' in 'b<u>u</u>ry' and the 'ay' in 's<u>ay</u>s'. So, you might mistakenly pronounce the 'a' in '<u>a</u>ny' as the TRAP vowel sound *(p.57 - as in '<u>a</u>nd')*, or the 'u' in 'b<u>u</u>ry' as the STRUT vowel sound *(p.35 - as in 'h<u>u</u>rry')*. But all these words, despite the variation in spelling, are pronounced with the DRESS vowel sound.

It is also typical for a speaker to have a certain spelling that they often associate with a vowel sound. For example, many speakers associate the spelling 'e' with the DRESS vowel sound. One might then hope that all words spelt with 'e' would be pronounced as the DRESS vowel sound. Sadly, this is not true, as the 'e' in '<u>E</u>ngland' should be pronounced as the longer KIT vowel sound *(p.70 - as in '<u>i</u>t')*, in 'th<u>e</u>se' it is pronounced as the FLEECE vowel sound *(p.65 - as in 's<u>ee</u>n')*, and in 's<u>e</u>rious' it is pronounced as the NEAR vowel sound *(p.74 - as in '<u>ear</u>')*. All of this might seem a bit overwhelming, but I have some simple and effective solutions that will help you: go to

> How do I change my habit?

 How do I encourage my lips to be slightly spread?

The only way to guarantee that you are slightly *spreading* your *lips* accurately instead of *rounding* them is to use a mirror when you practice. Otherwise, you can feel the movement in your *lips* by putting one finger in a vertical line over your *lips* – if your *lips* are *rounding* your finger will be pushed forwards; and if your *lips* are *neutral* or slightly *spreading* your finger will remain still. Say the following words, either looking in a mirror or with one finger on your *lips*, and encourage them to be slightly *spread* accurately:

    dr<u>e</u>ss   W<u>e</u>dnesday   st<u>e</u>p   y<u>e</u>s   thr<u>ea</u>t   sw<u>ea</u>t   spr<u>ea</u>d   d<u>ea</u>f   l<u>eo</u>pard
    L<u>eo</u>nard   fr<u>ie</u>nd   s<u>ai</u>d   ag<u>ai</u>n   <u>a</u>ny   m<u>a</u>ny   b<u>u</u>ry   s<u>ay</u>s

 How do I find the accurate tongue position for the DRESS vowel sound?

The position of the *tongue* and *lips* for the DRESS vowel sound is similar to their positions for the TRAP vowel sound *(p.57)* and KIT vowel sound *(p.70)*, so it might be helpful to compare them. Look in a mirror as you say 'h<u>a</u>d', 'h<u>ea</u>d' and 'h<u>i</u>d' (angle yourself towards a light or use a very small torch). It might be helpful to say the vowel sounds on their own after saying the words, in order to see the *tongue* more clearly. For 'h<u>a</u>d' (the TRAP vowel sound) encourage the *lips* to be slightly *spread*, the *front of the tongue* to be *low* in the

dress

phonetic symbol - e

front of the mouth and the sound to be *short* in duration. For 'head' (this is the target DRESS vowel sound) encourage the *lips* to be equally as *spread*, the sound to be equally as *short* in duration, but the *front of the tongue* to be in the *middle* of the *front of the mouth*. And for 'hid' (the KIT vowel sound) encourage the *lips* to be equally as *spread*, the sound to be equally as *short* in duration, but the *front of the tongue* to be slightly *higher* still in the *front of the mouth*.

259

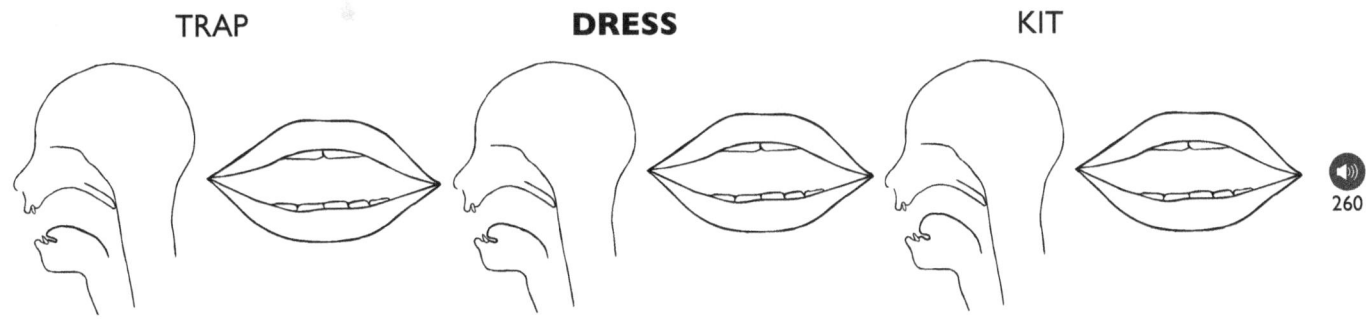

260

This TRAP, DRESS and KIT vowel sound sequence can be heard in the following sets of three words. Play with these words and encourage the *front of your tongue* to remain in between the positions for the TRAP and KIT vowel sounds. In all three sounds, encourage the *lips* to be slightly *spread* and the sound to be *short* in duration. Listen to the audio to help you imitate the sound accurately:

p<u>a</u>t p<u>e</u>t p<u>i</u>t   b<u>a</u>t b<u>e</u>t b<u>i</u>t   gn<u>a</u>t n<u>e</u>t n<u>i</u>t   p<u>a</u>n p<u>e</u>n p<u>i</u>n   s<u>a</u>t s<u>e</u>t s<u>i</u>t

261

If your habit is to replace the DRESS vowel sound with the KIT vowel sound, essentially, your *tongue* position is too *high*. For this reason, it might be helpful to say words with the TRAP vowel sound (which is made with the *tongue lower*) before saying words with the DRESS vowel sound, in order to encourage your *tongue* into a *lower* position. For example:

p<u>a</u>t p<u>e</u>t   b<u>a</u>t b<u>e</u>t   gn<u>a</u>t n<u>e</u>t   p<u>a</u>n p<u>e</u>n   s<u>a</u>t s<u>e</u>t   l<u>a</u>d l<u>ea</u>d   v<u>a</u>t v<u>e</u>t

262

Similarly, if your habit is to replace the DRESS vowel sound with the TRAP vowel sound, then your *tongue* position is too *low*. For this reason, it might be helpful to say words with the KIT vowel sound (which is made with the *tongue higher*) before saying words with the DRESS vowel sound, in order to encourage your *tongue* into a *higher* position. For example:

p<u>i</u>t p<u>e</u>t   b<u>i</u>t b<u>e</u>t   n<u>i</u>t n<u>e</u>t   p<u>i</u>n p<u>e</u>n   s<u>i</u>t s<u>e</u>t   l<u>i</u>t l<u>e</u>t   p<u>i</u>ck p<u>e</u>ck

263

Lastly, here's another game to play: say the DRESS vowel sound on its own before saying each word, to help you hear whether or not you are pronouncing it accurately and also to give you a reference for how it should sound in the word. Listen to the audio to help you imitate the sound accurately:

eh... dr<u>e</u>ss   W<u>e</u>dnesday   st<u>e</u>p   y<u>e</u>s   thr<u>ea</u>t   sw<u>ea</u>t   spr<u>ea</u>d   d<u>ea</u>f   l<u>eo</u>pard
L<u>eo</u>nard   fr<u>ie</u>nd   s<u>ai</u>d   ag<u>ai</u>n   <u>a</u>ny   m<u>a</u>ny   b<u>u</u>ry   s<u>a</u>ys

264

dress

phonetic symbol - **e**

🔧 *How do I avoid being guided by the spelling?*

Once you have used the exercises above to help you achieve an accurate pronunciation of this vowel sound, go to the *Lexical Sets* subsection *(p.16)* for advice on how to avoid being guided by the spelling.

🎤 ***Practice words and typical spellings for the DRESS vowel sound***

e	step	bet	yes	neck	fetch	Jeff	mess	mesh	ebb	bed	egg
edge	rev	fez	hem	pen	bell	depend	shelf	hemp	tent	separate	
theft	best	men	sex	next	effort	method	terror	tenor	jelly	centre	
pester	quest	red	mental	Wednesday	**ea**	threat	sweat	spread	deaf		
death	bread	dead	head	health	realm	meant	breast	ready	jealous		
pleasant	weather	treacherous	**eo**	Leonard	leopard	**ie**	friends				
ai	said	again	**a**	any	anything	many	**u**	bury	**ay**	says	

265

🎤 ***Practice Sentences for the DRESS vowel sound***

- The weather is terrible this weekend again! I envy Meg – she emigrates to Mexico in December!
- I regret sending that letter to Jeff. He's been a friend for years! He meant well… I'll make amends.
- She explained everything. I can empathise. Greg left me in September after eleven years!
- Every September we collect everything we own and together we sell it to have a fresh start.

266

Am I pronouncing it accurately?

Get a personalised assessment of every vowel, consonant and aspect of intonation to find out how well you're doing, exactly what to focus on and what you need to do to speak in this accent accurately and naturally:

https://www.ashleyhoward.me/pronunciation-evaluation

face

phonetic symbol - eɪ

This sound is pronounced in words like:

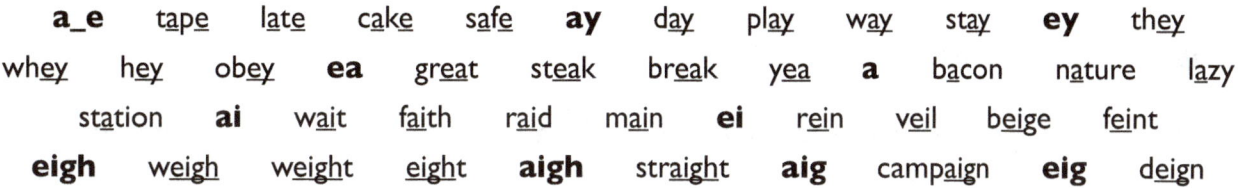

> ***How is the FACE vowel sound made in an RP accent?***

The FACE vowel sound is a *diphthong* – a combination of two vowel sounds where one slides into the other. The FACE vowel sound starts as the DRESS vowel sound *(p.78 - where the tongue tip is behind the bottom teeth, the front of the tongue is in the middle of the front of the mouth, and the lips are slightly spread)* which slides into a slightly *shorter* version of the FLEECE vowel sound *(p.65 - where the tongue tip stays behind the bottom teeth, the lips continue to be slightly spread but the front of the tongue slides slightly higher into the front of the mouth).* The *jaw* is loose, the *teeth* are apart, and the sound is *long* in duration.

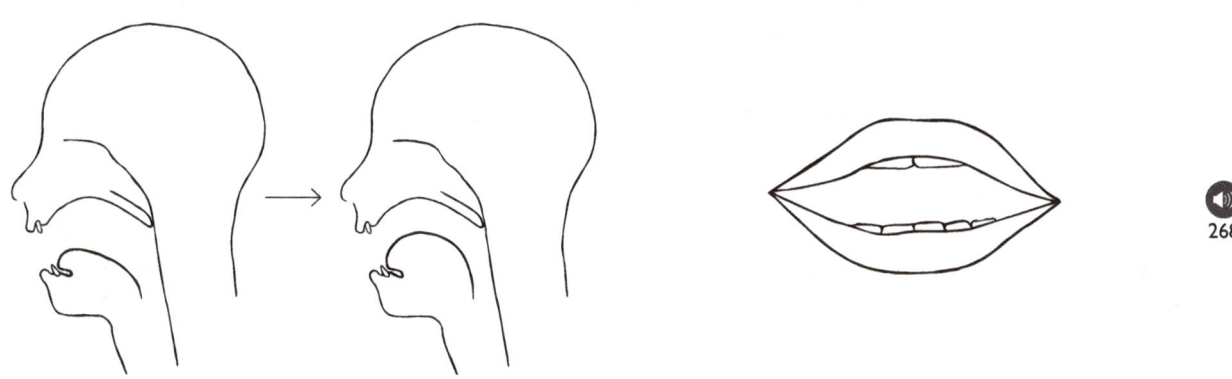

> ***What do I do habitually?***

- Do your lips remain neutral or rounded throughout the whole diphthong?

Some speakers move their *tongue* through the accurate positions and make the sound *long* in duration, but their *lips* are *neutral* or *rounded* instead of slightly *spread,* which impacts on the quality and tone of the sound. Listen to the following words, firstly spoken with the *lips rounded*, then *neutral*, and then slightly *spread,* as they should be in RP: 'late', 'day', 'they', 'great', 'lazy', 'wait', 'feint', 'weight', 'straight', 'campaign' and 'deign'. If you do this, go to

- Are you making this diphthong too long or too short in duration?

Some speakers move their *tongue* and *lips* through the accurate positions but they make the *diphthong* too *short* or too *long* in duration, which impacts on the quality and tone of the sound. If you are making the *diphthong* too *long,* either both vowel sounds in the *diphthong* will be too *long*, which will make it sound like two syllables instead of one, or one of the vowel sounds in the *diphthong* will be too *long*. Listen to the following words, firstly spoken with the *diphthong* too *short* in duration, then with both vowel sounds too *long*, then with the first vowel sound too *long*, then with the second vowel sound too *long*, and finally

face

phonetic symbol - **eɪ**

as they should be in RP: 'l<u>a</u>te', 'd<u>ay</u>', 'th<u>ey</u>', 'gr<u>ea</u>t', 'l<u>a</u>zy', 'w<u>ai</u>t', 'f<u>ei</u>nt', 'w<u>ei</u>ght', 'str<u>aigh</u>t', 'camp<u>aig</u>n' and 'd<u>eig</u>n'. If you do this, go to 🔧

- Are you replacing the first vowel sound with the TRAP vowel sound?

Some speakers replace the first vowel sound (DRESS) with the TRAP vowel sound *(p.57)*, which is made with the *front of the tongue low* in the *front of the mouth*. The *lips* are equally as *spread* for both vowel sounds. Listen to the following words, firstly spoken with the TRAP vowel sound at the beginning of this *diphthong* and then with the DRESS vowel sound at the beginning, as they should be in RP: 'l<u>a</u>te', 'd<u>ay</u>', 'th<u>ey</u>', 'gr<u>ea</u>t', 'l<u>a</u>zy', 'w<u>ai</u>t', 'f<u>ei</u>nt', 'w<u>ei</u>ght', 'str<u>aigh</u>t', 'camp<u>aig</u>n' and 'd<u>eig</u>n'. If you do this, go to 🔧

- Are you replacing the first vowel sound with the STRUT vowel sound?

Some speakers replace the first vowel sound (DRESS) with the STRUT vowel sound *(p.35)*, which is made with the *middle of the tongue low* in the *centre of the mouth* and the *lips* are *neutral*. Listen to the following words, firstly spoken with the STRUT vowel sound at the beginning of this *diphthong* and then with the DRESS vowel sound at the beginning, as they should be in RP: 'l<u>a</u>te', 'd<u>ay</u>', 'th<u>ey</u>', 'gr<u>ea</u>t', 'l<u>a</u>zy', 'w<u>ai</u>t', 'f<u>ei</u>nt', 'w<u>ei</u>ght', 'str<u>aigh</u>t', 'camp<u>aig</u>n' and 'd<u>eig</u>n'. If you do this, go to 🔧

- Are you only saying the DRESS vowel sound and making it too long in duration?

Some speakers replace this *diphthong* with a *longer* version of the DRESS vowel sound *(p.78)*. Listen to the following words, firstly spoken with a *longer* version of the DRESS vowel sound, and then the FACE vowel sound, as they should be in RP: 'l<u>a</u>te', 'd<u>ay</u>', 'th<u>ey</u>', 'gr<u>ea</u>t', 'l<u>a</u>zy', 'w<u>ai</u>t', 'f<u>ei</u>nt', 'w<u>ei</u>ght', 'str<u>aigh</u>t', 'camp<u>aig</u>n' and 'd<u>eig</u>n'. If you do this, go to 🔧

- Is your pronunciation guided by the spelling?

Many non-native speakers use the spelling of a word as a guide to its pronunciation. But because British English is not written phonetically, one vowel sound can be represented by numerous spellings. For this reason, the spelling in British English cannot be trusted for vowel pronunciation. For example, the FACE vowel sound can be represented as the 'a_e' in 'l<u>a</u>te', the 'ay' in 'd<u>ay</u>', the 'ey' in 'th<u>ey</u>', the 'ea' in 'gr<u>ea</u>t', the 'ai' in 'w<u>ai</u>t', and the 'aigh' in 'str<u>aigh</u>t'. So, you might mistakenly pronounce the 'ea' in 'great' as the FLEECE vowel sound *(p.65 - as in 'm<u>ea</u>t')*. But all these words, despite the variation in spelling, are pronounced with the FACE vowel sound.

It is also typical for a speaker to have a certain spelling that they often associate with a vowel sound. For example, many speakers associate the spelling 'ei' with the FACE vowel sound. One might then hope that all words spelt with 'ei' would be pronounced as the FACE vowel sound. Sadly, this is not true, as the 'ei' in 'rec<u>ei</u>ve' should be pronounced as the FLEECE vowel sound *(p.65 - as in 'h<u>e</u>')*, in 'kal<u>ei</u>doscope' and 'h<u>eigh</u>t' it is pronounced as the PRICE vowel sound *(p.39 - as in '<u>eye</u>')*, and in 'Mad<u>ei</u>ra' it is pronounced as the NEAR vowel sound *(p.74 - as in '<u>ear</u>')*. All of this might seem a bit overwhelming, but I have some simple and effective solutions that will help you: go to 🔧

face

phonetic symbol - eɪ

> How do I change my habit?

 How do I find the accurate tongue position for the FACE vowel sound?

Firstly, ensure that you are accurately pronouncing the two component vowel sounds in this *diphthong* by following the exercises in the sections entitled *How do I find the accurate tongue position for the DRESS vowel sound? (p.75)* and *How do I find the accurate tongue position for the FLEECE vowel sound? (p.64)*.

Once you feel confident with how to make each vowel sound, your *tongue* needs to slide from one into the other to make the *diphthong*. Say each sound on its own, one after the other, with a brief pause between them. Watch your *tongue* and *lips* in a mirror and then take out the pause, sliding them into one another. All *diphthongs* are made with the first vowel slightly more *stressed* than the second. This being said, it is only *slightly* more *stressed* and should be observed with care. And remember that the two vowel sounds in a *diphthong* make a single *syllable*: the *tongue* slides smoothly but swiftly and the sound is *long*, but not too *long*.

Play with the following exercise. It offers you an opportunity to check whether you are accurately pronouncing the first vowel sound in the *diphthong* - DRESS. Listen to the audio to help you imitate the sound accurately:

| l<u>e</u>... | l<u>a</u>te | d<u>e</u>... | d<u>ay</u> | th<u>e</u>... | th<u>ey</u> | gr<u>e</u>... | gr<u>ea</u>t | l<u>e</u>... | l<u>a</u>zy | w<u>e</u>... | w<u>ai</u>t |
| f<u>e</u>... | f<u>ei</u>nt | w<u>e</u>... | w<u>ei</u>ght | str<u>e</u>... | str<u>ai</u>ght | camp<u>e</u>... | camp<u>ai</u>gn | d<u>e</u>... | d<u>ei</u>gn | | |

276

 How do I avoid being guided by the spelling?

Once you have used the exercises above to help you achieve an accurate pronunciation of this vowel sound, go to the *Lexical Sets* subsection *(p.16)* for advice on how to avoid being guided by the spelling.

> Anything Else?

- The LAYER triphthong: phonemic symbol eɪə

There are five of the eight *diphthongs* that can be extended with a final SCHWA vowel sound *(p.17)* which turns the *diphthong* into a *triphthong* – a combination of three vowel sounds where one slides into another. The FACE vowel sound is one such *diphthong*, so words like 'l<u>ayer</u>', 'pl<u>ayer</u>' and 'sl<u>ayer</u>' are pronounced with the FACE vowel sound followed by a SCHWA vowel sound. The *lips* relax back to *neutral* and the *tongue* slides from being in the *front of the mouth* to the *middle* of the *centre of the mouth*.

277

Some RP speakers add a YOD *(book 2 - Consonants)* to link the FACE vowel sound to the SCHWA vowel sound. This makes words like 'l<u>ayer</u>', 'pl<u>ayer</u>' and 'sl<u>ayer</u>' sound like two syllable words instead of one. In this version, the *tongue* moves quite suddenly into the SCHWA. Other speakers do not add a YOD. Instead they make the transition of their *tongue* from the FACE vowel sound to the SCHWA vowel sound much more smoothly, which makes the words above sound more like one syllable.

278

This variation in pronunciation is in part to do with the evolving nature of accents. And unfortunately

face

phonetic symbol - eɪ

these variations are not accounted for in a reliable dictionary. In some ways, this ambiguity could be seen as a frustrating, but another perspective would be to say that is allows for choice, as both are considered correct. Listen to the following words, firstly spoken with the YOD and then without:

layer   player   slayer   payer   conveyor   surveyor

279

And lastly, many words with these *triphthongs* have a written 'r' in the spelling, which should not be spoken, unless they are followed by a spoken vowel sound. Encourage your *tongue tip* to remain down, touching the *bottom front teeth* at the end of the *triphthong*.

Practice words and typical spellings for the FACE vowel sound

a_e	tape	late	cake	safe	case	spade	babe	fade	vague	hate	age
wave	bathe	craze	name	mane	vale	cage	change	ace	amaze	waste
ay	day	play	hay	way	Sunday	stay	gray	**ey**	they	whey	hey
obey	**ea**	great	steak	break	yea	**a**	taper	bacon	nature	lazy
station	amazing	lady	raven	invasion	April	bass (guitar)	**au**	gauge
ao	gaol	**ai**	jail	wait	waiter	faith	plaice	aitch	raid	Spain	nail
main	faint	sprain	**ei**	rein	veil	beige	feint	reindeer	**eigh**	weigh
weight	eight	**aigh**	straight	**aig**	campaign	**eig**	deign

280

Practice Sentences for the FACE vowel sound

- What days are you available? Monday? Would eight o'clock be too late? Great – it's a date!
- I'm amazed they renewed his contract! He is so lazy! April's figures were outrageous!
- After the play we went to a café. We waited for ages, so they gave out cake. We didn't say no!
- What a waste of time! I've complained! Just be straight with us – should we stay or go?

281

sq<u>ua</u>re

phonetic symbol - eə

⏱ 20min

This sound is pronounced in words like:

ar	sc<u>ar</u>ce	**are**	c<u>are</u>	sh<u>are</u>	st<u>are</u>	comp<u>are</u>	**air**	f<u>air</u>	h<u>air</u>	p<u>air</u>
	st<u>air</u>	**a**	v<u>a</u>ry	M<u>a</u>ry	v<u>a</u>rious	<u>a</u>rea	**ai**	d<u>ai</u>ry	pr<u>ai</u>rie	f<u>ai</u>ry
ear	w<u>ear</u>	b<u>ear</u>	p<u>ear</u>	sw<u>ear</u>	**eir**	h<u>eir</u>	th<u>eir</u>	**ere**	th<u>ere</u>	wh<u>ere</u>
	other	pr<u>ay</u>er	m<u>ayor</u>	<u>ae</u>rial

🔊 282

> ### How is the SQUARE vowel sound made in an RP accent?

The SQUARE vowel sound is a *diphthong* – a combination of two vowel sounds where one slides into the other. The SQUARE vowel sound starts as the DRESS vowel sound *(p.78 - where the tongue tip is behind the bottom teeth, the front of the tongue is in the middle of the front of the mouth, and the lips are slightly spread)* which slides into the SCHWA vowel sound *(p.17 - where the tongue tip stays behind the bottom teeth, the lips release back to neutral and the middle of the tongue slides back into the middle of the centre of the mouth)*. The *jaw* is loose, the *teeth* are apart, and the sound is *long* in duration.

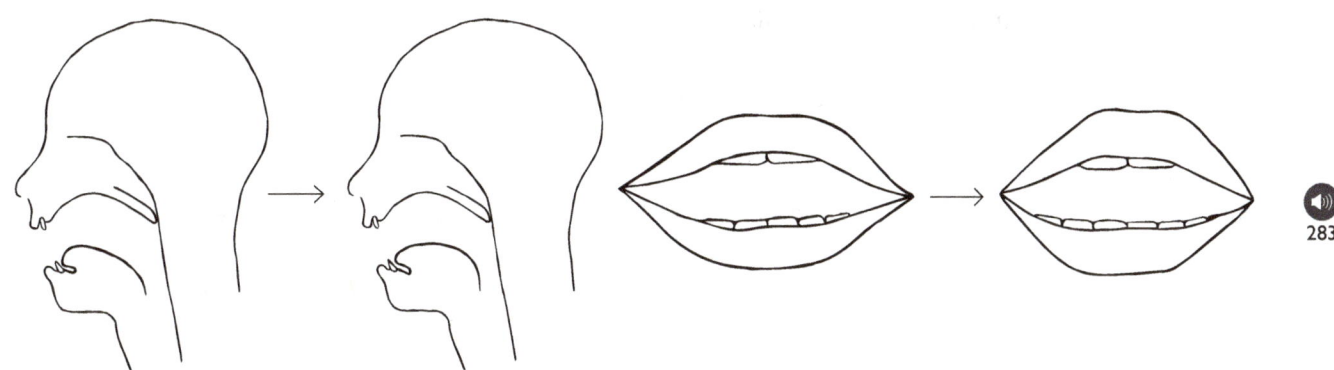

🔊 283

> ### What do I do habitually?

- Are you pronouncing every written 'r'?

If you are a *rhotic* speaker *(book 2 - Consonants)*, your habit is to pronounce every written 'r'. The SQUARE vowel sound is often spelt with a written 'r', as in 'sc<u>ar</u>ce', 'c<u>are</u>', 'f<u>air</u>', 'w<u>ear</u>' 'th<u>eir</u>', 'th<u>ere</u>' and 'pr<u>ayer</u>'. But RP is a *non-rhotic* accent so a written 'r' is only pronounced when it is followed by a spoken vowel sound. Listen to the words above, firstly spoken with the R sound and then without, as they should be in RP. If you do this, go to

🔊 284

- Do your lips remain rounded, neutral or spread throughout the whole diphthong?

Some speakers move their *tongue* through the accurate positions and make the sound *long* in duration, but their *lips* remain *rounded*, *neutral* or *spread* throughout instead of sliding from slightly *spread* to *neutral*, which impacts on the quality and tone of the sound. Listen to the following words, firstly spoken with the *lips rounded*, then *neutral*, then *spread,* and then sliding from slightly *spread* to *neutral,* as they should be in RP: 'sc<u>ar</u>ce', 'c<u>are</u>', 'f<u>air</u>', 'w<u>ear</u>' 'th<u>eir</u>', 'th<u>ere</u>', 'pr<u>ay</u>er', 'v<u>a</u>ry' and 'd<u>ai</u>ry'. If you do this, go to

🔊 285

square

phonetic symbol - eə

- Are you making this diphthong too short or too long in duration?

Some speakers move their *tongue* and *lips* through the accurate positions but they make the *diphthong* too *short* or too *long* in duration, which impacts on the quality and tone of the sound. If you are making the *diphthong* too *long*, either both vowel sounds in the *diphthong* will be too *long*, which will make it sound like two *syllables* instead of one, or one of the vowel sounds in the *diphthong* will be too *long*. Listen to the following words, firstly spoken with the *diphthong* too *short* in duration, then with both vowel sounds too *long*, then with the first vowel sound too *long*, then with the second vowel sound too *long*, and finally as they should be in RP: 'sc<u>ar</u>ce', 'c<u>are</u>', 'f<u>air</u>', 'w<u>ear</u>' 'th<u>eir</u>', 'th<u>ere</u>', 'pr<u>ayer</u>', 'v<u>ar</u>y' and 'd<u>air</u>y'. If you do this then, go to 286

- Are you replacing the first vowel sound with the KIT vowel sound?

Some speakers replace the first vowel sound (DRESS) with the KIT vowel sound *(p.70)* which is made with the *front of the tongue* slightly *higher* in the *front of the mouth*. The *lips* are equally as *spread* for both vowel sounds. Listen to the following words, firstly spoken with the KIT vowel sound at the beginning of this *diphthong* and then with the DRESS vowel sound at the beginning, as they should be in RP: 'sc<u>ar</u>ce', 'c<u>are</u>', 'f<u>air</u>', 'w<u>ear</u>' 'th<u>eir</u>', 'th<u>ere</u>', 'pr<u>ayer</u>', 'v<u>ar</u>y' and 'd<u>air</u>y'. If you do this, go to 287

- Are you only pronouncing the DRESS vowel sound and making it too long in duration?

Some speakers only say the DRESS vowel sound *(p.78 -* which is made with the *front of the tongue* in the *middle* of the *front of the mouth* and the *lips* slightly *spread)* but they also make the sound *long* in duration. And there are some RP speakers who do do this. Listen to the following words, firstly spoken with the lengthened DRESS vowel sound and then with the SQUARE vowel sound, as they should be in RP: 'sc<u>ar</u>ce', 'c<u>are</u>', 'f<u>air</u>', 'w<u>ear</u>' 'th<u>eir</u>', 'th<u>ere</u>', 'pr<u>ayer</u>', 'v<u>ar</u>y' and 'd<u>air</u>y'. If you do this, go to 288

- Are you replacing the second vowel sound with the STRUT vowel sound?

Some speakers replace the final vowel sound (SCHWA) with the STRUT vowel sound *(p.35)* – which is made with the *middle of the tongue low* in the *centre of the mouth* and the *lips* equally as *neutral*. Listen to the following words, firstly spoken with the STRUT vowel sound as the final vowel sound of this *diphthong*, and then with the SCHWA vowel sound as the final vowel sound, as they should be in RP: 'c<u>are</u>', 'f<u>air</u>', 'w<u>ear</u>' 'th<u>eir</u>', 'th<u>ere</u>', 'pr<u>ayer</u>'. If you do this, go to 289

- Is your pronunciation guided by the spelling?

Many non-native speakers use the spelling of a word as a guide to its pronunciation. But because British English is not written phonetically, one vowel sound can be represented by numerous spellings. For this reason, the spelling in British English cannot be trusted for vowel pronunciation. For example, the SQUARE vowel sound can be represented as the 'ar' in 'sc<u>ar</u>ce', the 'ayer' in 'pr<u>ayer</u>', the 'ayor' in 'm<u>ayor</u>', the 'ear' as in 'w<u>ear</u>' and the 'ae' in '<u>ae</u>rial'. So, you might mistakenly pronounce the 'eir' in 'th<u>eir</u>' as the NEAR vowel sound *(p.74 -* as in 'w<u>ei</u>rd'). But all these words, despite the variation in spelling, are pronounced with the SQUARE vowel sound.

290

sq<u>ua</u>re

phonetic symbol - eə

It is also typical for a speaker to have a certain spelling that they often associate with a vowel sound. For example, many speakers associate the spelling 'air' with the SQUARE vowel sound. And thankfully words spelt with 'air' tend only to be pronounced with the SQUARE vowel sound, as in 'st<u>air</u>', 'h<u>air</u>' and 'f<u>air</u>'. This means that when you see the spelling 'air' we can say almost certainly that you should use the SQUARE vowel sound. All of this might seem a bit overwhelming, but I have some simple and effective solutions that will help you: go to

291

> How do I change my habit?

How do I avoid pronouncing a written 'r' that should not be pronounced?

Firstly, encourage your *tongue tip* to stay down, touching the *bottom front teeth* when you are saying the vowel sound. Secondly, unless the vowel sound is followed by another consonant, encourage the *tongue* to stay completely still throughout, avoiding any movement at the end of the sound. When it is followed by a consonant that needs the *tongue tip*, encourage the *tongue* to move directly to the position for that consonant, and not to pronounce an R sound just before. Listen to the audio to help you imitate the sound accurately and watch your *tongue* in a mirror:

        sc<u>a</u>rce   c<u>a</u>re   f<u>ai</u>r   w<u>ea</u>r   th<u>ei</u>r   th<u>e</u>re   pr<u>ay</u>er

292

How do I find the accurate tongue position for the SQUARE vowel sound?

Firstly, ensure that you are accurately pronouncing the two component vowel sounds in this *diphthong* by following the exercises in the sections entitled *How do I find the accurate tongue position for the DRESS vowel sound? (p.75)* and *How do I find the accurate tongue position for the SCHWA vowel sound? (p.18).*

Once you feel confident with how to make each vowel sound, your *tongue* needs to slide from one into the other to make the *diphthong*. Say each sound on its own, one after the other, with a brief pause between them. Watch your *tongue* and *lips* in a mirror and then take out the pause, sliding them into one another. All *diphthongs* are made with the first vowel slightly more *stressed* than the second. This being said, it is only *slightly* more *stressed* and should be observed with care. And remember that the two vowel sounds in a *diphthong* make a single *syllable*: the *tongue* slides smoothly but swiftly and the sound is *long*, but not too *long*.

Play with the following exercise. It offers you an opportunity to check whether you are accurately pronouncing the first vowel sound in the *diphthong* – DRESS. Listen to the audio to help you imitate the sound accurately:

    sce... sc<u>a</u>rce   ce... c<u>a</u>re   fe... f<u>ai</u>r   we... w<u>ea</u>r   the... th<u>ei</u>r
        the... th<u>e</u>re   pre... pr<u>ay</u>er   ve... v<u>a</u>ry   de... d<u>ai</u>ry

293

How do I avoid being guided by the spelling?

Once you have used the exercises above to help you achieve an accurate pronunciation of this vowel sound, go to the *Lexical Sets* subsection *(p.16)* for advice on how to avoid being guided by the spelling.

square

phonetic symbol - eə

🎤 **Practice words and typical spellings for the SQUARE vowel sound**

ar	scarce	**are**	hare	care	share	mare	bare	stare	compare
air	air	fair	flair	hair	pair	stair	**a**	vary	canary	Mary	aquarium
	various	precarious	rarity	area	Pharaoh	**ai**	dairy	prairie	fairy
ear	wear	bear	pear	swear	**eir**	heir	their	**ere**	there	where
	other spellings	Ayr	Eyre	prayer	mayor	aerial	Eire

294

🎤 **Practice Sentences for the SQUARE vowel sound**

- We've shared a house for years. We're quite fair. We fight here and there, but he's bearable.
- Did you compare the figures? They really vary! It's scary. In what areas can we improve?
- Where are we going? What should I wear? Should I do my hair? Who's going to be there?
- I've been very careful to make everyone aware of the precarious state of the stairs.

295

 20min

goose
phonetic symbol - Uː

This sound is pronounced in words like:

oo	f<u>oo</u>d	pr<u>oo</u>f	l<u>oo</u>se	m<u>oo</u>d	**o_e**	m<u>ove</u>	pr<u>ove</u>	l<u>ose</u>	wh<u>ose</u>
oe	sh<u>oe</u>	**o**	d<u>o</u>	m<u>o</u>vie	wh<u>o</u>	tw<u>o</u>	**ou**	gr<u>ou</u>p	y<u>ou</u>th	gh<u>ou</u>l	y<u>ou</u>
ough	thr<u>ough</u>	**u**	pr<u>u</u>dent	fl<u>u</u>	l<u>u</u>cid	cr<u>u</u>cial	**ui**	br<u>ui</u>se	fr<u>ui</u>t	j<u>ui</u>ce
cr<u>ui</u>se	**ue**	bl<u>ue</u>	gl<u>ue</u>	tr<u>ue</u>	r<u>ue</u>	**eu**	sl<u>eu</u>th	d<u>eu</u>ce	f<u>eu</u>d	n<u>eu</u>tral
ew	n<u>ew</u>t	n<u>ew</u>	f<u>ew</u>	kn<u>ew</u>	v<u>iew</u>	rev<u>iew</u>	**eau**	b<u>eau</u>ty	b<u>eau</u>tiful

 296

> ### How is the GOOSE vowel sound made in an RP accent?

The *tongue tip* is behind the *bottom teeth* and the *back of the tongue* is *high* in the *back of the mouth*. The *lips* are *rounded*, the *jaw* is loose and the *teeth* are apart. The GOOSE vowel sound is *long* in duration. Compared to all other vowel sounds, the *back of the tongue* is most *high* and *back* for the GOOSE vowel sound.

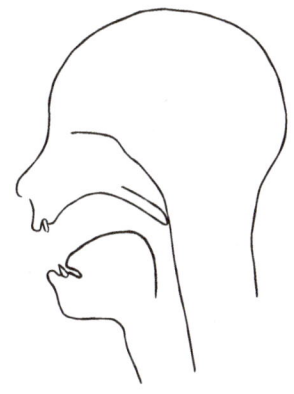 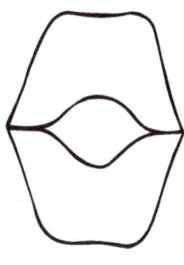

297

> ### Some words are preceded by a YOD

Some words that are pronounced with the GOOSE vowel sound are often preceded by a YOD *(book 2 - Consonants)*, as in 'd<u>eu</u>ce', 'f<u>eu</u>d', 'n<u>eu</u>tral', 'n<u>ew</u>', 'f<u>ew</u>', 'v<u>iew</u>', 'rev<u>iew</u>', 'am<u>u</u>se' and 'b<u>eau</u>ty'. Whilst there is no conclusive spelling pattern that will help you to know when to use the YOD, one way to be sure is to look at the phonetic transcription in a reliable dictionary. When listening to the audio examples in this section, pay attention to the presence or absence of the YOD so as to avoid mispronunciation.

 298

> ### What do I do habitually?

- Are your lips spread or neutral instead of rounded?

Some speakers have their *tongue* in an accurate position and make the sound *short* in duration, but their *lips* are *neutral* or *spread* instead of *rounded*, which impacts on the quality and tone of the sound. Listen to the following words, firstly spoken with the *lips spread*, then *neutral*, and then *rounded*, as they should be in RP: 'f<u>oo</u>d', 'm<u>ove</u>', 'sh<u>oe</u>', 'd<u>o</u>', 'gr<u>ou</u>p', 'thr<u>ough</u>', 'fl<u>u</u>', 'fr<u>ui</u>t', 'bl<u>ue</u>', 'n<u>eu</u>tral', 'n<u>ew</u>', 'tw<u>o</u>', 'b<u>eau</u>ty' and 'v<u>iew</u>'. If you do this, go to 🔧

 299

goose

phonetic symbol - **Uː**

- Are you replacing the GOOSE vowel sound with the FOOT vowel sound?

Some speakers replace the GOOSE vowel sound with the FOOT vowel sound *(p.94)*, which is made with the *back of the tongue* slightly *lower* in the *back of the mouth*, the *lips* slightly less *rounded* and the sound *short* in duration. So words like 'L<u>u</u>ke' sound more like 'l<u>oo</u>k', and 'w<u>oo</u>ed' sounds more like 'w<u>oo</u>d'. If you do this, go to

300

- Are you replacing the GOOSE vowel sound with the THOUGHT vowel sound?

Some speakers replace the GOOSE vowel sound with the THOUGHT vowel sound *(p.48)*, which is made with the *back of the tongue* in the *middle* of the *back of the mouth*, the *lips* slightly less *rounded* and the sound equally as *long* in duration. So words like 's<u>oo</u>n' sound more like 's<u>aw</u>n', and 'm<u>oo</u>n' sounds more like 'm<u>our</u>n'. If you do this, go to

301

- Is your pronunciation guided by the spelling?

Many non-native speakers use the spelling of a word as a guide to its pronunciation. But because British English is not written phonetically, one vowel sound can be represented by numerous spellings. For this reason, the spelling in British English cannot be trusted for vowel pronunciation. For example, the GOOSE vowel sound can be represented as the 'o_e' in 'm<u>o</u>ve', the 'o' in 'wh<u>o</u>', the 'ou' in 'gr<u>ou</u>p', the 'ough' in 'thr<u>ough</u>', the 'ui' in 'fr<u>ui</u>t', the 'ue' in 'tr<u>ue</u>', the 'eu' in 'n<u>eu</u>tral', the 'ew' in 'n<u>ew</u>', the 'eau' in 'b<u>eau</u>ty', and the 'iew' in 'rev<u>iew</u>'. So, you might mistakenly pronounce the 'o' in 'm<u>o</u>ve' as the LOT vowel sound *(p.43 - as in 'o<u>f</u>')*, or the 'ough' in 'thr<u>ough</u>' as the GOAT vowel sound *(p.26 - as in 'alth<u>ough</u>')*. But all these words, despite the variation in spelling, are pronounced with the GOOSE vowel sound.

302

It is also typical for a speaker to have a certain spelling that they often associate with a vowel sound. For example, many speakers associate the spelling 'oo' with the GOOSE vowel sound. One might then hope that all words spelt with 'oo' would be pronounced as the GOOSE vowel sound. Sadly, this is not true, as the 'oo' in bl<u>oo</u>d' is pronounced as the STRUT vowel sound *(p.35 - as in 'c<u>u</u>p')*, in 'g<u>oo</u>d' it is pronounced as the FOOT vowel sound *(p.94 - as in 'sh<u>ou</u>ld')*, and in 'br<u>oo</u>ch' it is pronounced as the GOAT vowel sound *(p.26 - as in 'n<u>o</u>')*. All of this might seem a bit overwhelming, but I have some simple and effective solutions that will help you: go to

303

> **How do I change my habit?**

 How do I encourage my lips to be rounded?

The only way to guarantee that your *lips* are *rounded* accurately instead of being *neutral* or *spread* is to use a mirror when you practice. Otherwise, you can feel the movement in your *lips* by putting one finger in a vertical line over your *lips* – if your *lips* are *rounding* your finger will be pushed forwards; and if your *lips* are *neutral* or slightly *spreading* your finger will remain still. Say the following words, either looking in a mirror or with one finger on your *lips*, and encourage them to be *rounded* accurately:

| f<u>oo</u>d | pr<u>oo</u>f | m<u>o</u>ve | pr<u>o</u>ve | sh<u>oe</u> | d<u>o</u> | wh<u>o</u> | gr<u>ou</u>p | y<u>ou</u>th | thr<u>ough</u> | fl<u>u</u> |
| cr<u>u</u>cial | fr<u>ui</u>t | j<u>ui</u>ce | bl<u>ue</u> | gl<u>ue</u> | f<u>eu</u>d | n<u>eu</u>tral | n<u>ew</u> | f<u>ew</u> | b<u>eau</u>ty | b<u>eau</u>tiful |

304

goose

phonetic symbol - **Uː**

 How do I find the accurate tongue position for the GOOSE vowel sound?

The position of the *tongue* and *lips* for the GOOSE vowel sound is similar to their positions for the THOUGHT vowel sound *(p.48)* and FOOT vowel sound *(p.94)*, so it might be helpful to compare them. Look in a mirror as you say 'h<u>oar</u>d', 'h<u>oo</u>d' and 'wh<u>o</u>' (angle yourself towards a light or use a very small torch – although you might still struggle to see the *back of the tongue* because the *lips* need to be *rounded* when saying these vowel sounds). It might be helpful to say the vowel sounds on their own after saying the words, in order to see the *tongue* more clearly. For 'h<u>oar</u>d' (the THOUGHT vowel sound) encourage the *lips* to be *rounded*, the *back of the tongue* to be in the *middle* of the *back of the mouth* and the sound to be *long* in duration. For 'h<u>oo</u>d' (the FOOT vowel sound) encourage the *lips* to be more *rounded*, the *back of the tongue* to be very slightly *higher* in the *back of the mouth* and the sound to be *short* in duration. And for 'wh<u>o</u>' (this is the target GOOSE vowel sound) encourage the *lips* to be more *rounded* still, the *back of the tongue* to be *higher* still in the *back of the mouth* and the sound to be *long* in duration.

305

THOUGHT 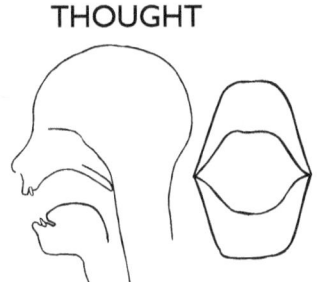   FOOT 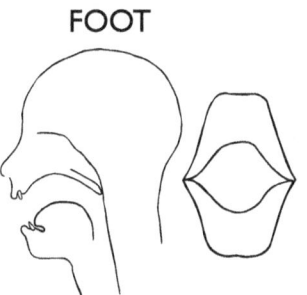   **GOOSE**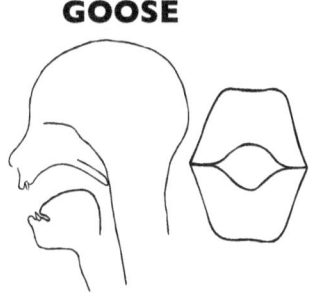

306

This THOUGHT, FOOT and GOOSE vowel sound sequence can be heard in the following sets of three words. Play with these words and encourage the *back of your tongue* to be higher and the lips to be more rounded than the FOOT vowel sound. Encourage the sound to be *long* in duration. Listen to the audio to help you imitate the sound accurately:

    w<u>ar</u>d   w<u>oo</u>d   w<u>ooe</u>d   c<u>or</u>d   c<u>ou</u>ld   c<u>ooe</u>d   sh<u>or</u>e   sh<u>oo</u>k   sh<u>oe</u>

307

Here's another game to play: say the GOOSE vowel sound on its own before saying each word, to help you hear whether or not you are pronouncing it accurately and also to give you a reference for how it should sound in the word. Listen to the audio to help you imitate the sound accurately:

f<u>oo</u>d   pr<u>oo</u>f   m<u>ove</u>   pr<u>ove</u>   sh<u>oe</u>   d<u>o</u>   wh<u>o</u>   gr<u>ou</u>p   y<u>ou</u>th   thr<u>ough</u>   fl<u>u</u>
cr<u>u</u>cial   fr<u>ui</u>t   j<u>ui</u>ce   bl<u>ue</u>   gl<u>ue</u>   f<u>eu</u>d   n<u>eu</u>tral   n<u>ew</u>   f<u>ew</u>   b<u>eau</u>ty   b<u>eau</u>tiful

308

 How do I avoid being guided by the spelling?

Once you have used the exercises above to help you achieve an accurate pronunciation of this vowel sound, go to the *Lexical Sets* subsection *(p.16)* for advice on how to avoid being guided by the spelling.

> ***Anything Else?***

This is a very minor detail, but sometimes, when the GOOSE vowel sound is followed by a dark L (book

goose

phonetic symbol - uː

2 - Consonants) a written L that is followed by a consonant sound or by a pause) some RP speakers now use a slightly hybrid vowel sound that is a cross between the GOOSE vowel sound and THOUGHT vowel sound *(p.48)*, so something between 'r<u>ue</u>' and 'r<u>oar</u>'.

This can be heard in words like 'f<u>oo</u>l', 'sch<u>oo</u>l', 'p<u>oo</u>l', 'r<u>u</u>le', 'm<u>u</u>le', 't<u>oo</u>l', 'st<u>oo</u>l', 'c<u>oo</u>l' and 'f<u>ue</u>l'. So 'r<u>u</u>le' is being pronounced a bit like 'r<u>oar</u>' with an L sound on the end: 'r<u>oar</u>-l' (it's tricky to describe this, so listen to the audio). This is not indicated in pronunciation dictionaries as it only occurs in a handful of words, namely the ones above. As I said, this is a very minor detail and would add further specificity to your pronunciation, but if you were to continue to pronounce the GOOSE vowel sound in words like these, you will still be clearly understood and your pronunciation will lie within the RP canon.

🎤 Practice words and typical spellings for the GOOSE vowel sound

oo	l<u>oo</u>p	sh<u>oo</u>t	sp<u>oo</u>k	sm<u>oo</u>ch	f<u>oo</u>d	pr<u>oo</u>f	l<u>oo</u>se	m<u>oo</u>d	gr<u>oo</u>ve
sm<u>oo</u>th	ch<u>oo</u>se	b<u>oo</u>m	sp<u>oo</u>n	f<u>oo</u>l	t<u>oo</u>	b<u>oo</u>st	s<u>oo</u>ner	b<u>oo</u>ty	t<u>oo</u>th
r<u>oo</u>f	h<u>oo</u>f	**o_e**	m<u>o</u>ve	pr<u>o</u>ve	l<u>o</u>se	wh<u>o</u>se	r<u>u</u>de	pl<u>u</u>me	**oe**	sh<u>oe</u>
o	t<u>o</u>mb	d<u>o</u>	m<u>o</u>vie	wh<u>o</u>	tw<u>o</u>	**ou**	gr<u>ou</u>p	y<u>ou</u>th	gh<u>ou</u>l	y<u>ou</u>
ough	thr<u>ough</u>	**u**	l<u>u</u>cre	pr<u>u</u>dent	fl<u>u</u>	l<u>u</u>cid	cr<u>u</u>cial	l<u>u</u>dicrous	l<u>u</u>natic
d<u>u</u>pe	m<u>u</u>te	d<u>u</u>ke	tr<u>u</u>th	obt<u>u</u>se	c<u>u</u>be	f<u>u</u>gue	h<u>u</u>ge	t<u>u</u>na	am<u>u</u>se	t<u>u</u>ne
f<u>u</u>neral	d<u>u</u>ty	p<u>u</u>pil	m<u>u</u>cus	conf<u>u</u>sion	m<u>u</u>sic	h<u>u</u>man	n<u>u</u>de	**ui**	br<u>ui</u>se
fr<u>ui</u>t	j<u>ui</u>ce	cr<u>ui</u>se	n<u>ui</u>sance	**ue**	bl<u>ue</u>	gl<u>ue</u>	tr<u>ue</u>	r<u>ue</u>	**eu**	sl<u>eu</u>th
d<u>eu</u>ce	f<u>eu</u>d	n<u>eu</u>tral	f<u>eu</u>dal	<u>eu</u>nuch	**ew**	n<u>ew</u>t	n<u>ew</u>	f<u>ew</u>	kn<u>ew</u>
s<u>e</u>wage	thr<u>ew</u>	**wo**	tw<u>o</u>	**eau**	b<u>eau</u>ty	b<u>eau</u>tiful	**ie**	v<u>ie</u>w	rev<u>ie</u>w

🎤 Practice Sentences for the GOOSE vowel sound

- The dresses are t<u>oo</u> b<u>eau</u>tiful to ch<u>oo</u>se between. I'm conf<u>u</u>sed! What to d<u>o</u>? I'll get tw<u>o</u>!
- He thr<u>ew</u> the t<u>oo</u>ls on the floor, called me a l<u>u</u>dicrous n<u>ui</u>sance and ran out thr<u>ough</u> the hall!
- Very f<u>ew</u> things m<u>o</u>ve me like these sal<u>u</u>brious Per<u>u</u>vian t<u>u</u>nes and L<u>u</u>ke's am<u>u</u>sing anecdotes.
- I think it's cr<u>u</u>cial to begin s<u>oo</u>n. Y<u>ou</u> get the st<u>u</u>dents, I'll start the m<u>u</u>sic and we'll concl<u>u</u>de.

⏱ 20min

foot
phonetic symbol - ʊ

This sound is pronounced in words like:

| u | p**u**t | b**u**sh | f**u**ll | b**u**tcher | oo | g**oo**d | st**oo**d | w**oo**d | w**oo**l | f**oo**t | l**oo**k |
| o | w**o**man *sing.* | w**o**lf | b**o**som | | ou | c**ou**ld | sh**ou**ld | w**ou**ld | sh**ou**ldn't | | |

🔊 313

> ### How is the FOOT vowel sound made in an RP accent?

The *tongue tip* is behind the *bottom teeth* and the *back of the tongue* is *high* in the *back* of the mouth. The *lips* are *rounded*, the *jaw* is loose and the *teeth* are apart. The FOOT vowel sound is *short* in duration.

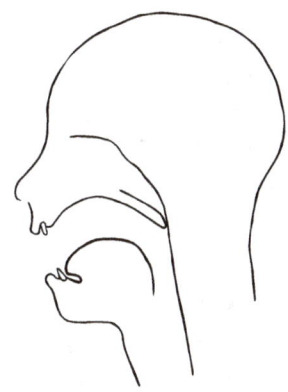
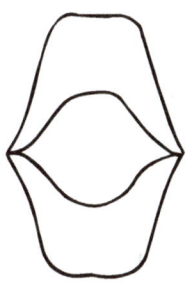

🔊 314

> ### What do I do habitually?

- Are your lips spread or neutral instead of rounded?

Some speakers have their *tongue* in an accurate position and make the sound *short* in duration, but their *lips* are *neutral* or *spread* instead of *rounded*, which impacts on the quality and tone of the sound. Listen to the following words, firstly spoken with the *lips spread*, then *neutral*, and then *rounded*, as they should be in RP: 'put', 'full', 'good', 'look', 'woman' (*sing.*), 'wolf', 'could' and 'shouldn't'. If you do this, go to 🔧

🔊 315

- Are you replacing the FOOT vowel sound with the SCHWA vowel sound?

Some speakers replace the FOOT vowel sound with the SCHWA vowel sound *(p.17)*, which is made with the *middle of the tongue* in the *middle* of the *centre of the mouth*, the *lips neutral* and the sound equally as *short* in duration. It is tricky to directly compare words with the SCHWA vowel sound, as it is the sound that tends to represent the *weak syllable* in a word *(book 3 - Intonation)*, and so it can be spelt in many ways. It is the sound that ends words like 'pizz**a**' and 'tun**a**'. Listen to the following words, firstly spoken with the SCHWA vowel sound, then with the FOOT vowel sound, as they should be in RP: 'put', 'full', 'good', 'look', 'woman' (*sing.*), 'wolf', 'could' and 'shouldn't'. If you do this, go to 🔧

🔊 316

- Are you replacing the FOOT vowel sound with the GOOSE vowel sound?

Some speakers replace the FOOT vowel sound with the GOOSE vowel sound *(p.90)* – especially when it is spelt 'oo' as in 'good' and 'stood' - which is made with the *back of the tongue* slightly *higher* in the *back of the mouth*, the sound *longer* in duration, and the *lips* very slightly more *rounded*. So words like 'w**oo**d' sound more like 'wooed', and 'l**oo**k' sounds more like 'Luke'. If you do this, go to 🔧

🔊 317

94

foot

phonetic symbol - ʊ

- Are you replacing the FOOT vowel sound with the THOUGHT vowel sound?

Some speakers replace the FOOT vowel sound with the THOUGHT vowel sound *(p.48)*, which is made with the *back of the tongue* very slightly *lower* in the *back of the mouth*, and the sound *longer* in duration. So words like 'h<u>oo</u>k' sound more like 'h<u>aw</u>k', 'c<u>ou</u>ld' sounds more like 'c<u>or</u>d', 'c<u>oo</u>k' sounds more like 'c<u>or</u>k' and 't<u>oo</u>k' sounds more like 't<u>al</u>k'. If you do this, go to 318

- Is your pronunciation guided by the spelling?

Many non-native speakers use the spelling of a word as a guide to its pronunciation. But because British English is not written phonetically, one vowel sound can be represented by numerous spellings. For this reason, the spelling in British English cannot be trusted for vowel pronunciation. For example, the FOOT vowel sound can be represented as the 'oo' in 'g<u>oo</u>d', the 'o' in the singular of 'w<u>o</u>man' and the 'ou' in 'sh<u>ou</u>ld'. So, you might mistakenly pronounce the 'oo' in 'g<u>oo</u>d' as the GOOSE vowel sound *(p.90 - as in 'f<u>oo</u>d')*. But all these words, despite the variation in spelling, are pronounced with the FOOT vowel sound. 319

It is also typical for a speaker to have a certain spelling that they often associate with a vowel sound. For example, many speakers associate the spelling 'u' with the FOOT vowel sound. One might then hope that all words spelt with 'u' would be pronounced as the FOOT vowel sound. Sadly, this is not true, as the 'u' in 'c<u>u</u>t' should be pronounced as the STRUT vowel sound *(p.35 - as in 'sh<u>u</u>t')*, in 'b<u>u</u>sy' it is pronounced as the KIT vowel sound *(p.70 - as in '<u>i</u>t')*, in 'b<u>u</u>ry' it is pronounced as the DRESS vowel sound *(p.78 - as in 'l<u>e</u>t')*, in 'h<u>u</u>ge' it is pronounced as the GOOSE vowel sound *(p.90 - as in 'f<u>oo</u>d')*, and in 'sec<u>u</u>rity' it is pronounced as the CURE vowel sound *(p.98 - as in 'man<u>u</u>re')*. All of this might seem a bit overwhelming, but I have some simple and effective solutions that will help you: go to 320

> How do I change my habit?

How do I encourage my lips to be rounded?

The only way to guarantee that your *lips* are *rounded* accurately instead of being *neutral* or *spread* is to use a mirror when you practice. Otherwise, you can feel the movement in your *lips* by putting one finger in a vertical line over your *lips* – if your *lips* are *rounding* your finger will be pushed forwards; and if your *lips* are *neutral* or slightly *spreading* your finger will remain still. Say the following words, either looking in a mirror or with one finger on your *lips*, and encourage them to be *rounded* accurately:

p<u>u</u>t   b<u>u</u>sh   f<u>u</u>ll   b<u>u</u>tcher   g<u>oo</u>d   st<u>oo</u>d   w<u>oo</u>d   w<u>oo</u>l   f<u>oo</u>t   l<u>oo</u>k

w<u>o</u>man *sing.*   w<u>o</u>lf   b<u>o</u>som   c<u>ou</u>ld   sh<u>ou</u>ld   w<u>ou</u>ld   sh<u>ou</u>ldn't

 321

How do I find the accurate tongue position for the FOOT vowel sound?

The position of the *tongue* and *lips* for the FOOT vowel sound is similar to their positions for the THOUGHT vowel sound *(p.48)* and GOOSE vowel sound *(p.90)*, so it might be helpful to compare them. Look in a mirror as you say 'h<u>oa</u>rd', 'h<u>oo</u>d' and 'wh<u>o</u>' (angle yourself towards a light or use a very small torch – although you might still struggle to see the *back of the tongue* because the *lips* need to be *rounded* when saying these vowel sounds). It might be helpful to say the vowel sounds on their own after saying

foot

phonetic symbol - ʊ

the words, in order to see the *tongue* more clearly. For 'hoard' (the THOUGHT vowel sound) encourage the *lips* to be *rounded*, the sound to be *long* in duration, and the *back of the tongue* to be in the *middle* of the *back of the mouth*. For 'hood' (this is the target FOOT vowel sound) encourage the *lips* to be slightly more *rounded*, the *back of the tongue* to be very slightly *higher* in the *back of the mouth*, and the sound to be *short* in duration. And for 'who' (the GOOSE vowel sound) encourage the *lips* to be slightly more *rounded*, the *back of the tongue* to be very slightly *higher* still in the *back of the mouth*, and the sound to be *longer* in duration.

322

THOUGHT   FOOT   GOOSE

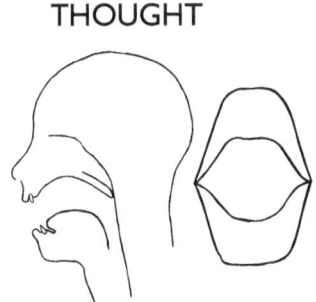 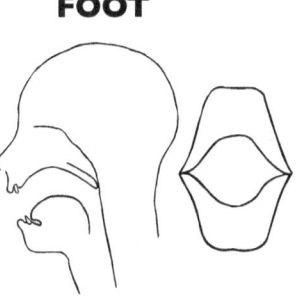 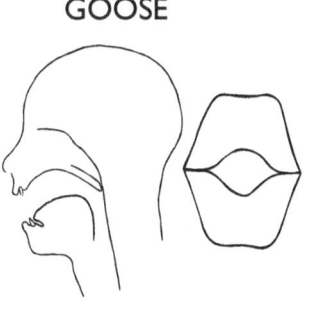

323

This THOUGHT, FOOT and GOOSE vowel sound sequence can be heard in the following sets of three words. Play with these words and encourage the *back of your tongue* and *lips* to remain in between the positions for the THOUGHT and GOOSE vowel sounds. Encourage the sound to be *short* in duration. Listen to the audio to help you imitate the sound accurately:

l<u>aw</u>n   l<u>oo</u>k   L<u>u</u>ke   s<u>aw</u>n   s<u>oo</u>t   s<u>oo</u>n   b<u>ough</u>t   b<u>oo</u>k   b<u>oo</u>t   sh<u>or</u>n   sh<u>oo</u>k   sh<u>oe</u>

324

If your habit is to replace the FOOT vowel sound with the GOOSE vowel sound, essentially, your *tongue* position is too *high*. For this reason, it might be helpful to say words with the THOUGHT vowel sound (which is made with the *tongue lower*) before saying words with the FOOT vowel sound, in order to encourage your *tongue* into a *lower* position. For example:

l<u>aw</u>n   l<u>oo</u>k   s<u>aw</u>n   s<u>oo</u>t   b<u>ough</u>t   b<u>oo</u>k   sh<u>or</u>n   sh<u>oo</u>k   c<u>or</u>k   c<u>oo</u>k   h<u>oar</u>d   h<u>oo</u>d

325

Similarly, if your habit is to replace the FOOT vowel sound with the SCHWA or THOUGHT vowel sound, then your *tongue* position is too *low* or *central*. For this reason, it might be helpful to say words with the GOOSE vowel sound (which is made with the *tongue higher* in the *back of the mouth*) before saying words with the FOOT vowel sound, in order to encourage your *tongue* into a position that is *higher* and further *back*. For example:

L<u>u</u>ke   l<u>oo</u>k   s<u>oo</u>n   s<u>oo</u>t   b<u>oo</u>t   b<u>oo</u>k   sh<u>oe</u>   sh<u>oo</u>k   w<u>oo</u>ed   w<u>oo</u>d

326

Lastly, here's another game to play: say the FOOT vowel sound on its own before saying each word, to help you hear whether or not you are pronouncing it accurately and also to give you a reference for how it should sound in the word. Listen to the audio to help you imitate the sound accurately:

p<u>u</u>t   b<u>u</u>sh   f<u>u</u>ll   b<u>u</u>tcher   g<u>oo</u>d   st<u>oo</u>d   w<u>oo</u>d   w<u>oo</u>l   f<u>oo</u>t   l<u>oo</u>k   w<u>o</u>man *sing*.   w<u>o</u>lf   b<u>o</u>som   c<u>ou</u>ld   sh<u>ou</u>ld   w<u>ou</u>ld   sh<u>ou</u>ldn't

327

foot

phonetic symbol - ʊ

🔧 *How do I avoid being guided by the spelling?*

Once you have used the exercises above to help you achieve an accurate pronunciation of this vowel sound, go to the *Lexical Sets* subsection *(p.16)* for advice on how to avoid being guided by the spelling.

🎙 *Practice words and typical spellings for the FOOT vowel sound*

u	p<u>u</u>t	b<u>u</u>sh	f<u>u</u>ll	b<u>u</u>tcher	c<u>u</u>shion	p<u>u</u>dding	b<u>u</u>llet	p<u>u</u>sh	p<u>u</u>ll	s<u>u</u>gar
oo	g<u>oo</u>d	st<u>oo</u>d	w<u>oo</u>d	w<u>oo</u>l	c<u>oo</u>k	l<u>oo</u>k	sh<u>oo</u>k	f<u>oo</u>t	h<u>oo</u>d
o	w<u>o</u>man *sing.*	w<u>o</u>lf	b<u>o</u>som	**ou**	c<u>ou</u>ld	sh<u>ou</u>ld	w<u>ou</u>ld	sh<u>ou</u>ldn't

328

🎙 *Practice Sentences for the FOOT vowel sound*

- I c<u>ou</u>ld just b<u>u</u>lly my way to the top, but I w<u>ou</u>ldn't establish any g<u>oo</u>d will – I'd l<u>oo</u>k stupid.
- Our local b<u>u</u>tcher c<u>oo</u>ked a roast for us on Sunday. He was so f<u>u</u>ll of g<u>oo</u>d humor.
- The w<u>oo</u>ds are beautiful. I'd take a w<u>oo</u>ly jumper and g<u>oo</u>d f<u>oo</u>twear. You will love it, trust me!
- I sh<u>ou</u>ldn't have any more s<u>u</u>gar. I l<u>oo</u>k awf<u>u</u>l. Give me a c<u>u</u>shion w<u>ou</u>ld you? I need to lie down.

329

Am I pronouncing it accurately?

Get a personalised assessment of every vowel, consonant and aspect of intonation to find out how well you're doing, exactly what to focus on and what you need to do to speak in this accent accurately and naturally:

https://www.ashleyhoward.me/pronunciation-evaluation

⏱ 20min

cure

phonetic symbol - ʊə

This sound is pronounced in words like:

our g<u>our</u>met t<u>our</u>niquet **oor** sp<u>oor</u> **ure** man<u>ure</u> mat<u>ure</u> p<u>ure</u>
sec<u>ure</u> **u** r<u>u</u>ral c<u>u</u>rious f<u>u</u>rious lux<u>u</u>rious **eu** <u>Eu</u>rope n<u>eu</u>ron pl<u>eu</u>risy
330

> ### How is the CURE vowel sound made in an RP accent?

The CURE vowel sound is a *diphthong* – a combination of two vowel sounds where one slides into the other. The CURE vowel sound starts as the FOOT vowel sound *(p.94 - where the tongue tip is behind the bottom teeth, the back of the tongue is high in the back of the mouth, and the lips are rounded)* which slides into the SCHWA vowel sound *(p.17 - where the tongue tip stays behind the bottom teeth, the lips release back to neutral and the middle of the tongue slides back into the middle of the centre of the mouth)*. The *jaw* is loose, the *teeth* are apart, and the sound is *long* in duration.

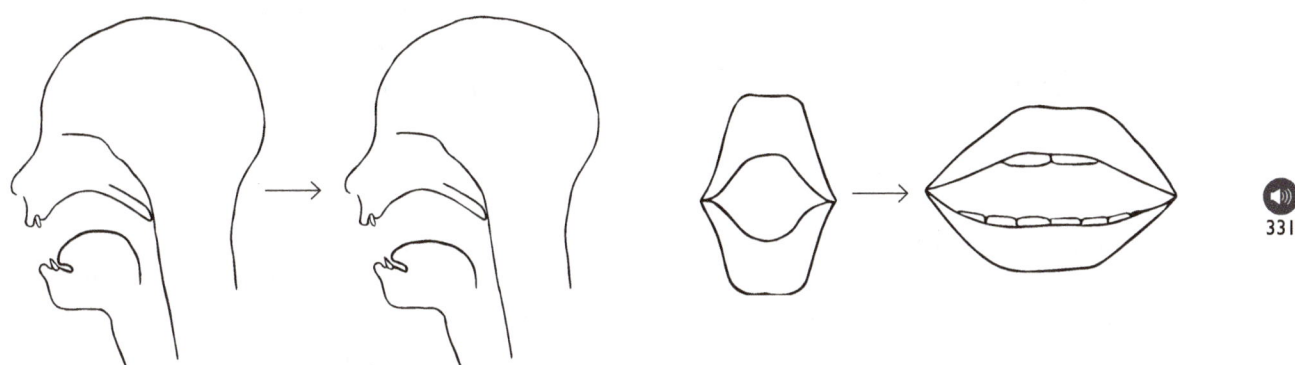

331

> ### Some words are preceded by a YOD

Some words that are pronounced with the CURE vowel sound are often preceded by a YOD *(book 2 - Consonants)*, as in 'end<u>ure</u>', 'man<u>ure</u>', 'obsc<u>ure</u>', 'p<u>ure</u>', 'sec<u>ure</u>', 'c<u>u</u>rious', 'f<u>u</u>rious', '<u>Eu</u>rope', 'n<u>eu</u>ral' and 'n<u>eu</u>ron'. Whilst there is no conclusive spelling pattern that will help you to know when to use the YOD, one way to be sure is to look at the phonetic transcription in a reliable dictionary. When listening to the audio examples in this section, pay attention to the presence or absence of the YOD so as to avoid mispronunciation.   332

> ### What do I do habitually?

- Are you pronouncing every written 'r'?

If you are a *rhotic* speaker *(book 2 - Consonants)* your habit is to pronounce every written 'r'. The CURE vowel sound is often spelt with a written 'r' as in 'g<u>our</u>met', 'sp<u>oor</u>', 'end<u>ure</u>', 'man<u>ure</u>' and 'mat<u>ure</u>'. But RP is a *non-rhotic* accent so a written 'r' is only pronounced when it is followed by a spoken vowel sound. Listen to the words above, firstly spoken with the R sound and then without, as they should be in RP. If you do this, go to

333

98

cure

phonetic symbol - ʊə

- Do your lips remain rounded, neutral or spread throughout the whole diphthong?

Some speakers move their *tongue* through the accurate positions and make the sound *long* in duration, but their *lips* remain *rounded, neutral* or *spread* throughout instead of sliding from being *rounded* to *neutral,* which impacts on the quality and tone of the sound. Listen to the following words, firstly spoken with the *lips rounded,* then *neutral,* then *spread,* and then sliding from being *rounded* to *neutral,* as they should be in RP: 'g<u>our</u>met', 'f<u>ur</u>ious', 'end<u>ure</u>', 'r<u>ur</u>al' and 'E<u>ur</u>ope'. If you do this, go to

- Are you making this diphthong too long or too short in duration?

Some speakers move their *tongue* and *lips* through the accurate positions but they make the *diphthong* too *short* or too *long* in duration, which impacts on the quality and tone of the sound. If you are making the *diphthong* too *long,* either both vowel sounds in the *diphthong* will be too *long,* which will make it sound like two *syllables* instead of one, or one of the vowel sounds in the *diphthong* will be too *long.* Listen to the following words, firstly spoken with the *diphthong* too *short* in duration, then with both vowel sounds too *long,* then with the first vowel sound too *long,* then with the second vowel sound too *long,* and finally as they should be in RP: 'g<u>our</u>met', 'f<u>ur</u>ious', 'end<u>ure</u>', 'r<u>ur</u>al' and 'E<u>ur</u>ope'. If you do this, go to

- Are you replacing the CURE vowel sound with the LOT vowel sound?

Some speakers replace the CURE vowel sound with the LOT vowel sound *(p.43),* which is made with the *back of the tongue low* in the *back of the mouth,* the *lips* slightly *rounded* and the sound *short* in duration. Listen to the following words, firstly spoken with the LOT vowel sound, and then with the CURE vowel sound, as they should be in RP: 'g<u>our</u>met', 'f<u>ur</u>ious', 'end<u>ure</u>', 'r<u>ur</u>al' and 'E<u>ur</u>ope'. If you do this, go to

- Are you replacing the CURE vowel sound with the NURSE vowel sound?

Some speakers replace the CURE vowel sound with the NURSE vowel sound *(p.21),* which is made with the *middle of the tongue* in the *middle* of the *centre of the mouth,* the *lips neutral* and the sound *long* in duration. Listen to the following words, firstly spoken with the NURSE vowel sound, and then with the CURE vowel sound, as they should be in RP: 'g<u>our</u>met', 'f<u>ur</u>ious', 'end<u>ure</u>', 'r<u>ur</u>al' and 'E<u>ur</u>ope'. If you do this, go to

- Are you replacing the CURE vowel sound with the THOUGHT vowel sound?

Some speakers replace the CURE vowel sound with the THOUGHT vowel sound *(p.48),* which is made with the *back of the tongue* in the *middle* of the *back of the mouth,* the *lips rounded* and the sound *long* in duration. Listen to the following words, firstly spoken with the THOUGHT vowel sound, and then with the CURE vowel sound, as they should be in RP: 'g<u>our</u>met', 'f<u>ur</u>ious', 'end<u>ure</u>', 'r<u>ur</u>al' and 'E<u>ur</u>ope'. If you do this, go to

The CURE vowel sound has been evolving for some years, and there are some words in this *lexical set (p.16)* now pronounced with the THOUGHT vowel sound by most RP speakers, partly because they share many of the same spellings. For example 'p<u>ure</u>' is most commonly pronounced with the CURE vowel sound, whereas many speakers now pronounce 's<u>ure</u>' with the THOUGHT vowel sound, as in 'sh<u>ore</u>'. See the *Anything Else? (p.97)* section below for more information about this.

cure

phonetic symbol - ʊə

- Are you replacing the second vowel sound with the STRUT or DRESS vowel sound?

Some speakers replace the final vowel sound (SCHWA) with the STRUT vowel sound *(p.35 - which is made with the middle of the tongue low in the centre of the mouth and the lips equally as neutral)* or with the DRESS vowel sound *(p.78 - which is made with the front of the tongue in the middle in the front of the mouth and the lips slightly spread)*. Listen to the following words, firstly spoken with the STRUT vowel sound as the final vowel sound of the *diphthong*, then with the DRESS vowel sound as the final vowel sound, and lastly with the SCHWA vowel sound as the final vowel sound, as they should be in RP: 'p<u>ure</u>', 'sp<u>oor</u>', 'end<u>ure</u>', 'man<u>ure</u>', 'sec<u>ure</u>' and 'mat<u>ure</u>'. If you do this, go to

- Is your pronunciation guided by the spelling?

Many non-native speakers use the spelling of a word as a guide to its pronunciation. But because British English is not written phonetically, one vowel sound can be represented by numerous spellings. For this reason, the spelling in British English cannot be trusted for vowel pronunciation. For example, the CURE vowel sound can be represented as the 'our' in 'g<u>our</u>met', the 'oor' in 'sp<u>oor</u>', the 'u' in 'r<u>u</u>ral', and the 'eu' in '<u>Eu</u>rope'. So, you might mistakenly pronounce the 'u' in 'f<u>u</u>ry' as the STRUT vowel sound *(p.35 - as in* 'h<u>u</u>rry'). But all these words, despite the variation in spelling, are pronounced with the CURE vowel sound.

It is also typical for a speaker to have a certain spelling that they often associate with a vowel sound. For example, many speakers associate the spelling 'ure' with the CURE vowel sound. One might then hope that all words spelt with 'ure' would be pronounced as the CURE vowel sound. Sadly, this is not true, as the 'ure' in 's<u>ure</u>' can be pronounced as the THOUGHT vowel sound *(p.48 - as in* 'sh<u>ore</u>'), and when it's a weak syllable as in 'nat<u>ure</u>' it is pronounced as the SCHWA vowel sound *(p.17 - as in* 'tun<u>a</u>'). All of this might seem a bit overwhelming, but I have some simple and effective solutions that will help you: go to

> How do I change my habit?

🔧 *How do I avoid pronouncing a written 'r' that should not be pronounced?*

Firstly, encourage your *tongue tip* to stay down, touching the *bottom front teeth* when you are saying the vowel sound. Secondly, unless the vowel sound is followed by another consonant, encourage the *tongue* to stay completely still throughout, avoiding any movement at the end of the sound. When it is followed by a consonant that needs the *tongue tip*, encourage the *tongue* to move directly to the position for that consonant, and not to pronounce an R sound just before. Listen to the audio to help you imitate the sound accurately and watch your *tongue* in a mirror:

        g<u>our</u>met   p<u>ure</u>   sp<u>oor</u>   end<u>ure</u>   man<u>ure</u>   sec<u>ure</u>   mat<u>ure</u>

🔧 *How do I find the accurate tongue position for the CURE vowel sound?*

Firstly, ensure that you are accurately pronouncing the two component vowel sounds in this *diphthong* by following the exercises in the sections entitled *How do I find the accurate tongue position for the FOOT vowel sound? (p.91)* and *How do I find the accurate tongue position for the SCHWA vowel sound? (p.18)*.

Once you feel confident with how to make each vowel sound, your *tongue* needs to slide from one into the

cure

phonetic symbol - ʊə

other to make the *diphthong*. Say each sound on its own, one after the other, with a brief pause between them. Watch your *tongue* and *lips* in a mirror and then take out the pause, sliding them into one another. All *diphthongs* are made with the first vowel slightly more *stressed* than the second. This being said, it is only *slightly* more *stressed* and should be observed with care. And remember that the two vowel sounds in a *diphthong* make a single *syllable*: the *tongue* slides smoothly but swiftly and the sound is *long*, but not too *long*.

Play with the following exercise. It offers you an opportunity to check whether you are accurately pronouncing the first vowel sound in the *diphthong* – FOOT. Listen to the audio to help you imitate the sound accurately:

    gu... g<u>ou</u>rmet   spu... sp<u>oo</u>r   endu... end<u>ure</u>   ru... r<u>u</u>ral   u... <u>Eu</u>rope

344

🔧 How do I avoid being guided by the spelling?

Once you have used the exercises above to help you achieve an accurate pronunciation of this vowel sound, go to the *Lexical Sets* subsection *(p.16)* for advice on how to avoid being guided by the spelling.

> Anything Else?

- The evolving CURE vowel sound

The CURE vowel sound has been evolving for a number of years, and there are some words in this *lexical set* that some RP speakers pronounce with the THOUGHT vowel sound. For example, '<u>sure</u>' can be pronounced with the THOUGHT vowel sound, as in 'sh<u>ore</u>'. Thankfully, there are very few words in the CURE *lexical set*. And most speakers now pronounce the examples given below with the THOUGHT vowel sound, and you may come across others. This is not to say that pronouncing them with the CURE vowel sound is incorrect, but simply that it is a slightly more traditional pronunciation often associated with older speakers. Listen to the following words, firstly spoken with the THOUGHT vowel sound and then the CURE vowel sound:

our	t<u>our</u>	g<u>our</u>d	**ou**	t<u>ou</u>rism	t<u>ou</u>rist	**oor**	m<u>oor</u>	p<u>oor</u>
oo	b<u>oo</u>rish	**ure**	s<u>ure</u>ly	ass<u>ure</u>	ens<u>ure</u>	ins<u>ure</u>		
	s<u>ure</u>	abj<u>ure</u>	end<u>ure</u>	**u**	ass<u>u</u>rance	ins<u>u</u>rance		

345

- '*tourney*' and '*tournament*'

Some speakers pronounce words like '<u>tour</u>ney' and '<u>tour</u>nament' with the NURSE vowel sound *(p.21)* some with the THOUGHT vowel sound *(p.48)* and some with the CURE vowel sound.

346

> Practice words and typical spellings for the CURE vowel sound

our	am<u>our</u>	b<u>our</u>se	b<u>our</u>geois	g<u>our</u>mand	g<u>our</u>met	t<u>our</u>niquet	
oor sp<u>oor</u>	**ure**	adj<u>ure</u>	all<u>ure</u>	dem<u>ure</u>	end<u>ure</u>	imm<u>ure</u>	in<u>ure</u>	l<u>ure</u>

347

c<u>u</u>re

phonetic symbol - ʊə

🎙️ **Practice words and typical spellings for the CURE vowel sound (cont.)**

man<u>ure</u>   mat<u>ure</u>   **u**   angost<u>u</u>ra   brav<u>u</u>ra   b<u>u</u>reau   caes<u>u</u>ra   inc<u>u</u>rable

m<u>u</u>ral   j<u>u</u>ry   l<u>u</u>rid   mat<u>u</u>rity   obsc<u>u</u>rity   p<u>u</u>rify   p<u>u</u>rity   sec<u>u</u>rity   sulph<u>u</u>ric

eu   <u>Eu</u>rope   n<u>eu</u>ral   n<u>eu</u>ron   pl<u>eu</u>risy

347

🎙️ **Practice Sentences for the CURE vowel sound**

- The room was lux<u>u</u>rious, but M<u>u</u>riel was rather c<u>u</u>rious about the large m<u>u</u>ral of r<u>u</u>ral France.
- I just hope there is a c<u>u</u>re. End<u>u</u>ring any more of this obsc<u>u</u>re treatment will make me f<u>u</u>rious!
- I sold the b<u>u</u>reau to a mat<u>u</u>re gentleman d<u>u</u>ring the war. He was a n<u>eu</u>rosurgeon!
- She was a dem<u>u</u>re lady, with a kind and p<u>u</u>re nature. The j<u>u</u>ry felt sec<u>u</u>re in their judgement.

348

> Bonus Material!

Great news – there's a FREE online video about the CURE on my YouTube channel:

https://www.youtube.com/@ashleyhowardvoicecoach

Take the next step...

Congratulations, you did it!
Well Done!

You're a third of your way on the journey. This is book 1 of a 3 part series. So what do you want to master next? Consonants or intonation?

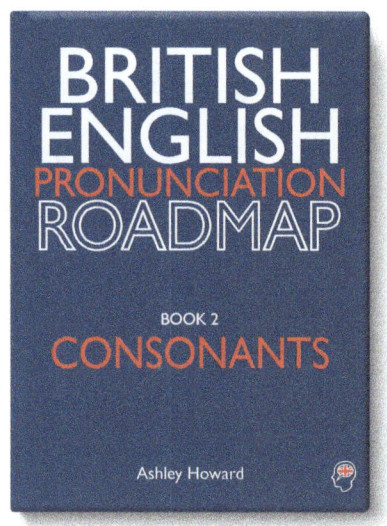

Book 2 - Consonants

- Step-by-step guide to help you perfect the 24 consonant sounds in English - particular help with NG, TH, R, L and other difficult sounds
- 4 hours of audio to practice with
- Clear illustrations of the tongue and lip positions.
- Colour-coded icons to guide you to specific exercises for your specific habits
- AND some special bonus material...

Available online.

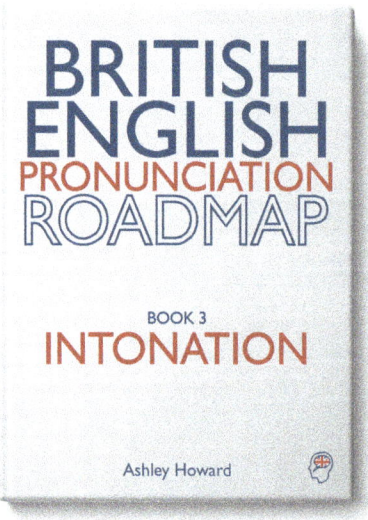

Book 3 - Intonation

Covers all this and MORE:

- Word and sentence stress - creating meaning
- Rising and falling intonation patterns
- Weak forms and unstressed syllables
- Rhythm and pitch - adding feeling and intention
- Connected speech - elision, contractions, assimilation
- Asking questions, making statements, apologising, sarcasm, quoting and paraphrasing...
- Linking and intrusive consonants
- Prefixes and suffixes
- AND much, much more...

Available online.

How do I Integrate these New Habits into Live Speech

> Repetition, repetition, repetition

It sounds obvious and potentially quite boring, but it is the only sure way to build muscle memory and enable these new habits to manifest in live speech. However, here are three main ways in which you can practice:

- Sit, listen and imitate

Set aside a period of time, as regularly as you can, to sit down with the book, and practice the areas that you found challenging. Take your time, repeat the exercises, listen to the audio, imitate the examples whilst watching yourself in a mirror and record yourself.

- Listen, listen, listen

Most of us live very busy lives, and even finding ten minutes to practice can be challenging. But we all have time while we are doing other things, like travelling, eating, cleaning, cooking, waiting etc… where we could do some listening. Even when we can't actually practice aloud, just listening can be very productive! I won't bore you with the science, but the brain and body engage in some very sophisticated imitative processes while listening, and so open the audio on your computer or mobile device and listen to it. Have it on in the background while you're cooking or cleaning. Have it on your phone and listen on your headphones if you're travelling on a train or bus or taxi. Just surround yourself with the sounds that you're hoping to inhabit.

- Stealing the 'best bits'

Look and listen out for speakers who embody the pronunciation and intonation habits that you're hoping to inhabit. These might be friends and colleagues, or people in the media, who you might be able to hear regularly and steal some of what they're doing really well. It's nothing to do with becoming them, but simply having a reference to inspire and guide you.

- Expand your word banks and rehearse phrases

Hopefully, you've been building a *word bank* for each new sound and feature that you've explored through the book. Take time to reflect on the language you use day to day, and expand those word banks to focusing your practice on words and phrases that you can then use in daily speech. Build these words into typical phrases and expressions that you use regularly, for example, 'I'll be home at six', 'what time is the meeting?' or 'do you want to go for lunch?'. Rehearsing these phrases might enable you to have greater control of how you pronounce the vowels and consonants, and which stresses and intonation you use, so that when you speak it is less like a game of roulette, and more specific and confident.

- Have a 'second take'

After any conversation, meeting or presentation, you'll be surprised at how you will have identified some words and phrases that you weren't happy with in terms of pronunciation or intonation. 'Strike while the iron is hot' as we would say – find a couple of minutes to note down some of those words or phrases and immediately give them another go or a 'second take'. Get really specific about what could have been better, maybe check their phonetic transcription in a reliable dictionary and play with them over the following days and weeks.

⏱ 10min

Practice Pages - n<u>ur</u>se

phonetic symbol - 3:

🎤 Ex. 1 - Spot the NURSE vowel sound (p.21)

"The first thing to say, is that you've all worked really hard. And on Thursday, we found out that we're now third in the country, competing with the likes of Earnest Worthing and Scott Burns! The purpose of our recent advertisement was to raise the profile and start the next part of our journey. We've come a long way in thirteen years, mostly due to your commitment. Those early starts have paid off, and every person here is part of this success. The question is – how do we become first in the country? We need to learn more, assert ourselves and cause a stir in the industry. We'll reinvent this firm and in doing so, you'll all earn a bit more money!"

🔊 349

🎤 Ex. 2 - Everyday words

b<u>ir</u>th	b<u>ur</u>st	c<u>ur</u>ve	<u>ear</u>th	p<u>ur</u>pose	s<u>er</u>vant	t<u>ur</u>n	v<u>er</u>se	w<u>or</u>d	w<u>or</u>k
b<u>ir</u>d	ch<u>ur</u>ch	c<u>ir</u>cle	c<u>ur</u>tain	g<u>ir</u>l	n<u>er</u>ve	sh<u>ir</u>t	sk<u>ir</u>t	w<u>or</u>m	f<u>er</u>tile	c<u>er</u>tain
d<u>ir</u>ty	p<u>ur</u>pose	h<u>ur</u>t	fl<u>ir</u>t	b<u>ur</u>n	<u>ear</u>n	al<u>er</u>t	s<u>ear</u>ch	w<u>or</u>th	f<u>ir</u>st	em<u>er</u>gency
conc<u>er</u>n	l<u>ur</u>king	s<u>ur</u>f	p<u>ur</u>pose	transf<u>er</u>	f<u>ur</u>	f<u>ur</u>ther	f<u>ir</u>m	m<u>ur</u>der	t<u>er</u>m
g<u>er</u>ms	p<u>er</u>manent	disc<u>er</u>n	p<u>er</u>m	ch<u>ur</u>n	s<u>ir</u>	th<u>ir</u>sty	th<u>ir</u>ty	th<u>ir</u>d	h<u>er</u>

🔊 350

- Ex. 3 – Create phrases from the words above

Create 6 phrases that you might use containing words from Ex. 2 above.

1 .... 2 ....
3 .... 4 ....
5 .... 6 ....

- Ex. 4 - My Word Bank

What are your 12 most frequently used words containing the NURSE vowel sound?

1 .... 2 .... 3 .... 4 ....
5 .... 6 .... 7 .... 8 ....
9 .... 10 .... 11 .... 12 ....

- Ex. 5 - My Phrase Bank

What are your 6 most frequently used phrases containing the NURSE vowel sound?

1 .... 2 ....
3 .... 4 ....
5 .... 6 ....

Practice Pages - g<u>oa</u>t

10min

phonetic symbol – əʊ

Ex. 1 - Spot the GOAT vowel sound (p.26)

"I got a new coat today. I know, I should be saving up for the boat trip with Owen but it was on offer and I couldn't say no! It's mauve with roses sewn onto the pockets. They were about to close, and they only had one left and it was in my size. I don't treat myself very often, and it's so warm I can wear it when we're out cruising on the ocean. I should go home and show Owen. He doesn't go back on the road until tomorrow."

351

Ex. 2 - Everyday words

<u>o</u>ver	n<u>o</u>	th<u>ough</u>	s<u>o</u>	bl<u>ow</u>	gr<u>ow</u>th	h<u>o</u>pe	m<u>o</u>tion	n<u>o</u>te	<u>o</u>wner	pr<u>o</u>cess
pr<u>o</u>se	pr<u>o</u>test	sl<u>o</u>pe	sm<u>o</u>ke	sn<u>ow</u>	s<u>oa</u>p	st<u>o</u>ne	b<u>o</u>ne	c<u>o</u>mb	g<u>oa</u>t
n<u>o</u>se	thr<u>oa</u>t	t<u>oe</u>	br<u>o</u>ken	<u>o</u>pen	l<u>ow</u>	sl<u>ow</u>	g<u>o</u>	sh<u>ow</u>	gl<u>oa</u>t	c<u>oa</u>t	t<u>oa</u>st
r<u>oa</u>st	b<u>oa</u>st	m<u>o</u>st	ph<u>o</u>ne	ph<u>o</u>to	ph<u>o</u>tograph	b<u>oa</u>t	cl<u>o</u>se	c<u>o</u>de	cond<u>o</u>ne
gr<u>oa</u>n	p<u>o</u>ke	s<u>oa</u>k	str<u>o</u>ke	l<u>oa</u>n	al<u>o</u>ne	kn<u>ow</u>	y<u>o</u>ke	envel<u>o</u>pe	p<u>o</u>st

352

- Ex. 3 – Create phrases from the words above

Create 6 phrases that you might use containing words from Ex. 2 above.

1 .... 2 ....
3 .... 4 ....
5 .... 6 ....

- Ex. 4 - My Word Bank

What are your 12 most frequently used words containing the GOAT vowel sound?

1 .... 2 .... 3 .... 4 ....
5 .... 6 .... 7 .... 8 ....
9 .... 10 .... 11 .... 12 ....

- Ex. 5 - My Phrase Bank

What are your 6 most frequently used phrases containing the GOAT vowel sound?

1 .... 2 ....
3 .... 4 ....
5 .... 6 ....

Practice Pages - b<u>a</u>th, p<u>a</u>lm, st<u>ar</u>t

10min

phonetic symbol – ɑː

Ex. 1 - Spot the BATH vowel sound (p.31)

"I agree, but the answer is not to sack the staff. The branch has no clear direction… Don't laugh – They all work very hard… Please don't interrupt me. They all work hard - without any appreciation I might add – the issue is poor management. Arthur is not a leader. From the very start he has been argumentative; he's clueless about the state of the market; he's not part of the team. For example, I asked him to talk to Martha to reassure her that we'll support her through these difficult circumstances. He refused and made some alarming remark about hormones and barged past. The answer is to sack Arthur."

353

Ex. 2 - Everyday words

after	far	argument	art	brass	chance	example	father	glass	grass
harbour	harmony	mark	plant	arch	arm	army	basket	bath	card	cart
farm	garden	heart	parcel	star	hard	sharp	dark	last	pass	grasp
last	fast	nasty	fasten	disaster	advance	answer	demand	advantage	dance
grant	ask	daft	banana	sample	branch	contrast			

354

- Ex. 3 – Create phrases from the words above

Create 6 phrases that you might use containing words from Ex. 2 above.

1 ………………………………………… 2 …………………………………………
3 ………………………………………… 4 …………………………………………
5 ………………………………………… 6 …………………………………………

- Ex. 4 - My Word Bank

What are your 12 most frequently used words containing the BATH vowel sound?

1 ………………… 2 ………………… 3 ………………… 4 …………………
5 ………………… 6 ………………… 7 ………………… 8 …………………
9 ………………… 10 ……………… 11 ……………… 12 ………………

- Ex. 5 - My Phrase Bank

What are your 6 most frequently used phrases containing the BATH vowel sound?

1 ………………………………………… 2 …………………………………………
3 ………………………………………… 4 …………………………………………
5 ………………………………………… 6 …………………………………………

p.124

Practice Pages - str**u**t

phonetic symbol - ʌ

Ex. 1 - Spot the STRUT vowel sound *(p.35)*

"Could you pick up the kids from school today? Come on Duncan! I seldom ask you for anything, and I'm under so much pressure. I've got to run through the agenda for Monday, do some number crunching, and then collect the cupcakes from Mum for the fund raiser on Sunday. It's just this once! After this month it'll all be done. I love you. Please don't punish me. It'll be summer soon. We'll have such fun in London. Kate's son is coming, and your brother is always such great company. I'll make it up to you, I promise!"

355

Ex. 2 - Everyday words

am**o**ng   **u**nder   **o**ther   s**o**me   s**u**ch   b**u**t   en**ou**gh   adj**u**stment   bl**oo**d   b**u**tter
c**o**lour   c**o**mfort   c**ou**ntry   c**o**ver   cr**u**sh   c**u**rrent   destr**u**ction   disc**o**very
disc**u**ssion   disg**u**st   d**u**st   fr**o**nt   g**o**vernment   j**u**dge   j**u**mp   m**o**ney   m**o**ther
r**u**b   r**u**n   str**u**cture   s**u**bstance   th**u**nder   t**ou**ch   tr**ou**ble   br**u**sh   b**u**cket
b**u**d   b**u**tton   c**u**p   gl**o**ve   g**u**n   m**o**nkey   m**u**scle   n**u**t   **o**ven   p**u**mp   sp**o**nge
st**o**mach   s**u**n   th**u**mb   t**o**ngue   c**u**t   s**u**dden   y**ou**ng   p**u**blic   r**ou**gh   sh**u**t

356

- Ex. 3 – Create phrases from the words above

Create 6 phrases that you might use containing words from Ex. 2 above.

1 .... 2 ....
3 .... 4 ....
5 .... 6 ....

- Ex. 4 - My Word Bank

What are your 12 most frequently used words containing the STRUT vowel sound?

1 ....   2 ....   3 ....   4 ....
5 ....   6 ....   7 ....   8 ....
9 ....   10 ....   11 ....   12 ....

- Ex. 5 - My Phrase Bank

What are your 6 most frequently used phrases containing the STRUT vowel sound?

1 .... 2 ....
3 .... 4 ....
5 .... 6 ....

Practice Pages - pr<u>i</u>ce

phonetic symbol - ɑɪ

🕙 10min

🎙️ **Ex. 1 - Spot the PRICE vowel sound** (p.39)

"We've been to Venice tw<u>i</u>ce this year! Eileen told us to go to see the s<u>igh</u>ts and taste the food, and both were wonderful. The fl<u>igh</u>t over is easy and we always pack l<u>igh</u>t. It's expensive, but the experience is pr<u>i</u>celess. And the people are so k<u>i</u>nd and fr<u>ie</u>ndly, I cr<u>ie</u>d when we said goodbye! But on our last n<u>igh</u>t we tr<u>ie</u>d a new restaurant. The food wasn't good and there was a f<u>igh</u>t outside, so next t<u>i</u>me we'll f<u>i</u>nd somewhere n<u>i</u>cer." 357

🎙️ **Ex. 2 - Everyday words**

b<u>y</u>	<u>I</u>	wh<u>i</u>le	wh<u>y</u>	q<u>ui</u>te	b<u>i</u>te	cr<u>i</u>me	cr<u>y</u>	des<u>ig</u>n	dr<u>i</u>ving	f<u>igh</u>t	g<u>ui</u>de
<u>i</u>ce	<u>i</u>ron	l<u>igh</u>t	m<u>i</u>nd	m<u>i</u>ne	m<u>igh</u>t	pr<u>i</u>ce	r<u>i</u>ce	sc<u>i</u>ence	s<u>i</u>de	s<u>ig</u>n	s<u>i</u>ze
sk<u>y</u>	sm<u>i</u>le	soc<u>ie</u>ty	surpr<u>i</u>se	t<u>i</u>me	w<u>i</u>ne	wr<u>i</u>te	<u>eye</u>	fl<u>y</u>	<u>i</u>sland	kn<u>i</u>fe	
l<u>i</u>brary	l<u>i</u>ne	p<u>i</u>pe	br<u>igh</u>t	h<u>igh</u>	l<u>i</u>ke	pr<u>i</u>vate	q<u>uie</u>t	r<u>igh</u>t	t<u>igh</u>t	w<u>i</u>de	
w<u>i</u>se	dr<u>y</u>	wh<u>i</u>te									

358

- Ex. 3 – Create phrases from the words above

Create 6 phrases that you might use containing words from Ex. 2 above.

1 .... 2 ....
3 .... 4 ....
5 .... 6 ....

- Ex. 4 - My Word Bank

What are your 12 most frequently used words containing the PRICE vowel sound?

1 .... 2 .... 3 .... 4 ....
5 .... 6 .... 7 .... 8 ....
9 .... 10 .... 11 .... 12 ....

- Ex. 5 - My Phrase Bank

What are your 6 most frequently used phrases containing the PRICE vowel sound?

1 .... 2 ....
3 .... 4 ....
5 .... 6 ....

Practice Pages - l<u>o</u>t, cl<u>o</u>th

phonetic symbol - ɒ

⏱ 10min

🎤 Ex. 1 - Spot the LOT vowel sound *(p.43)*

"I've got a new job! I've been at Hobsons for too long, it wasn't satisfying me any more. So, I got the paper and saw an opportunity at Godrey's Locksmiths in Gloucester. I applied, went down to their offices, talked about my experience and they offered it to me on the spot! I said 'could I get back to you tomorrow? I'm just considering my options'. What else was I to do? They told me that I've got to do some more training in October, and I'll be on probation for six months, but Oscar works there and he said that offers like this don't come along that often and I should take it. So I did!"

🔊 359

🎤 Ex. 2 - Everyday words

acr<u>o</u>ss	fr<u>o</u>m	<u>o</u>ff	<u>o</u>n	<u>o</u>f	bec<u>au</u>se	n<u>o</u>t	tom<u>o</u>rrow	auth<u>o</u>rity	b<u>o</u>dy	cl<u>o</u>th
c<u>o</u>pper	c<u>o</u>py	c<u>o</u>tton	c<u>ou</u>gh	kn<u>ow</u>ledge	l<u>o</u>ss	p<u>o</u>lish	pr<u>o</u>fit	pr<u>o</u>perty
qu<u>a</u>lity	s<u>a</u>lt	sh<u>o</u>ck	s<u>o</u>ng	st<u>o</u>p	t<u>o</u>p	w<u>a</u>sh	b<u>o</u>ttle	b<u>o</u>x	cl<u>o</u>ck	c<u>o</u>llar
d<u>o</u>g	dr<u>o</u>p	h<u>o</u>spital	kn<u>o</u>t	<u>o</u>range	p<u>o</u>cket	p<u>o</u>t	r<u>o</u>d	s<u>o</u>ck	st<u>o</u>cking	w<u>a</u>tch
c<u>o</u>mmon	c<u>o</u>mplex	c<u>o</u>nscious	h<u>o</u>llow	l<u>o</u>ng	p<u>o</u>ssible	pr<u>o</u>bable	resp<u>o</u>nsible
str<u>o</u>ng	f<u>a</u>lse	<u>o</u>pposite	s<u>o</u>ft	s<u>o</u>lid	wr<u>o</u>ng

🔊 360

- Ex. 3 – Create phrases from the words above

Create 6 phrases that you might use containing words from Ex. 2 above.

1 .... 2 ....
3 .... 4 ....
5 .... 6 ....

- Ex. 4 - My Word Bank

What are your 12 most frequently used words containing the LOT vowel sound?

1 .... 2 .... 3 .... 4 ....
5 .... 6 .... 7 .... 8 ....
9 .... 10 .... 11 .... 12 ....

- Ex. 5 - My Phrase Bank

What are your 4 most frequently used phrases containing the LOT vowel sound?

1 .... 2 ....
3 .... 4 ....

 10min

Practice Pages - th<u>ou</u>ght, n<u>or</u>th, f<u>or</u>ce

phonetic symbol - ɔː

🎤 Ex. 1 - Spot the THOUGHT vowel sound (p.48)

"Do you have to work tonight Paul? Why don't we go for a walk? Or order a takeaway? I thought I could get a couple of bottles of wine, you could hire a film, and we could just relax for a bit. I've found things so stressful recently. Work has been mad. I've been given all these reports to do, and I'm not coping with it very well. George starts high school next week. Laura is organising an auction at the village hall and wants me to give a talk…. I need a holiday, that's what I need. Come on - it's just one night… If I take the kids out tomorrow morning you could work then instead." 361

🎤 Ex. 2 - Everyday words

bef<u>ore</u>	f<u>or</u>	<u>a</u>ll	<u>or</u>	f<u>or</u>ward	<u>a</u>lmost	n<u>or</u>th	c<u>au</u>se	ch<u>a</u>lk	c<u>or</u>k	d<u>au</u>ghter
f<u>a</u>ll	f<u>or</u>ce	l<u>a</u>w	<u>or</u>nament	p<u>or</u>ter	rec<u>or</u>d v.	rew<u>ar</u>d	s<u>or</u>t	st<u>or</u>y	supp<u>or</u>t	
th<u>ou</u>ght	w<u>ar</u>	w<u>a</u>ter	b<u>a</u>ll	b<u>oar</u>d	c<u>or</u>d	d<u>oo</u>r	dr<u>aw</u>	fl<u>oor</u>	f<u>or</u>k	h<u>or</u>n
h<u>or</u>se	st<u>ore</u>	w<u>a</u>ll	imp<u>or</u>tant	n<u>or</u>mal	p<u>oor</u>	t<u>a</u>ll	w<u>ar</u>m	sh<u>or</u>t	sm<u>a</u>ll	
t<u>a</u>lk	ass<u>or</u>t	dist<u>or</u>t	f<u>or</u>m	t<u>or</u>ture	<u>or</u>thodox	<u>or</u>gan	w<u>ar</u>drobe	ign<u>ore</u>	p<u>or</u>k	t<u>or</u>n

362

- Ex. 3 – Create phrases from the words above

Create 6 phrases that you might use containing words from Ex. 2 above.

1 …………………………………………………… 2 ……………………………………………………
3 …………………………………………………… 4 ……………………………………………………
5 …………………………………………………… 6 ……………………………………………………

- Ex. 4 - My Word Bank

What are your 12 most frequently used words containing the THOUGHT vowel sound?

1 ………………… 2 ………………… 3 ………………… 4 …………………
5 ………………… 6 ………………… 7 ………………… 8 …………………
9 ………………… 10 ………………… 11 ………………… 12 …………………

- Ex. 5 - My Phrase Bank

What are your 6 most frequently used phrases containing the THOUGHT vowel sound?

1 …………………………………………………… 2 ……………………………………………………
3 …………………………………………………… 4 ……………………………………………………
5 …………………………………………………… 6 ……………………………………………………

Practice Pages - ch**oi**ce

phonetic symbol - ɔɪ

🎤 **Ex. 1 - Spot the CHOICE vowel sound** *(p.53)*

I've been getting really annoyed at Joy. She's always spoiling things by talking rudely, and the toys she got Lloyd are so inappropriate. Why can't she just employ some common sense? She'll upset everyone if she keeps going like this, but it's her choice. Anyway I shouldn't loiter here any longer, you've got potatoes to boil and the kids to put to bed. It was a lovely party, and the soy-yoghurts went down well! No need for my paranoia after all.

🎤 **Ex. 2 - Everyday words**

j**oi**n   n**oi**se   **oi**l   p**oi**nt   p**oi**son   v**oi**ce   b**oy**   c**oi**n   t**oi**l   v**oi**d   s**oi**l   tabl**oi**d
h**oi**st   av**oi**d   m**oi**st   ster**oi**d   j**oy**   t**oy**   dec**oy**   env**oy**   ann**oy**   **oy**ster
v**oy**age   empl**oy**   destr**oy**   depl**oy**   c**oi**l   s**oi**l   sp**oi**l   p**oi**se   j**oi**st   j**oi**nt
t**oi**let   embr**oi**led   an**oi**nt   rej**oi**ce   l**oi**ter   ch**oi**ce   hemorrh**oi**d   f**oi**l   thyr**oi**d
paran**oi**d   embr**oi**dery   aster**oi**d

- Ex. 3 – Create phrases from the words above

Create 6 phrases that you might use containing words from Ex. 2 above.

1 ....   2 ....
3 ....   4 ....
5 ....   6 ....

- Ex. 4 - My Word Bank

What are your 12 most frequently used words containing the CHOICE vowel sound?

1 ....   2 ....   3 ....   4 ....
5 ....   6 ....   7 ....   8 ....
9 ....   10 ....   11 ....   12 ....

- Ex. 5 - My Phrase Bank

What are your 6 most frequently used phrases containing the CHOICE vowel sound?

1 ....   2 ....
3 ....   4 ....
5 ....   6 ....

Practice Pages - tr**a**p

10min

phonetic symbol - æ

Ex. 1 - Spot the TRAP vowel sound (p.57)

"We're going to a tango dance class on Saturday, would you like to come? Andrew is coming. So is Mathew, Andrea and Sam. Come on, we just stomp around for a bit. It's great! It's mad but such a laugh. And the man that leads it is very attractive. He isn't married, and he has a waxed chest!! Then we'll head back to mine, have a glass or two and then go down to the Fat Cat – that pub on the corner of Ashford road, near Amber's house. There's a band playing – they're called the Mad Hatters I think. How does that sound?"

365

Ex. 2 - Everyday words

at	as	than	act	animal	attack	back	balance	canvas	comparison	crack
damage	expansion	fact	family	land	language	manager	mass	reaction
sand	smash	tax	transport n.	value	angle	ant	apple	bag	camera
carriage	flag	hammer	hand	map	match	rat	acid	angry	automatic
black	elastic	flat	hanging	happy	natural	parallel	bad	narrow	sad

366

- Ex. 3 – Create phrases from the words above

Create 6 phrases that you might use containing words from Ex. 2 above.

1 .... 2 ....
3 .... 4 ....
5 .... 6 ....

- Ex. 4 - My Word Bank

What are your 12 most frequently used words containing the TRAP vowel sound?

1 .... 2 .... 3 .... 4 ....
5 .... 6 .... 7 .... 8 ....
9 .... 10 .... 11 .... 12 ....

- Ex. 5 - My Phrase Bank

What are your 6 most frequently used phrases containing the TRAP vowel sound?

1 .... 2 ....
3 .... 4 ....
5 .... 6 ....

p.126

Practice Pages - m<u>ou</u>th

phonetic symbol - aʊ

🎤 **Ex. 1 - Spot the MOUTH vowel sound** *(p.61)*

I can't believe we sold the house! We should celebrate! The MacCleods seem like a nice family. We should leave the towel rail and I doubt we'll need the dishwasher. Do you remember there's that brown stain on the bath? We need to get that out. It'll be strange to leave this town, but I'm sure it'll be lovely down south. We've looked around, it's a good area.

🔊 367

🎤 **Ex. 2 - Everyday words**

ab<u>ou</u>t	h<u>ow</u>	n<u>ow</u>	<u>ou</u>t	acc<u>ou</u>nt	am<u>ou</u>nt	m<u>ou</u>ntain	p<u>ow</u>der	s<u>ou</u>nd
w<u>ou</u>nd *(past tense of the verb 'wind')*			cl<u>ou</u>d	c<u>ow</u>	f<u>ow</u>l	m<u>ou</u>th v.	pl<u>ough</u>	tr<u>ou</u>sers
r<u>ou</u>nd	l<u>ou</u>d	ast<u>ou</u>nd	gr<u>ou</u>nd	m<u>ou</u>nd	s<u>ou</u>nd	gr<u>ow</u>l	f<u>ou</u>l	r<u>ou</u>se	n<u>ou</u>n
st<u>ou</u>t	p<u>ou</u>ch	m<u>ou</u>se	m<u>ou</u>nt	g<u>ou</u>ge	c<u>ou</u>ch	f<u>ou</u>nd	p<u>ou</u>nd	dev<u>ou</u>t	l<u>ou</u>nge
s<u>ou</u>th	c<u>ou</u>nt	pron<u>ou</u>nce	c<u>ou</u>ncil	b<u>ou</u>ndary	cr<u>ow</u>d	br<u>ow</u>se	all<u>ow</u>		

🔊 368

- Ex. 3 – Create phrases from the words above

Create 6 phrases that you might use containing words from Ex. 2 above.

1 .... 2 ....
3 .... 4 ....
5 .... 6 ....

- Ex. 4 - My Word Bank

What are your 12 most frequently used words containing the MOUTH vowel sound?

1 .... 2 .... 3 .... 4 ....
5 .... 6 .... 7 .... 8 ....
9 .... 10 .... 11 .... 12 ....

- Ex. 5 - My Phrase Bank

What are your 6 most frequently used phrases containing the MOUTH vowel sound?

1 .... 2 ....
3 .... 4 ....
5 .... 6 ....

Practice Pages - fl<u>ee</u>ce

phonetic symbol - iː

🎤 **Ex. 1 - Spot the FLEECE vowel sound** (p.65)

"Are you free next week? I've got this meeting on Wednesday evening and I'm feeling so uneasy about it. Could you come round, read my notes and then give me some feedback? I'd really appreciate it! It's about the team's recent performance figures. We had three people quit last month and they want me to give some reasons why I think they left, and it's in front of the chief exec. Maxine will be there, which is a relief. But nonetheless, I'm a complete wreck! I've been dreaming about it for weeks. Even Steven noticed that I've been acting sheepish recently, and that's something!"

🎤 **Ex. 2 - Everyday words**

k<u>ee</u>p	s<u>ee</u>m	b<u>e</u>	s<u>ee</u>	betw<u>ee</u>n	th<u>e</u>	h<u>e</u>	<u>ea</u>st	pl<u>ea</u>se	agr<u>ee</u>ment	bel<u>ie</u>f
degr<u>ee</u>	d<u>e</u>tail	dis<u>ea</u>se	fi<u>e</u>ld	h<u>ea</u>t	incr<u>ea</u>se v.	l<u>ea</u>d	mach<u>i</u>ne	m<u>ea</u>l	m<u>ea</u>t	
n<u>ee</u>d	p<u>ea</u>ce	r<u>ea</u>ding	s<u>ea</u>	sl<u>ee</u>p	sn<u>ee</u>ze	st<u>ea</u>m	st<u>ee</u>l	t<u>ea</u>ching	w<u>ee</u>k	
b<u>ee</u>	ch<u>ee</u>se	k<u>e</u>y	kn<u>ee</u>	l<u>ea</u>f	rec<u>ei</u>pt	s<u>ee</u>d	str<u>ee</u>t	tr<u>ee</u>	wh<u>ee</u>l	
ch<u>ea</u>p	cl<u>ea</u>n	d<u>ee</u>p	<u>e</u>qual	fr<u>ee</u>	fr<u>e</u>quent adj.	sw<u>ee</u>t	f<u>e</u>male	f<u>ee</u>ble	gr<u>ee</u>n	
s<u>e</u>cret										

- Ex. 3 – Create phrases from the words above

Create 6 phrases that you might use containing words from Ex. 2 above.

1 .... 2 ....
3 .... 4 ....
5 .... 6 ....

- Ex. 4 - My Word Bank

What are your 12 most frequently used words containing the FLEECE vowel sound?

1 .... 2 .... 3 .... 4 ....
5 .... 6 .... 7 .... 8 ....
9 .... 10 .... 11 .... 12 ....

- Ex. 5 - My Phrase Bank

What are your 4 most frequently used phrases containing the FLEECE vowel sound?

1 .... 2 ....
3 .... 4 ....

Practice Pages - k*i*t

phonetic symbol - **ɪ**

10min

Ex. 1 - Spot the K*I*T vowel sound *(p.70)*

"I've been given this extra work to do, but I don't think it's fair. Jim has never taken any work home in the last four years and it's frustrating not to have even been acknowledged for putting in additional evenings and weekends. He just goes to the gym every night. I've helped Flynn build this business! He can't manage his staff. If it doesn't change soon, I'll be looking for a new job, that's for sure!"

371

Ex. 2 - Everyday words

w*i*ll   *i*n   w*i*th   t*i*ll   st*i*ll   l*i*ttle   add*i*tion   b*i*t   compet*i*tion   cond*i*tion   dec*i*sion
d*i*stance   d*i*vision   dr*i*nk   ex*i*stence   f*i*ction   gr*i*p   h*i*story   *i*mpulse   *i*ncrease *n.*
*i*ndustry   *i*nsect   *i*nstrument   *i*nterest   k*i*ck   k*i*ss   l*i*ft   l*i*mit   l*i*nen   l*i*quid
l*i*st   m*i*ddle   m*i*lk   m*i*nute   m*i*st   op*i*nion   pos*i*tion   pr*i*nt   rel*i*gion   rh*y*thm
r*i*ver   s*i*lver   s*i*ster   sl*i*p   st*i*tch   sw*i*m   s*y*stem   th*i*ng   t*i*n   tr*i*ck   tw*i*st
w*i*nd   w*i*nter   br*i*ck   sh*i*p   sk*i*n   spr*i*ng   st*i*ck   t*i*cket   wh*i*stle   w*i*ndow   w*i*ng
f*i*xed   l*i*ving   m*i*litary   ph*y*sical   pol*i*tical   qu*i*ck   st*i*cky   st*i*ff   th*i*ck   b*i*tter
d*i*fferent   *i*ll   m*i*xed

372

- Ex. 3 – Create phrases from the words above

Create 6 phrases that you might use containing words from Ex. 2 above.

1 .... 2 ....
3 .... 4 ....
5 .... 6 ....

- Ex. 4 - My Word Bank

What are your 12 most frequently used words containing the KIT vowel sound?

1 ....   2 ....   3 ....   4 ....
5 ....   6 ....   7 ....   8 ....
9 ....   10 ....   11 .... 12 ....

- Ex. 5 - My Phrase Bank

What are your 4 most frequently used phrases containing the KIT vowel sound?

1 .... 2 ....
3 .... 4 ....

Practice Pages - n<u>ear</u>

phonetic symbol - ɪə

10min

🎤 Ex. 1 - *Spot the NEAR vowel sound* (p.74)

He's handed in his notice at the museum. He wants to pursue a career in medicine! He's got so much studying to do, but he really is serious about it. I don't want to interfere. I think it's clear in his mind and that's all that matters. It's weird to think he'll be going back to university after all these years. I fear change – I don't think I could do it.

373

🎤 Ex. 2 - *Everyday words*

h<u>ere</u>	n<u>ear</u>	exp<u>e</u>rience	h<u>ea</u>ring	id<u>ea</u>	th<u>eo</u>ry	y<u>ear</u>	<u>ear</u>	mat<u>e</u>rial	s<u>e</u>rious
d<u>ear</u>	t<u>ear</u>	s<u>ear</u>	g<u>ear</u>	sh<u>ear</u>	bl<u>ear</u>y	dr<u>ear</u>y	app<u>ear</u>	m<u>ere</u>	we'<u>re</u>	adh<u>ere</u>
sph<u>ere</u>	coh<u>e</u>rent	sev<u>ere</u>	rev<u>ere</u>	aust<u>ere</u>	sinc<u>ere</u>	persev<u>ere</u>	car<u>eer</u>

374

- Ex. 3 – *Create phrases from the words above*

Create 6 phrases that you might use containing words from Ex. 2 above.

1 .... 2 ....
3 .... 4 ....
5 .... 6 ....

- Ex. 4 - *My Word Bank*

What are your 12 most frequently used words containing the NEAR vowel sound?

1 .... 2 .... 3 .... 4 ....
5 .... 6 .... 7 .... 8 ....
9 .... 10 .... 11 .... 12 ....

- Ex. 5 - *My Phrase Bank*

What are your 6 most frequently used phrases containing the NEAR vowel sound?

1 .... 2 ....
3 .... 4 ....
5 .... 6 ....

Practice Pages - dr<u>e</u>ss

phonetic symbol - e

🎤 Ex. 1 - Spot the DRESS vowel sound *(p.78)*

"Have you heard about Emily? You know that she's been applying to different universities to do her PHD? Well, she got in! Guess where! Oxford! She's thrilled. A bit overwhelmed no doubt, but so happy. The selection process is rigorous. I hope she's ready!? I'm so envious! Greg is over the moon. He's taking her to Edinburgh for a special celebratory weekend away together!" 375

🎤 Ex. 2 - Everyday words

g<u>e</u>t   l<u>e</u>t   s<u>e</u>nd   <u>a</u>ny   <u>e</u>very   wh<u>e</u>n   <u>e</u>ver   th<u>e</u>n   v<u>e</u>ry   y<u>e</u>sterday   w<u>e</u>st
y<u>e</u>s   att<u>e</u>mpt   att<u>e</u>ntion   br<u>ea</u>d   br<u>ea</u>th   conn<u>e</u>ction   cr<u>e</u>dit   d<u>ea</u>th   d<u>e</u>bt
dev<u>e</u>lopment   dig<u>e</u>stion   dir<u>e</u>ction   <u>e</u>dge   <u>e</u>ffect   <u>e</u>nd   <u>e</u>rror   <u>e</u>vent   <u>e</u>xpert
fr<u>ie</u>nd   h<u>e</u>lp   inv<u>e</u>ntion   j<u>e</u>lly   l<u>ea</u>ther   l<u>e</u>tter   l<u>e</u>vel   m<u>ea</u>sure   m<u>e</u>mory   m<u>e</u>tal
pl<u>ea</u>sure   qu<u>e</u>stion   r<u>e</u>cord *n.*   regr<u>e</u>t   requ<u>e</u>st   resp<u>e</u>ct   r<u>e</u>st   s<u>e</u>cretary   s<u>e</u>lf 376
s<u>e</u>nse   s<u>e</u>x   sm<u>e</u>ll   st<u>e</u>p   str<u>e</u>tch   sugg<u>e</u>stion   t<u>e</u>ndency   t<u>e</u>st   v<u>e</u>ssel   w<u>ea</u>ther
b<u>e</u>d   b<u>e</u>ll   b<u>e</u>rry   ch<u>e</u>st   sh<u>e</u>lf   st<u>e</u>m   thr<u>ea</u>d   umbr<u>e</u>lla   ch<u>e</u>mical   dep<u>e</u>ndent
el<u>e</u>ctric   g<u>e</u>neral   h<u>ea</u>lth   m<u>e</u>dical   n<u>e</u>cessary   pr<u>e</u>sent *n.*   pr<u>e</u>sent *v.*   r<u>e</u>gular
irr<u>e</u>gular   s<u>e</u>cond   s<u>e</u>parate *adj.*   s<u>e</u>parate *v.*   w<u>e</u>t   y<u>e</u>llow   d<u>ea</u>d   d<u>e</u>licate   l<u>e</u>ft

- Ex. 3 – Create phrases from the words above

Create 6 phrases that you might use containing words from Ex. 2 above.

1 .... 2 ....
3 .... 4 ....
5 .... 6 ....

- Ex. 4 - My Word Bank

What are your 12 most frequently used words containing the DRESS vowel sound?

1 ....   2 ....   3 ....   4 ....
5 ....   6 ....   7 ....   8 ....
9 ....   10 ....   11 ....   12 ....

- Ex. 5 - My Phrase Bank

What are your 4 most frequently used phrases containing the DRESS vowel sound?

1 .... 2 ....
3 .... 4 ....

Practice Pages - face

phonetic symbol - eɪ

Ex. 1 - Spot the FACE vowel sound (p.82)

"I've been at the station for hours. I think the train is delayed. I'm so sorry. It's just started to rain as well! What a crazy day! Sorry for the wait! Are you free in April, could I come and stay then? Great! And I won't be late! We'll have an amazing time! I think I'll go by plane next time."

Ex. 2 - Everyday words

make   take   say   may   again   apparatus   base   behaviour   change   danger
education   exchange   flame   grain   hate   name   nation   observation   operation
organisation   page   pain   paint   paper   paste   payment   place   play   range
rate   ray   relation   representation   scale   shade   shake   shame   space   stage
statement   taste   trade   wave   way   weight   baby   basin   blade   brain
brake   cake   chain   drain   face   nail   plate   potato   rail   sail   snake
spade   table   trail   train   tray   able   grey   male   same   straight   awake
safe   strange

- Ex. 3 – Create phrases from the words above

Create 6 phrases that you might use containing words from Ex. 2 above.

1 .... 2 ....
3 .... 4 ....
5 .... 6 ....

- Ex. 4 - My Word Bank

What are your 12 most frequently used words containing the FACE vowel sound?

1 ....   2 ....   3 ....   4 ....
5 ....   6 ....   7 ....   8 ....
9 ....   10 ....   11 ....   12 ....

- Ex. 5 - My Phrase Bank

What are your 6 most frequently used phrases containing the FACE vowel sound?

1 .... 2 ....
3 .... 4 ....
5 .... 6 ....

Practice Pages - sq**uare**

phonetic symbol - **eə**

⏱ 10min

🎙 **Ex. 1 - Spot the SQUARE vowel sound** *(p.86)*

"We went to the fayre today. Mary absolutely loved it. There were various tents and stalls. There was one selling homemade pear cider. I bought five bottles! What you can buy in the supermarket just doesn't compare to this. There was a whole area that had been turned into a fairy grotto. And there was a very precarious looking tree house. I was worried when the children were running up and down those stairs, but no one was hurt and it did look beautiful. Whoever designed it has a lot of artistic flair!" 🔊 379

🎙 **Ex. 2 - Everyday words**

wh**ere**	**air**	c**are**	h**air**	squ**are**	sh**are**	w**ear**	r**are**	f**air**	comp**are**	f**are**
d**are**	sw**ear**	sc**are**	bl**are**	aw**are**	fl**are**	bew**are**	decl**are**	prep**are**	ensn**are**	
nightm**are**	p**air**	fl**air**	aff**air**	écl**air**	st**airs**	d**airy**	can**ary**	million**aire**	Cl**aire**	
desp**air**	b**are**	h**eir**	p**ear**	sc**arce**	v**ary**					

🔊 380

- Ex. 3 – Create phrases from the words above

Create 6 phrases that you might use containing words from Ex. 2 above.

1 .... 2 ....
3 .... 4 ....
5 .... 6 ....

- Ex. 4 - My Word Bank

What are your 12 most frequently used words containing the SQUARE vowel sound?

1 .... 2 .... 3 .... 4 ....
5 .... 6 .... 7 .... 8 ....
9 .... 10 .... 11 .... 12 ....

- Ex. 5 - My Phrase Bank

What are your 6 most frequently used phrases containing the SQUARE vowel sound?

1 .... 2 ....
3 .... 4 ....
5 .... 6 ....

⏱ 10min

Practice Pages - g<u>oo</u>se

phonetic symbol - ʊː

🎤 Ex. 1 - Spot the GOOSE vowel sound (p.90)

"How was your holiday? Where did you go? Sounds beautiful! No, we stayed here. I'm working really hard trying to get this assignment finished. I think I'm losing my mind – it's gruelling! I'm getting up at six… It's true! I'm out by seven then I'm either writing, proofreading or editing up until half five everyday day. It's hard to get in the groove, you know? I'm still doing my private work but when I do, if I'm honest, I just can't focus on anything. The deadline is looming and who knows if I'll be done. It's two weeks today! Who knew that writing and thinking could be so exhausting! I'll be done soon. Once I've finished, I think I'll sleep for a week!"

🔊 381

🎤 Ex. 2 - Everyday words

thr<u>ough</u>	t<u>o</u>	am<u>u</u>sement	appr<u>o</u>val	distrib<u>u</u>tion	f<u>oo</u>d	fr<u>ui</u>t	gr<u>ou</u>p	h<u>u</u>mour
m<u>o</u>ve	m<u>u</u>sic	n<u>e</u>ws	prod<u>u</u>ce	r<u>oo</u>m	r<u>u</u>le	s<u>ou</u>p	<u>u</u>nit	<u>u</u>se	v<u>ie</u>w	w<u>ou</u>nd
(injury)	b<u>oo</u>t	j<u>e</u>wel	m<u>oo</u>n	r<u>oo</u>f	r<u>oo</u>t	sch<u>oo</u>l	scr<u>e</u>w	sh<u>oe</u>	sp<u>oo</u>n
t<u>oo</u>th	n<u>ew</u>	sm<u>oo</u>th	bl<u>ue</u>	cr<u>ue</u>l	f<u>oo</u>lish	f<u>u</u>ture	l<u>o</u>se	rev<u>iew</u>	j<u>ui</u>ce
n<u>ui</u>sance	conf<u>u</u>sion	cr<u>u</u>cial	thr<u>ough</u>	t<u>oo</u>th	ch<u>oo</u>se	b<u>oo</u>st

🔊 382

- Ex. 3 – Create phrases from the words above

Create 6 phrases that you might use containing words from Ex. 2 above.

1 .... 2 ....
3 .... 4 ....
5 .... 6 ....

- Ex. 4 - My Word Bank

What are your 12 most frequently used words containing the GOOSE vowel sound?

1 .... 2 .... 3 .... 4 ....
5 .... 6 .... 7 .... 8 ....
9 .... 10 .... 11 .... 12 ....

- Ex. 5 - My Phrase Bank

What are your 6 most frequently used phrases containing the GOOSE vowel sound?

1 .... 2 ....
3 .... 4 ....
5 .... 6 ....

Practice Pages - f<u>oo</u>t

phonetic symbol - ʊ

🎤 Ex. 1 - Spot the FOOT vowel sound *(p.94)*

"I shouldn't be here. I'm sorry. I know how awkward it makes you. I couldn't make it last week, because I was at that book fair in town. I stood for hours. It was good though, but the host was awful - so full of himself... Do you want a cushion? That bed looks so uncomfortable... How do you feel now? That woman next door looks grumpy... How's the food? Would you like me to cook you something?"

🎤 Ex. 2 - Everyday words

p<u>u</u>t	l<u>oo</u>k	p<u>u</u>ll	p<u>u</u>sh	s<u>u</u>gar	w<u>oo</u>d	w<u>oo</u>l	f<u>oo</u>t	h<u>oo</u>k	c<u>ou</u>ld	sh<u>ou</u>ld
w<u>ou</u>ldn't	sh<u>ou</u>ldn't	sh<u>oo</u>k	cr<u>oo</u>k	t<u>oo</u>k	h<u>oo</u>d	sh<u>oo</u>k	c<u>oo</u>kie	b<u>u</u>sh		

- Ex. 3 – Create phrases from the words above

Create 6 phrases that you might use containing words from Ex. 2 above.

1 .... 2 ....
3 .... 4 ....
5 .... 6 ....

- Ex. 4 - My Word Bank

What are your 12 most frequently used words containing the FOOT vowel sound?

1 .... 2 .... 3 .... 4 ....
5 .... 6 .... 7 .... 8 ....
9 .... 10 .... 11 .... 12 ....

- Ex. 5 - My Phrase Bank

What are your 6 most frequently used phrases containing the FOOT vowel sound?

1 .... 2 ....
3 .... 4 ....
5 .... 6 ....

Practice Pages - c<u>u</u>re

phonetic symbol - ʊə

🎤 Ex. 1 - Spot the CURE vowel sound *(p.98)*

"The doctors say it's incurable. I was furious at first, but I'm coming to terms with it now. She doesn't want to have to endure any more tests. She's so calm and mature about it. She's very inspiring. I'm not coping as well, but I think she feels very secure in the home and they're doing everything they can for her. Her room's quite luxurious, and it's good that it's so rural, she can watch the deer from her window." 385

🎤 Ex. 2 - Everyday words

ins<u>u</u>rance   ass<u>u</u>re   imp<u>u</u>re   obsc<u>u</u>re   proc<u>u</u>re   p<u>u</u>re   sec<u>u</u>re   c<u>u</u>re   pl<u>u</u>ral   r<u>u</u>ral
Tr<u>u</u>ro   cent<u>u</u>rion   c<u>u</u>rious   f<u>u</u>rious   inj<u>u</u>rious   lux<u>u</u>rious   m<u>u</u>ral   pen<u>u</u>rious   386
sp<u>u</u>rious   c<u>u</u>rate   d<u>u</u>ring   f<u>u</u>ry

- Ex. 3 – Create phrases from the words above

Create 6 phrases that you might use containing words from Ex. 2 above.

1 ....   2 ....
3 ....   4 ....
5 ....   6 ....

- Ex. 4 - My Word Bank

What are your 12 most frequently used words containing the CURE vowel sound?

1 ....   2 ....   3 ....   4 ....
5 ....   6 ....   7 ....   8 ....
9 ....   10 ....   11 ....   12 ....

- Ex. 5 - My Phrase Bank

What are your 6 most frequently used phrases containing the CURE vowel sound?

1 ....   2 ....
3 ....   4 ....
5 ....   6 ....

Practice Pages - Answers

> ### *the NURSE vowel sound*

- *Ex. 1 - Spot the NURSE vowel sound (p.105)*

"The f<u>ir</u>st thing to say, is that you've all w<u>or</u>ked really hard. And on Th<u>ur</u>sday, we found out that we're now th<u>ir</u>d in the country, competing with the likes of <u>Ear</u>nest W<u>or</u>thing and Scott B<u>ur</u>ns! The p<u>ur</u>pose of our recent adv<u>er</u>tisement was to raise the profile of the company and start the next part of our j<u>our</u>ney. We've come a long way in th<u>ir</u>teen years, mostly due to your commitment. Those <u>ear</u>ly starts have paid off, and every p<u>er</u>son here is part of this success. The question is – how do we become f<u>ir</u>st in the country? We need to l<u>ear</u>n more, ass<u>er</u>t ourselves and cause a st<u>ir</u> in the industry. We'll reinvent this f<u>ir</u>m and in doing so, you'll all <u>ear</u>n a bit more money!" ₃₄₉

> ### *the GOAT vowel sound*

- *Ex. 1 - Spot the GOAT vowel sound (p.106)*

"I g<u>o</u>t a new c<u>oa</u>t today. I kn<u>ow</u>, I should be saving up for the b<u>oa</u>t trip with <u>O</u>wen but it was on offer and I couldn't say n<u>o</u>! It's m<u>au</u>ve with r<u>o</u>ses s<u>ew</u>n onto the pockets. They were about to cl<u>o</u>se, and they <u>o</u>nly had one left and it was in my size. I d<u>o</u>n't treat myself very often, and it's s<u>o</u> warm I can wear it when we're out cruising on the <u>o</u>cean. I should g<u>o</u> h<u>o</u>me and sh<u>ow</u> <u>O</u>wen. He doesn't g<u>o</u> back on the r<u>oa</u>d until tomorr<u>ow</u>." ₃₅₁

> ### *the BATH, PALM, START vowel sound*

- *Ex. 1 - Spot the BATH vowel sound (p.107)*

"I agree, but the <u>a</u>nswer is not to sack the st<u>a</u>ff. The br<u>a</u>nch has no clear direction... Don't l<u>au</u>gh – They all work very h<u>ar</u>d... Please don't interrupt me. They all work h<u>ar</u>d - without any appreciation I might add – the issue is poor management. <u>Ar</u>thur is not a leader. From the very st<u>ar</u>t he has been <u>ar</u>gumentative; he's clueless about the state of the m<u>ar</u>ket; he's not p<u>ar</u>t of the team. For ex<u>a</u>mple, I <u>a</u>sked him to talk to M<u>ar</u>tha to reassure her that we'll support her through these difficult circumst<u>a</u>nces. He refused and made some al<u>ar</u>ming rem<u>ar</u>k about hormones and b<u>ar</u>ged p<u>a</u>st. The <u>a</u>nswer is to sack <u>Ar</u>thur." ₃₅₃

Practice Pages - Answers

> ### *the STRUT vowel sound*

- Ex. 1 - Spot the TRAP vowel sound (p.108)

"Could you pick <u>u</u>p the kids from school today? C<u>o</u>me on D<u>u</u>ncan! I seldom ask you for anything, and I'm <u>u</u>nder so m<u>u</u>ch pressure. I've got to r<u>u</u>n through the agenda for M<u>o</u>nday, do s<u>o</u>me n<u>u</u>mber cr<u>u</u>nching, and then collect the c<u>u</u>pcakes from M<u>u</u>m for the f<u>u</u>ndraiser on S<u>u</u>nday. It's j<u>u</u>st this <u>o</u>nce! After this m<u>o</u>nth it'll all be d<u>o</u>ne. I l<u>o</u>ve you. Please don't p<u>u</u>nish me. It'll be s<u>u</u>mmer soon. We'll have s<u>u</u>ch f<u>u</u>n in L<u>o</u>ndon. Kate's s<u>o</u>n is c<u>o</u>ming, and your br<u>o</u>ther is always s<u>u</u>ch great c<u>o</u>mpany. I'll make it <u>u</u>p to you, I promise!"

> ### *the PRICE vowel sound*

- Ex. 1 - Spot the PRICE vowel sound (p.109)

"We've been to Venice tw<u>i</u>ce this year! <u>Ei</u>leen told us to go to see the s<u>i</u>ghts and taste the food, and both were wonderful. The fl<u>i</u>ght over is easy and we always pack l<u>i</u>ght. It's expensive, but the experience is pr<u>i</u>celess. And the people are so k<u>i</u>nd and friendly, I cr<u>ie</u>d when we said goodb<u>ye</u>! But on our last n<u>i</u>ght we tried a new restaurant. The food wasn't good and there was a f<u>i</u>ght outs<u>i</u>de, so next t<u>i</u>me we'll find somewhere n<u>i</u>cer."

> ### *the LOT vowel sound*

- Ex. 1 - Spot the LOT vowel sound (p.110)

"I've g<u>o</u>t a new j<u>o</u>b! I've been at H<u>o</u>bsons for too l<u>o</u>ng, it w<u>a</u>sn't satisfying me any more. So, I g<u>o</u>t the paper and saw an <u>o</u>pportunity at G<u>o</u>drey's L<u>o</u>cksmiths in Gl<u>o</u>ucester. I applied, went down to their <u>o</u>ffices, talked about my experience and they <u>o</u>ffered it to me <u>o</u>n the sp<u>o</u>t! I said 'could I get back to you tom<u>o</u>rrow? I'm just considering my <u>o</u>ptions'. What else was I to do? They told me that I've g<u>o</u>t to do some more training in <u>O</u>ctober, and I'll be <u>o</u>n probation for six months, but <u>O</u>scar works there and he said that <u>o</u>ffers like this don't come al<u>o</u>ng that <u>o</u>ften and I should take it. So I did!"

Practice Pages - Answers

> ### the THOUGHT, NORTH, FORCE vowel sound

- Ex. 1 - Spot the THOUGHT vowel sound (p.111)

"Do you have to work tonight P<u>au</u>l? Why don't we go for a w<u>a</u>lk? <u>Or</u> <u>or</u>der a takeaway? I th<u>ough</u>t I could get a couple of bottles of wine, you could hire a film, and we could just relax for a bit. I've found things so stressful recently. Work has been mad. I've been given all these rep<u>or</u>ts to do, and I'm not coping with it very well. G<u>e</u>orge starts high school next week. Laura is <u>or</u>ganising an auction at the village h<u>a</u>ll and wants me to give a t<u>a</u>lk.... I need a holiday, that's what I need. Come on - it's just one night... If I take the kids out tomorrow m<u>or</u>ning you could work then instead." 361

> ### the CHOICE vowel sound

- Ex. 1 - Spot the CHOICE vowel sound (p.112)

"I've been getting really ann<u>oy</u>ed at J<u>oy</u>. She's always sp<u>oi</u>ling things by talking rudely, and the t<u>oy</u>s she got Ll<u>oy</u>d are so inappropriate. Why can't she just empl<u>oy</u> some common sense? She'll upset everyone if she keeps going on like this, but it's her ch<u>oi</u>ce. Anyway I shouldn't l<u>oi</u>ter here any longer, you've got potatoes to b<u>oi</u>l and the kids to put to bed. It was a lovely party, and the s<u>oy</u>-yoghurts went down well! No need for my paran<u>oi</u>a after all." 363

> ### the TRAP vowel sound

- Ex. 1 - Spot the TRAP vowel sound (p.113)

"We're going to a t<u>a</u>ngo dance class on S<u>a</u>turday, would you like to come? <u>A</u>ndrew is coming. So is M<u>a</u>thew, <u>A</u>ndrea and S<u>a</u>m. Come on, we just st<u>a</u>mp around for a bit. It's great! It's m<u>a</u>d but such a laugh. <u>A</u>nd the m<u>a</u>n that leads it is very attr<u>a</u>ctive. He isn't m<u>a</u>rried, <u>a</u>nd he h<u>a</u>s a w<u>a</u>xed chest!! Then we'll head b<u>a</u>ck to mine, h<u>a</u>ve a glass or two and then go down to the F<u>a</u>t C<u>a</u>t – th<u>a</u>t pub on the corner of <u>A</u>shford road, near <u>A</u>mber's house. There's a b<u>a</u>nd playing – they're called the M<u>a</u>d H<u>a</u>tters I think. How does th<u>a</u>t sound?" 365

> ### the MOUTH vowel sound

- Ex. 1 - Spot the MOUTH vowel sound (p.114)

"I can't believe we sold the h<u>ou</u>se! We should celebrate! The MacCle<u>o</u>ds seem like a nice family. We should leave the t<u>ow</u>el rail and I d<u>ou</u>bt we'll need the dishwasher. Do you remember there's that br<u>ow</u>n stain on the bath? We need to get that <u>ou</u>t. It'll be strange to leave this t<u>ow</u>n, but I'm sure it'll be lovely d<u>ow</u>n s<u>ou</u>th. We've looked ar<u>ou</u>nd, it's a good area." 367

126

Practice Pages - Answers

> ### *the FLEECE vowel sound*

- Ex. 1 - Spot the FLEECE vowel sound (p.115)

"Are you fr__ee__ next w__ee__k? I've got this m__ee__ting on Wednesday __e__vening and I'm f__ee__ling so un__ea__sy about it. Could you come round, r__ea__d my notes and then give m__e__ some f__ee__dback? I'd really appr__e__ciate it! It's about the t__ea__m's r__e__cent performance figures. W__e__ had thr__ee__ p__eo__ple quit last month and they want m__e__ to give some r__ea__sons why I think they left, and it's in front of the chi__ef__ exec. Max__i__ne will b__e__ there, which is a rel__ie__f. But nonetheless, I'm a complete wreck! I've been dr__ea__ming about it for w__ee__ks. __E__ven St__e__ven noticed that I've been acting sh__ee__pish r__e__cently, and that's something!"
369

> ### *the KIT vowel sound*

- Ex. 1 - Spot the KIT vowel sound (p.116)

"I've been g__i__ven th__is__ extra work to do, but I don't th__i__nk __it__'s fair. J__i__m has never taken any work home __i__n the last four years and __it__'s frustrating not to have even been acknowl__e__dged for putting __i__n add__i__tional even__i__ngs and weekends. He just goes to the g__y__m every night. I've helped Fl__y__nn bu__i__ld this business! He can't man__a__ge h__is__ staff. __If__ __i__t doesn't change soon, I'll be look__i__ng for a new job, that's for sure!"
371

> ### *the NEAR vowel sound*

- Ex. 1 - Spot the NEAR vowel sound (p.117)

"He's handed in his notice at the mus__eu__m. He wants to pursue a car__eer__ in medicine! He's got so much studying to do, but he r__ea__lly is s__e__rious about it. I don't want to interf__ere__. I think it's cl__ear__ in his mind and that's all that matters. It's w__ei__rd to think he'll be going back to university after all these y__ea__rs. I f__ear__ change – I don't think I could do it."
373

> ### *the DRESS vowel sound*

- Ex. 1 - Spot the DRESS vowel sound (p.118)

"Have you heard about __E__mily? You know that she's been applying to different universities to do her PHD? W__e__ll, she got in! G__ue__ss where! Oxford! She's thrilled. A bit overwh__e__lmed no doubt, but so happy. The sel__e__ction process is rigorous. I hope she's r__ea__dy!? I'm so __e__nvious! Gr__e__g is over the moon. He's taking her to __E__dinburgh for a sp__e__cial c__e__lebratory week__e__nd away together!"
375

127

Practice Pages - Answers

> ### the FACE vowel sound

- Ex. 1 - Spot the FACE vowel sound (p.119)

"I've been at the st<u>a</u>tion for hours. I think the tr<u>ai</u>n is del<u>ay</u>ed. I'm so sorry. It's just started to r<u>ai</u>n as well! What a cr<u>a</u>zy d<u>ay</u>! Sorry for the w<u>ai</u>t! Are you free in <u>A</u>pril, could I come and st<u>ay</u> then? Gr<u>ea</u>t! And I won't be l<u>a</u>te! We'll have an am<u>a</u>zing time! I think I'll go by pl<u>a</u>ne next time."
377

> ### the SQUARE vowel sound

- Ex. 1 - Spot the SQAURE vowel sound (p.120)

"We went to the f<u>ayre</u> today. Mary absolutely loved it. Th<u>ere</u> were v<u>a</u>rious tents and stalls. Th<u>ere</u> was one selling homemade p<u>ear</u> cider. I bought five bottles! What you can buy in the supermarket just doesn't comp<u>are</u> to this. There was a whole <u>a</u>rea that had been turned into a f<u>ai</u>ry grotto. And there was a very prec<u>a</u>rious looking tree house. I was worried when the children were running up and down those st<u>airs</u>, but no one was hurt and it did look beautiful. Whoever designed it has a lot of artistic fl<u>air</u>!"
379

> ### the GOOSE vowel sound

- Ex. 1 - Spot the GOOSE vowel sound (p.121)

"How was your holiday? Where did y<u>ou</u> go? Sounds b<u>eau</u>tiful! No, we stayed here. I'm working really hard trying to get this assignment finished. I think I'm l<u>o</u>sing my mind – it's gr<u>ue</u>lling! I'm getting up at six... It's tr<u>ue</u>! I'm out by seven then I'm either writing, pr<u>oo</u>freading or editing up until half five everyday day. It's hard to get in the gr<u>oo</u>ve, you know? I'm still d<u>o</u>ing my private work but when I d<u>o</u>, if I'm honest, I just can't focus on anything. The deadline is l<u>oo</u>ming and wh<u>o</u> knows if I'll be done. It's t<u>w</u>o weeks today! Wh<u>o</u> kn<u>ew</u> that writing and thinking could be so exhausting! I'll be done s<u>oo</u>n. Once I've finished, I think I'll sleep for a week!"
381

> ### the FOOT vowel sound

- Ex. 1 - Spot the FOOT vowel sound (p.122)

"I sh<u>ou</u>ldn't be here. I'm sorry. I know how awkward it makes you. I c<u>ou</u>ldn't make it last week, because I was at that b<u>oo</u>k fair in town. I st<u>oo</u>d for hours. It was g<u>oo</u>d though, but the host was awful - so f<u>u</u>ll of himself... Do you want a c<u>u</u>shion? That bed l<u>oo</u>ks so uncomfortable... How do you feel now? That w<u>o</u>man next door looks grumpy... How's the food? W<u>ou</u>ld you like me to c<u>oo</u>k you something?"
383

Practice Pages - Answers

> the CURE vowel sound

- Ex. 1 - Spot the CURE vowel sound (p.123)

"The doctors say it's inc<u>u</u>rable. I was f<u>u</u>rious at first, but I'm coming to terms with it now. She doesn't want to have to end<u>ure</u> any more tests. She's so calm and mat<u>ure</u> about it. She's very inspiring. I'm not coping as well, but I think she feels very sec<u>ure</u> in the home and they're doing everything they can for her. Her room's quite lux<u>u</u>rious, and it's good that it's so r<u>u</u>ral, she can watch the deer from her window."

Additional Resources - Phonetic Symbols

This is just a reference page, so refer to it when prompted.

Vowels		**Consonants**
		Find out in Book 2 - Consonants.

- ɪ   K<u>I</u>T *(p.70)*
- e   DR<u>E</u>SS *(p.78)*
- ʌ   STR<u>U</u>T *(p.35)*
- ʊ   F<u>OO</u>T *(p.94)*
- æ   TR<u>A</u>P *(p.57)*
- ɒ   L<u>O</u>T, CL<u>O</u>TH *(p.43)*
- ə   The Schwa *(p.17)*
- uː   G<u>OO</u>SE *(p.90)*
- ɔː   TH<u>OUGH</u>T, F<u>OR</u>CE, N<u>OR</u>TH *(p.48)*
- ɜː   N<u>UR</u>SE *(p.21)*
- ɑː   B<u>A</u>TH, P<u>AL</u>M, ST<u>A</u>RT *(p.31)*
- iː   FL<u>EE</u>CE *(p.65)*
- eɪ   F<u>A</u>CE *(p.82)*
- aɪ   PR<u>I</u>CE *(p.39)*
- ɔɪ   CH<u>OI</u>CE *(p.53)*
- əʊ   G<u>OA</u>T *(p.26)*
- aʊ   M<u>OU</u>TH *(p.61)*
- ɪə   N<u>EA</u>R *(p.74)*
- eə   SQU<u>ARE</u> *(p.86)*
- ʊə   C<u>URE</u> *(p.98)*
- eɪə   L<u>AYER</u> *(p.84)*
- aɪə   L<u>IAR</u> *(p.41)*
- ɔɪə   L<u>AWYER</u> *(p.55)*
- əʊə   L<u>OWER</u> *(p.29)*
- aʊə   H<u>OUR</u> *(p.63)*

Additional Resources - Tongue Height for Vowels

This is just a reference page, so refer to it when prompted.

Encouraging the tongue to move into a new position for a vowel sound requires physical awareness and an accurate picture of the tongue and the inside of the mouth. For many people this just takes a bit of time and practice, but you might find it helpful to use this picture. It shows a word for each vowel sound inside the mouth, and it's position indicates how high and in what position the tongue should be when speaking in a standard British English accent. In addition to this, it might also be helpful to see which vowel sounds are nearest one another in terms of the tongue's position, and how close/far apart the they are.

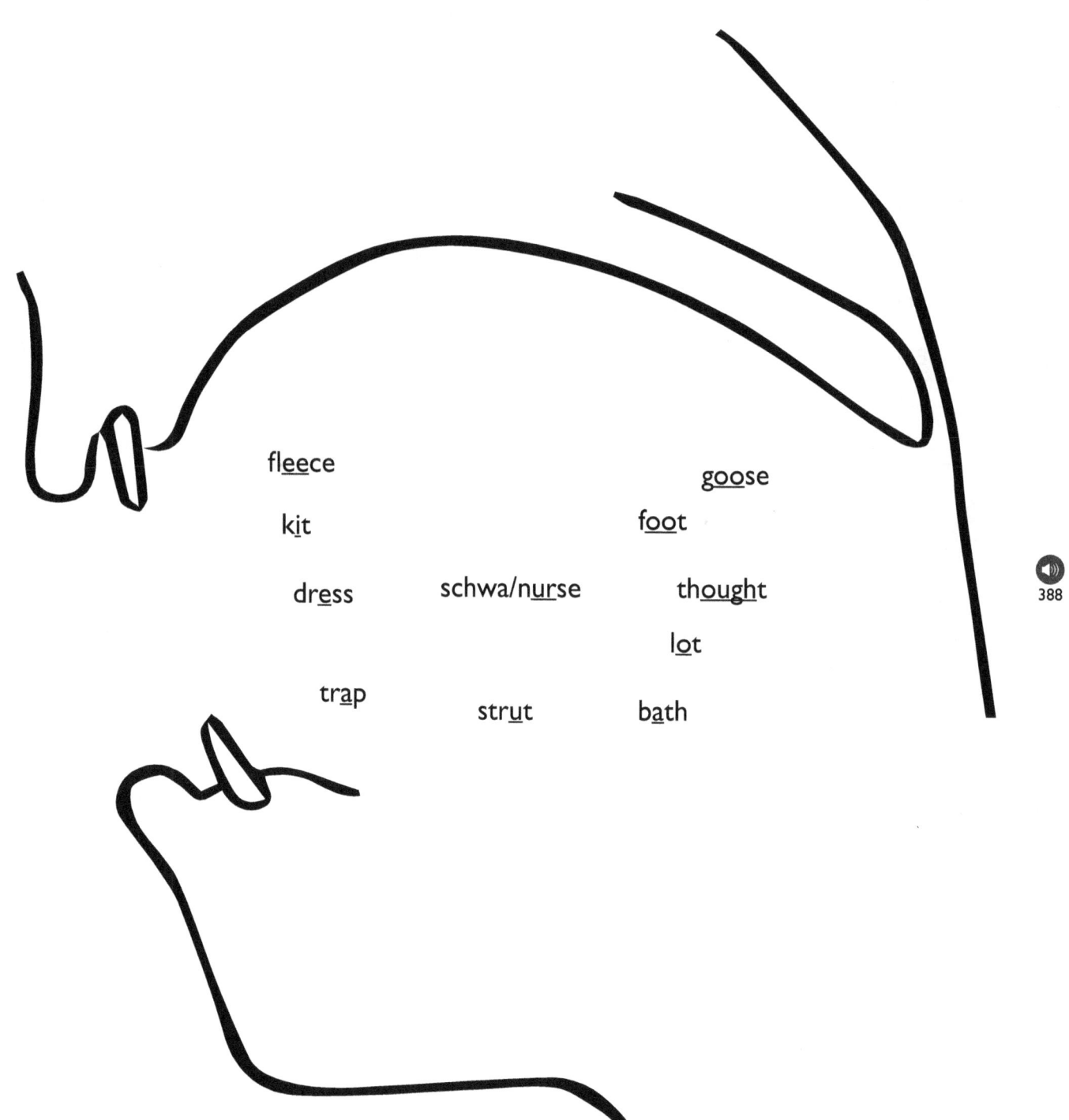

Bibliography and Recommended Reading

Bibliography

Daniel Jones, *English Pronouncing Dictionary* (CUP 1917)
Peter Roach, *English Phonetics and Phonology* (3rd. Ed. CUP, 2000)
J.C. Wells, *Accents of English: An Introduction* (CUP, 1982)

Recommended Reading

Clifford Turner, *Voice and Speech in the Theatre* (A & C Black, 1950)
J.C. Wells, *Accents of English: An Introduction* (CUP, 1982)
J.C. Wells, *Accents of English: The British Isles* (CUP, 1982)
J.C. Wells, *English Intonation, An Introduction* (CUP, 2006)
Peter Roach, *English Phonetics and Phonology* (3rd. Ed. CUP, 2000)
H. Ashton, S. Shepherd, *Work on your Accent* (Collins, 2012)
E. Sharpe, J.H. Rowles, *How To Do Accents* (Oberon Books, 2009)
OUP, *Oxford Advanced Learner's Dictionary* (OUP, 2015)
Daniel Jones, *Cambridge English Pronunciation Dictionary* (CUP, 2011)
Martin Hewings, *English Pronunciation in Use* (CUP, 2007)

Recommended Websites

www.oxfordlearnersdictionaries.com
www.wordfind.com
www.en.wikipedia.org/wiki/Lexical_set
https://en.wikipedia.org/wiki/Received_Pronunciation

You're a third of your way on the journey. This is book 1 of a 3 part series. So what do you want to master next? Consonants or intonation?

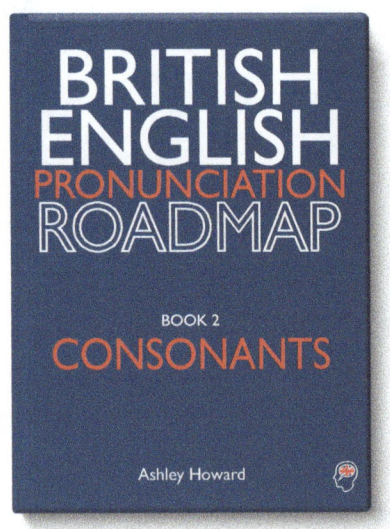

Book 2 - Consonants

- Step-by-step guide to help you perfect the 24 consonant sounds in English - particular help with NG, TH, R, L and other difficult sounds
- 4 hours of audio to practice with
- Clear illustrations of the tongue and lip positions.
- Colour-coded icons to guide you to specific exercises for your specific habits
- AND some special bonus material...

Available online.

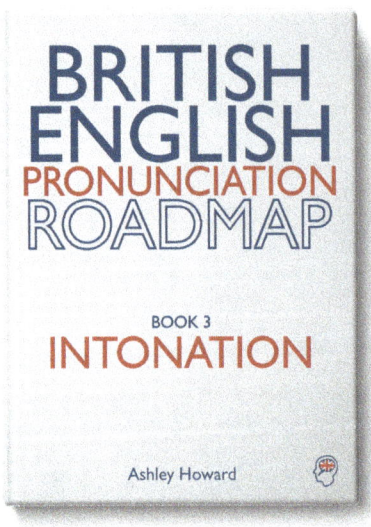

Book 3 - Intonation

Covers all this and MORE:

- Word and sentence stress - creating meaning
- Rising and falling intonation patterns
- Weak forms and unstressed syllables
- Rhythm and pitch - adding feeling and intention
- Connected speech - elision, contractions, assimilation
- Asking questions, making statements, apologising, sarcasm, quoting and paraphrasing...
- Linking and intrusive consonants
- Prefixes and suffixes
- AND much, much more...

Available online.